The Making of English Reading Audiences,
1790–1832

The Making of English Reading Audiences, 1790–1832

JON P. KLANCHER

The University of Wisconsin Press

Published 1987

The University of Wisconsin Press
114 North Murray Street
Madison, Wisconsin 53715

The University of Wisconsin Press, Ltd.
1 Gower Street
London WC1E 6HA, England

First printing

Printed in the United States of America

For LC CIP information see the colophon

ISBN 0-299-10780-9

Publication of this book was made possible in part
by a grant from the Andrew W. Mellon Foundation.

"Reading the Social Text" appeared in a slightly
different version in *Studies in Romanticism* 23
(Summer 1984): 183–204. Courtesy of the
Trustees of Boston University.

For my mother and father,
and for Emily

Contents

vii

Preface

THIS book examines a wide range of writings for diverse audiences, many of them unread since the early nineteenth century: periodical writings, political works, and travel diaries as well as Romantic theoretical texts. For cultural research in this era, there are few bibliographical aids of the kind Victorian scholars have developed, and those few give only a partial view of what was available to read. Periodicals alone represent an awesome task of critical reading; between 1790 and 1832 over four thousand journals were published in Britain, some in many dozens of volumes. To make these and other texts available for study, I have reproduced sometimes lengthy passages of prose for readers who would otherwise have difficulty finding them. This tactic provides, along the way, a very brief anthology of early-nineteenth-century discourse. Such writings, I have found, constantly surprise one; they range much further, in every conceivable cultural direction, than the limited canon of "Romantic" prose would lead one to expect. There is a huge, still largely unknown world of text-making to be read in writings of the early nineteenth century. To gain access to this world, however, means giving up the frequent methodological double standard that encourages interpreting or theorizing about canonical texts, but counting or averaging popular texts. It also means refusing any premature judgments of taste, since what is at issue is precisely the historical forming of taste as well as readers' interpretive modes.

Since the late seventeenth century, writers have attempted to name their own readers. That effort remains paradoxical today. In a newly published book about the use of signs, I find the following invocation to its public: "This collection will therefore aid the student, provoke the scholar, be of value to the businessman or woman, be of interest to people in politics, educate those in the media, and please and amuse the general reader."[1] This is an eighteenth-century sentence; it might, with more strain, have been written in the mid–nineteenth century, and it simply amuses us in the twentieth. But it could not have been written in the Romantic era, which knew no such serenity about the orders of reading. In this book I have written to different audiences, crossing the often well-guarded borders between empirical and interpretive discourse, narrative and tropological writing, description and polemic. My subject cuts across these categories and I have aimed to follow it where it leads. To interpret texts unread since the early nineteenth century, I reproduce passages of prose and investigate them with rhetorical and semiotic methods known best to literary critics; to relate them to the known canon, I raise some issues familiar mainly to Romanticists; to map their positions, I borrow from the sociology of writing, intellectual and social history, and the history of publishing; to make sense of them, I draw from certain poststructural and Marxist arguments. The early nineteenth century in England knew deep troughs of reaction and some startling moments of social and cultural change. Writing in another time of reaction, I have tried to recall that reading and writing themselves are agents, not reflexes, of individual, cultural, and social transformation.

My debt to my teachers and friends looms large. Robert Maniquis suggested undertaking a historical study of this kind; he guided its development and helped me sharpen its arguments. The impact of his teaching should be evident to him on every page. In long hours of discussion and reading, he provided the most responsive and diverse audience one could have. Jerome McGann gave me invaluable forms of support and, among his many contributions, challenged me to think out the implications of my historical efforts. Others improved the manuscript by giving their time to read various chapters: Max Novak, Marilyn Butler, John Sutherland, Peter Thorslev, Peter Manning, Norman Fruman, Lawrence Rainey. For invitations to test certain arguments on listening audiences, I thank Kathryn Shevelow, Richard Terdiman, Eve Stoddard, and Ellen Quandahl. Constance Coiner gave generously of her critical skill and sustaining friendship, and I also want to thank Geoffrey Goshgarian, Jens Kruse, Annette Leddy, Kathryne Lindberg, Jenny Shute, Ron Bush, Chris Adam, and Dan Hawkes. For irreplaceable support and patience I am very grateful to Karen Hilfman. My brother Chris lent me his irony at just the right times.

I also want to thank the California Institute of Technology for providing Mellon postdoctoral support and the environment I needed to complete this book. Librarians at the Henry Huntington Library and UCLA's Special Collections were indispensable to my researches. Dara Thornton and a kindly, knowledgeable staff at Caltech helped me prepare the manuscript for publication. I thank *ELH* for permission to reprint Chapter 3 in a slightly different form, and *Studies in Romanticism* for permission, courtesy of the Trustees of Boston University, to republish part of Chapter 2 in an expanded and altered form.

The Making of English Reading Audiences,
1790-1832

Introduction

Historical Audiences and Social Theory

THE English Romantics were the first to become radically uncertain of their readers, and they faced the task Wordsworth called "*creating* the taste" by which the writer is comprehended. The late eighteenth century ushered in a confusing, unsettled world of reading and writing. Ideas, signs, and styles had to cross new cultural and social boundaries, and the status consciousness of the eighteenth century was already becoming the class awareness of the nineteenth. No single, unified "reading public" could be addressed in such times, as Coleridge and his contemporaries well knew. This inchoate cultural moment compelled a great many writers to shape the interpretive and ideological frameworks of audiences they would speak to. They carved out new readerships and transformed old ones. This book explores the textual and social tensions they produced.

Literary studies have generally confined the question of reading to either the narrow textuality of "reception" criticism or an equally enclosed empirical sociology of literature. To clarify what is at stake in historical reading, I have drawn upon recent theoretical and methodological proposals in social history, intellectual history, and cultural anthropology, which so far have limited themselves to interpretive questions in preindustrial European societies (prerevolutionary France, the Italian peasantry) or to "primitive" cultures.[1] Such developments in the human sciences converge theoretically with problems of literary study posed by Bakhtin and his circle: the tension between conflicting discourses, the struggle over the uses of signs, and the transformation of texts as they cross barriers of culture and social class. Removed from the domains of the novelistic or purely intertextual play, these questions assume an intriguingly different shape—as in the cultural transformations of late-eighteenth- and early-nineteenth-century Britain. Those years embraced both a redefini-

3

tion of audiences and the emergence of social classes in the modern sense. Writers shaped audiences who developed awareness of social class as they acquired self-consciousness as readers. But as collective formations, "class" and "audience" gave rise to conflicting forms of collective awareness. This tension appears everywhere in texts written between 1790 and 1832. It also puts into focus the kind of questions a study of historical audiences and their making must raise.

This book might have begun with Wordsworth or Blake or Coleridge. As a journalist, preacher, poet, playwright, cultural critic, and social theorist, Coleridge was the most attentive and perhaps most profound of those Romantic writers who confronted "the luxuriant misgrowth of our activity: a Reading Public!" But forging new social and textual relations between writers and audiences was too complex a historical process to be viewed through the texts of a single writer. We need to see Romantic writers *in* the larger world of audience-making that preoccupied so many early-nineteenth-century writers. Here I attempt a more panoptic view than any one writer's work can afford by taking the British periodical to be a paradigm of audience-making. Periodical texts and their myriad writers give us a new way to see how "making audiences" meant evolving readers' interpretive frameworks and shaping their ideological awareness. The journals became agents of Coleridge's "luxuriant misgrowth" when writers began using them, in the wake of the French Revolution, to divide audiences and guide them to compete for position in social and cultural space. Always supremely conscious of the audiences their writers imagine, assert, or entice, periodicals provide perhaps the clearest framework for distinguishing the emerging publics of the nineteenth century. Both well-known and obscure prose writers made the public journals stylistic and semiotic modes of carving out readerships. Around the journals I have also interpreted political works, social commentaries, publishers' reports, travelers' diaries, and, not least, Romantic theoretical strategies to form audiences. Still, this book attempts no survey of all readerships between 1790 and 1832. Instead, it focuses rather intently upon four strategically crucial audiences: a newly self-conscious middle-class public, a nascent mass audience, a polemical radical readership, and the special institutional audience—what Coleridge called the clerisy—that assumed its first shape in this contentious time.

To students of Romanticism, the perspective and many of the texts I deploy will be decidedly unfamiliar. Wordsworth's 1815 "Essay, Supplementary to the Preface" established the view that has dominated Romantic scholarship for at least the last forty years: rejecting the social and historical audiences of his own time, Wordsworth imagined the distant prospect of an ideal audience, "the People, philosophically characterized, and . . . the embodied spirit of their knowledge." Modern Romantic critics have often taken Wordsworth's "People" to mean themselves. What Meyer Abrams remarked in 1953—"There is something fatal to the audience in the romantic point of view"—seems to justify using an ideal academic readership to displace the recalcitrant historical publics early-nineteenth-century writers faced.[2] The discourse of Romantic Imagination has been nourished by this inversion, which essentializes and thus mystifies what was in fact a troubled contention over power, signs, and the function of culture itself. We are used to reading, for instance, that Blake's painful isolation from a real audience was quintessentially Romantic, which means, as Morris Eaves explains it, that Blake triumphed over his circumstance by generating a gratifying imaginary audience from the poet's deepest self.[3] I cite this example as a particularly ingenious effort to resolve the problem of the Romantics' readers. It appeals to the pervasive idealism Jerome J. McGann has called the Romantic Ideology, "an uncritical absorption in Romanticism's own self-representations."[4] But not only Romantic critics and scholars have accepted the metaphysical victory over social and historical conflict the word *Romanticism* has come to signify. The notion of the protean "reader" that empowers so much contemporary criticism and cultural theory was an important outcome of the struggle for audiences in the Romantic period. The modern humanist academy regards itself as the only true audience of literary texts. But that confidence depends on forgetting the real shaping and dividing of social and historical audiences within which the "clerisy" first found its form.

Coleridge's clerics were meant to be, above all, masters of interpretation. What they faced in the early nineteenth century was social and textual interpretation on an unprecedented scale, a complex contention over a burgeoning culture's texts. To grasp the dynamic of this struggle over meaning and power, I have adopted the widest sense of what interpretation implies. Frank Kermode's definition is useful here: "Whoever expounds a text (no matter at what level) and whoever castigates a text, is an interpreter."[5] In an unusually intense time of expounding and castigating texts, the audiences emerging in the nineteenth century were not only exercising vastly different "tastes." They were also, more critically, taking shape as diverging collective interpreters whose "readings" of the social and intellectual world opened unbridgeable cultural conflicts. What Kermode calls the "institutional control of interpretation" is no recent requirement of cultural peace. In the early nineteenth century, it became a crucial means of governing the relations *between* these emerging audiences over whom, individually, no institution had any control. Because interpretation attends *all* uses of a text, it requires a guarantee of institutional authority capable of ruling in, and ruling out, the possible readings made by possible audiences. Today, fascination with this control and its mechanisms fills critical journals and scholarly conferences, spilling over from literary criticism to law and anthropology and intellectual or social history.[6] But in the early nineteenth century this question was taken up from the "lowest" levels of cultural activity to the "highest," acted out or dreamed up in a host of social and ideological contexts, a matter of consequence for the smallest and largest audiences just then becoming aware of themselves as distinct social and textual readers of all their collective representations.

I

Audiences are not simply aggregates of readers. They are complicated social and textual formations; they have interpretive tendencies and ideological contours. Studying them requires us to ask what kind of collective being they represent and how an individual reader becomes aware of belonging to a great social audience. These questions have been necessarily raised by a new cultural history that appeals, honorifically or critically, to the notion of historical *mentalités* as models of the collective mind. Since Durkheim, such mental frameworks have always posed implicit or open challenges to the Marxist understanding of ideology and class consciousness. But the most recent notion of "mentality" is not the immobile, asocial mental architecture of Lucien Febvre's "collective mentality" or Lévy-Bruhl's "primitive mind." Far from such universalized constructs, the new cultural history shows us semiotic mentalities, differential and ideologically charged. Clifford Geertz's "theatre state" of nineteenth-century Bali or Lynn Hunt's rhetorical study of the French Revolution, to take two recent and striking examples, represent history as the making and reading of powerful signs. This new cultural history makes a number of bold claims. Geertz's semiotic rewriting of history tries to make obsolete both Marxist discourse about class ideologies and liberal-pluralist talk of consensus and balancing interests. These older paradigms of political and historical study merely pay off in what Geertz calls "the worn coin of European ideological debate." Power appeared in Bali not as masked class interest but as the pomp of semiotic display, itself the product of a peculiar "turn of mind—hierarchical, sensory, symbolistic, and theatrical."[7] Likewise, the French Revolution appears to Lynn Hunt and François Furet as the making of a new "political class" devoted to producing political signs, not a bourgeois class revolutionizing the mode of production.[8] What the Marxist tradition construes as production or practice, the new cultural history presents instead—blurring the distinction between "production" and "consumption" —as historical acts of interpretation. The consequences of this high-tech historicism will be unmistakable to anyone who has faced the crisis of Marxism in the past ten years. History understood as the making and reading of signs now appears to escape the grasp of Marxist reconstructions, and the crucial category of "class" looks indeed like the most worn-out of European coins.

Marxists have not taken such arguments lightly. "The conception of social class," as Fredric Jameson admits, "is as impossible as it is indispensable."[9] Jameson argues for exercising as a method (class analysis) what can no longer be trusted as a concept (class categories). Other Marxists have demurred from the notion that social class can be inferred from political and cultural production. Gareth Stedman Jones argues persuasively with E. P. Thompson's belief that social history can explain ideological texts by the social class they reveal or betray. His recent essay "Rethinking Chartism" goes further: the long-honored place of Chartism as England's first protosocialist, working-class movement is based on the error, common since Engels, of deducing social composition from political and cultural compositions.[10] Adhering to the notion of class rather than, say, Foucault's micropolitics of decentered power, Marxists provide a wide target for the new cultural historians who seek to "rethink" history as the unfolding of the empire of signs.

But signs constitute strategies in real wars. When semiotic cultural history transforms *all* conflict into the clash of signs, the real social and cultural struggles of men and women begin to appear as war in the heaven of semiosis. Perhaps that is, as Lyotard argues, the "postmodern condition."[11] Yet it is surely a mistake to read a postmodern condition back into historical epochs that did not know the utter absorption in the frenetic production and reading of signs that marks our own time. In the early nineteenth century, writers and readers became highly self-conscious about interpreting, constituting, and struggling over signs. They were equally absorbed in the problem of social hierarchy, class structure, and the refashioning of a status-conscious society of "ranks" typical of the eighteenth century into the more modern, lateral solidarities and conflicts of social class in the nineteenth. Often, as one reads their texts, it is hard to tell which has priority—the conflicts of class or the struggle over signs. It is also unnecessary: social divisions among classes both constrained the use of signs and resulted from the use of signs. As social agents, readers and writers classified

one another and often tried to avoid being classified themselves. The social conflict of classes, as Pierre Bourdieu has argued, takes cultural form as
the contest over "classifications."[12] And when this is a matter of "signs,"
the classification known as "audience" becomes a crucial body of social
and cultural apprehension.

"Audience" is, in fact, the most unexamined assumption in the armory
of cultural history and criticism. Yet since the founding texts of critical theory—Plato's *Dialogues* and *The Republic* and Aristotle's *Poetics*—some theory
of audience has lurked in all cultural criticism and social modelling. Plato's
citizens could not be trusted to be a poet's audience if they were also to
form a rational state: a "public." Aristotle's more subtle notion of audience
identifies it as the social formation that enables the state to function by
transforming social and psychological impulses dangerous to its well-being.
Necessarily distinguished but often locked in a complex relationship, the
public as "state" and the public as "audience" cannot really be set apart. To
Coleridge, the state embodied England's hierarchic class order, and in *On
the Constitution of Church and State,* he constructs a clerisy located between
this class order and the classless, individual, moral order of the church.
When Shelley addressed *Prometheus Unbound* to cultivated middle-class
readers and its virtual translation, "The Masque of Anarchy," to a radical
artisan audience, he acknowledged in poetic language a structural division
among audiences shaped by their experience of social class. These were
hardly the only writers of their time to identify an audience somewhere between the unmistakable structure of social class and the ideally classless
realm of the moral and human. As we will see, a host of nineteenth-
century writers forced their audiences to negotiate that distance, and *how*
they did so helped constitute the peculiar self-consciousness of the audiences themselves. Class consciousness and the idea of classless humanity
are not simply notional opposites. In the nineteenth century, the idea of
classlessness could arise only out of an initial, compelling class awareness.
Audiences could neither be equated with social classes nor conceived apart
from them. Writers produced class awareness while they shaped audiences,
and thus they negotiated between these classifications a complex topography: that of the social text.

II

I have not forgotten the individual reader, who remains crucial. Yet
this is where the protean but unsituated "reader" must come down to
earth. "The real intellectual wealth of the individual," Marx argued, "de-

pends entirely on the wealth of his real connections."[13] But it has been the most ideal, disconnected reader who, in Romantic and post-Romantic discourse, has most boldly proclaimed his intellectual wealth. A certain notion of the "life of the mind" goes hand-in-hand with the claim to have severed all one's "real connections" to the social audience from which one has been raised up. The terms "reader" and "audience" are hardly neutral; they have come to mean, in post-Romantic critical discourse, two wholly contradictory and seemingly irreconcilable intellectual frameworks: the one hermeneutic or "critical," the other empiricist or "sociological." My analysis in this book is both critical and sociological, hermeneutic and empirical. But to restore the relation of these lines of approach, we need to ask why the "reader" has become historically detached from his audience in the first place.

The figure of the "reader," ubiquitous in contemporary criticism, most often appears as the fleshed-out principle of linguistic or literary competence, dressed as the implied, ideal, or projected reader of reader-response theory and *Rezeptionkritik*. He is the inverse of Baudelaire's *hypocrite lecteur*; he knows every gambit, reacts to the wiliest stylistic maneuver, "composes" the Joycean text that makes any one definitive reading impossible, reverses all his assumptions at the turn of a comma.[14] He is neither excessive nor inadequate to the text, and he displaces all historical readers who, like Baudelaire's, stubbornly maintain their otherness to it. He is the logical corollary to the "death of the author," since the "reader" holds open the space of free subjectivity unconstrained by anything other than the protocols of a Kantian critical community or Stanley Fish's "interpretive community."

Though clearly ahistorical, this ideal reader invites curious attempts to plant him into historical soil. Robert Darnton portrays Jean Ranson, an intense eighteenth-century reader of Rousseau's *La Nouvelle Heloise*, as an appealingly ideal, yet concrete historical reader of the kind Rousseau imagined in and for his text. But the historian cannot avoid an arbitrary choice of one or another historical subject to fill in the empty contour of an abstracted "reader."[15] What should have been explained—the far wider and more complex *social* desire to be absorbed by texts in the mid-to-late eighteenth century—would require something Darnton, himself a very good reader, seems unable to approach: that is, a social as well as interpretive conception of "reading" itself, a larger collective landscape of interpretive acts within which to situate the solitary reader.

Carlo Ginzburg almost accomplishes that in his portrait of a far more interesting historical reader, the sixteenth-century miller Menocchio in

Ginzburg's *The Cheese and the Worms*. Menocchio, unlike Jean Ranson, does not predictably fulfill his writer's fantasy, but powerfully misreads the texts of Scripture and Renaissance humanism as he responds to questions posed by his Christian Inquisitors. Menocchio's heretical reading transforms Christian accounts of Genesis into a peculiar, crude account of maggots emerging from rotting cheese. Here the agent of reading is less the individual subject than what Ginzburg hypothesizes as a "lost" peasant culture that must have provided the "materialist underbelly" for Menocchio's startling interpretation. Collectively mediated, Menocchio's "reading" appears far less arbitrary than the reading of Darnton's Ranson. In effect, Ginzburg explains it according to its relationship to the audience of literate peasants to which Menocchio must have belonged. Still, the audience is irrecoverable, the historical evidence for it lacking, the mediation only speculative, and Menocchio's "reading" just as likely eccentric as typical. Inferring something like a collective peasant mentality from a single text, Ginzburg cannot avoid the consequence of departing from the singular reader which troubles every account of textuality, whether it conceives that reader hermeneutically or historically.[16]

Meanwhile, Ginzburg's suggestive study short-circuits what the historical evidence could have provided him when he repeatedly seeks "a direct study of lower-class society free of intermediaries." His own sources—remarkable documents of Menocchio's confession to the Inquisitors—appear unusually "direct" because the intermediaries had no motive to distort the miller's odd story, since they used it to justify burning him at the stake. But by attempting to eliminate the mediations between the historian, his sources, texts, and subject, Ginzburg unavoidably presents as a singular "reading" what was in fact the mutual production of a reading by all its interlocutors—the Inquisitors, the miller, the peasant community, and Ginzburg himself. All this remains largely invisible to the eye trying to see past intermediaries rather than making them part of the subject itself. Ginzburg shares with many other students of "popular culture" the longing to discover that culture "in itself," in the purified state uncontaminated by authorities, institutions, or translators.

Wordsworth struggled to remake the middle-class audience of the early nineteenth century by borrowing the peasant's language of English rustics. That complex effort should remind us that no act of reading can be "free of intermediaries." As Paul Mann has put it in a stimulating essay on Blake's cultural production, "Audience is precisely a mediated term."[17] The cultural critic or historian must multiply the mediators, not eliminate them. He or she must excavate the cultural institutions, the competitive readings, the social and political constraints, and above all the intense mutualities and struggles in social space that guide and block the passage of signs among historical writers, readers, and audiences. This means that the notion of a historical audience cannot remain the inertly empirical category known to the sociology of literature—where it has been described, counted, documented in a dozen ways without ever becoming, for theory or cultural history, the active collective interpreter it once constituted in social life. But I think the distance between the isolated, textual "reader" and the empirical "audience" is more than an aberration of modern criticism. Rather, that distance is an outcome of the cultural history explored in the following chapters. The intense cultural politics of the Romantic period obliged writers not only to distinguish among conflicting audiences, but to do so by elaborating new relations *between* the individual reader and the collective audience. For a reader is just as surely constituted among audiences when he is apparently abstracted from *all* audience-belonging as when he is firmly embedded within it. It is this connection between reader and audience that so-called reception theory has never deduced—the vital but by no means simple relation between an act of reading and a location with a collective realm, an audience (social, ideological, historical).

That relation can be seen in texts; it was a central preoccupation of Mikhail Bakhtin and his colleague V. N. Voloshinov. In Voloshinov's work, "reported speech"—the way one social language cites and represents another—becomes the mechanism of what Bakhtin would later call *heteroglossia*, the play of social languages within the same national language and even the same text. One social language does not merely refer intertextually to another social language, as Julia Kristeva construed it: it represents another social language. Here Bakhtin and Voloshinov crucially recognize relationships of priority, power, engagement, and disengagement within discourse. Yet heteroglot language could not represent "other" social languages without also representing their relationships to *their* readers. Voloshinov's direct, indirect, and quasi-direct modes of "reported speech" represent not only another's speech, but another's relation to his audience as that speech enacts it.[18]

I can put this another way, from the standpoint of an individual reader. Recognizing the trace of a socially alien discourse in the language I read, I must also recognize evidence of a relationship to that discourse different from mine: competitive with mine, perhaps antithetical to mine. I thus become aware of myself as a reader situated in a particular social space—a reading space among differing reading acts. But I do not recognize this merely as an individual reader. This awareness dawns on me by putting me in the realm of a *kind* of reading act that I share with some but decidedly do not share with others. In short, I attain—however inchoately—some sense of the audience to which I belong by becoming conscious, through heteroglot encounter, of that audience to which I cannot or will not belong.

Audiences cannot be understood taxonomically; they are not simply distinct sectors of the cultural sphere. They are mutually produced as an otherness within one's own discourse. In order to form the mode of reception for one audience, the writer has to produce, at the same time, another audience-text relationship, and this exerts an internal pressure against which he defines his relation to his own readers. Bakhtin's work, from this standpoint, suggests that one's awareness of belonging to a particular public can only be acquired *relationally*. One encounters some other audience as a form of textual interference, as heteroglossia. Further, the "audience" itself mediates between one's singular reading and one's awareness of belonging to other collective formations—class, gender, race—which themselves become conscious by being textually represented.

Indeed the critical moment of Bakhtin's dialogic imagination seems to occur "where the dialogue of voices arises directly *out of* a social dialogue of 'languages,' where an alien utterance *begins to sound* like a socially alien language, where the orientation of the word among alien utterances *changes into* an orientation of the word among socially alien languages" (*Dialogic Imagination*, 284–85). Here it can be neither purely individual nor purely social dialogism, but the moment of transition—when one passes over into the other, in either direction—that one's orientation as individual "reader" shifts to an intimation of the larger "audience" in which one may be inscribed.

That a reader is constructed within a certain audience does not mean he becomes an automaton. His encounter with colliding social languages, like the writer's, demands choice. Bakhtin maneuvers here between the specious creativity imagined by one cultural tradition and the blind economism decreed by another:

Language is not a neutral medium that passes freely and easily into the private property of the speaker's intentions; it is populated—overpopulated—with the intentions of others. Expropriating it, forcing it to submit to one's own intentions and accents, is a difficult and com-

plicated process. . . . Consciousness finds itself inevitably facing the
necessity of *having to choose a language*. With each literary-verbal performance, consciousness must actively orient itself amidst heteroglossia, it must move in and occupy a position for itself within it, it
chooses, in other words, a "language." (*Dialogic Imagination*, 294–95)

This is a strategic rather than a functionalist notion of writing and reading.
It depends on Bakhtin's historical sense of a culture that has passed beyond
the immobilized language zones of church, home, vocation, and village to
a semiotic culture where these languages collide all at once. What Coleridge meant by the reading public as "luxuriant misgrowth" was, in part,
the confusion of those languages and their readings. Socially explosive,
such "misgrowth" demanded that British readers reorient themselves, find
a position to occupy, classify others in the act of situating themselves. Yet
this deliberative, strategic historical moment—the Romantic period in
England—would give rise to the great systemic culture whose battle lines,
much more firmly drawn, were those of high culture and mass culture, bourgeoisie and working class, the imperial nation-states of Europe—in short,
the Victorian and then modernist societies whose categories early-
nineteenth-writers and readers had only begun to glimpse.

For cultural analysis this historical transition has been hard to grasp.
High-cultural production invites the language of "reception," the symbolic
giving and receiving of texts between great writers and singular, sensitive
readers. Mass-cultural production yields up the harsher vocabulary of "consumption," supply and demand among innumerable writers and vast, faceless audiences. Theoretically, this analytic double standard finds its defense
in Kant's Third Critique, where the "pure taste" of aesthetic judgment spirals away from the crude material "interests" of less exalted tastes. Hence it
is inevitable that Pierre Bourdieu would mount his massive assault on *The
Critique of Judgment* by remorselessly exposing "good taste" to the embar-
rassments of a radical functional analysis in his *Distinction: A Social Critique
of the Judgment of Taste*. Bourdieu shows persuasively how Kantian taste
masks its absorption in a material "habitus," the prejudices and cultural dispositions that a particular group acquires by internalizing objective conditions that it has, more or less unwittingly, produced as historical agents in
the first place. Those who share a habitus may also constitute an "audience," with a set of predispositions to judge and interpret texts. Bourdieu
firmly attaches these tendencies to the experience of social class: they be-

come ways to turn "necessity into a virtue," social limits into cultural "preferences." But they also form a tangled repository of textual effects, the accumulated residue of innumerable cultural experiences that act as both a brake against social and cultural change and a selection mechanism for subsequent cultural encounters.[19]

By refusing to analyze "high culture" in its own Kantian terms, Bourdieu describes the logic of classifications that govern all cultural choices. This politics of cultural classification must also involve readers, who, by the same logic, cannot establish or enact their own relation to texts without also classifying others'. They would seem to do so through the textual recognition Bakhtin calls heteroglossia—by becoming aware, at varying levels of explicitness, of representations of discourse that conflict with their own kind of discourse. But this is a subtle, elastic awareness of social classifying. Compared to Bakhtin's complex sense of heteroglot encounter, Bourdieu's framework may appear to many readers altogether too determined, too functionalist, a closed and almost airless cultural system. It tries to explain cultural production by matching each of its modes unerringly to the "tastes" of a particular habitus. Yet we need to know how cultural production *forms* these collective apperceptions, how writers and institutions constitute the collective interpreters we know as audiences. As Jon Elster rightly objects, Bourdieu never shows a mechanism by which his social actors "internalize" their world in cultural terms. To show that would be to show what Elster calls the "unintended effects" of social and cultural action. And no effects are more often unintended than the audiences shaped by writers whose historical intentions often misfire.[20]

I raise this problem because it is endemic to the late-eighteenth- and early-nineteenth-century British culture I study here. What made it a particularly poignant moment of cultural transformation was that, perhaps for the last time, it was still possible to conceive the writer's relation to an audience in terms of a personal compact. The small, deliberative, strategic world of early-nineteenth-century reading and writing still allowed for Wordsworth to imagine the reading of a poem as a personal exchange of "power" between writer and reader, for Shelley to imagine rather intensely the "five or six readers" of *Prometheus Unbound,* or for Coleridge to scan the audience of his plays to recognize those who had also attended his lectures. Political and periodical writers shifted between this world of cultural strategy and that cultural epoch emerging everywhere around them, the one that Byron and Scott awakened to, a massive audience for which they would perform, but a public they had never attempted to make.

III

Coleridge himself organized the cultural field by "classes" of readers, a social map upon which he could travel textual and ideological roads firmly contested by others. To arrange this study in audience-making, I have used a similar map in order to reread its social texts. Chapter 1 explains how eighteenth-century writers used the periodical to organize audiences, but also why their "widening circle" of readers perceptibly fragmented in the political crisis of the 1790s. Jürgen Habermas calls this the age of England's "public sphere"—eighteenth-century periodical writing as a textual society unifying readers otherwise divided into hierarchic social ranks. I briefly examine eighteenth-century periodical practices to show how this textual society was thought to work. But I also argue the "public sphere" was deeply compromised from the start, no sooner projected than transformed into an image to consume by readers who did not frequent it. Burgeoning English audiences divided sharply when the "French Revolution debate" exerted pressure upon its writers and readers to redefine their relation in terms of the social text. Such pressure appears tellingly in Arthur Young's then-popular *Travels in France*, a sociology of culture written as a travel diary that records Young's unexpected collision with the Revolution. As Young opposes discourses that "circulate" to those that "disseminate," he outlines a problematic of social reading to preoccupy Coleridge and other writers well into the nineteenth century. Meanwhile, periodical writers develop contrasting styles to signal particular ideological principles, from the *Monthly Magazine's* "intellectual man" to the radical journal's disaffected artisan and the *Oeconomist's* dislocated provincial reader. In this largely narrative chapter, I map the intentions to form three great audiences that fully emerge only in the nineteenth century: a newly self-conscious middle class, a nascent mass audience, and an insurgent radical readership.

For a middle-class audience that must become self-conscious of its own cultural power—the subject of Chapter 2—writers for *Blackwood's Magazine,* the *New Monthly Magazine,* the *Edinburgh Review,* and other journals use language to intimate to their readers extraordinary powers of mind to be realized in the act of reading itself. They develop hermeneutic strategies to guide their readers toward an intense awareness of what it means to interpret social and cultural sign systems, whether unmasking fraudulent social signs or forging the master sign of cultural diagnosis to read through all visible "signs of the times." The product of their audience-making is ultimately the reader who spirals above all audience-belonging, penultimate reader of

the social text. Yet while they intimate the making of a unified English culture rising above social conflicts, such texts do not yet produce an audience
able, as Coleridge put it, to "walk in the light of [its] own knowledge." To
this fatal incapacity Coleridge's theory of the clerisy and Arnold's later
problematic of culture and anarchy were to be addressed.

Meanwhile, Coleridge's and Wordsworth's worst fears materialized as
texts for a nascent "mass" audience in the 1820s. Chapter 3 grasps the new
mass public in the form its writers used to render it legible, the discourse of
the urban crowd. Taking it over from earlier writers who made the crowd a
faceless rabble, the mass writers transform it into a human spectacle, mirroring all social and psychological types, a powerfully suggestive image of
their own audience. In this way, writers begin to negotiate the nineteenth
century's most awesome signs of historical change: industrial creation, the
powers of the machine, the empire-building city. In the *Hive*, the *Mirror of
Amusement, Literature, and Instruction, Chambers' Journal*, the *Penny Magazine* and others, the writer uses the mingling of classes revealed in the
crowd to show, beneath apparent class structure, an allegorical world of
communal attachment and human desire. A price must be paid: to become
visible, individuals in the crowd must also become unintelligible. Making
the human concourse "spectacular" also means rendering it silent, erasing
all dialogue. Architects of a mass discourse embracing hundreds of thousands of readers, these writers try to lead them toward a latent realm of the
human and natural hidden within the forbidding signs of historical change.

Both middle-class and mass audiences, Chapter 4 argues, acquired
their shape by contesting the strategies of the radical public first formed in
the 1790s. Radical writers equated the dominant culture's signs with oppressive power, and they deployed tactics which included Paine's antithetical tropes, Wooler's symbolic textual violence, and Cobbett's effort to
dismantle the language of hegemonic culture by ramming it against the
blunt facts of historical change. Central to radical discourse is the problem
of "representation." Radical writers demand political representation to circumscribe the power of the ancien régime; they transform the rhetoric of
classical tradition to represent their own readers to the greater public; they
write in a representational language Coleridge calls the "verbal truth" that
declines to transport their readers beyond the social order. Such acts of representation are attempts to resist the making and unmaking of signs altogether. But radical discourse always threatens to become a sign, and
Shelley's meditation on signs and power suggests why this double bind defines the ambiguity of the radicals' stance.

Chapter 5 shifts from interpretive to theoretical texts in two Romantic writers' efforts to forge a new audience for symbolic works. In his prefaces, supplements, and letters, Wordsworth imagines the possibilities of cultural transmission, and there he constructs the terms by which cultural exchanges since 1800 have been largely understood: the commodified "consumption" or the symbolic "reception" of texts; the bridging of cultures by representing their languages; a redefinition of "literature" as a discourse without social audiences. For Coleridge, who traverses all the institutions of reading and writing, Wordsworth's anthropology of reading must give way to the making of an institutional audience, a clerisy whose reader-writers will define the symbolic strategies, interpretive rules, and certifying procedures that adjudicate all the "readings" the new social audiences may produce. In *On the Constitution of Church and State*, *The Friend*, the *Logic*, and elsewhere, Coleridge formulates the strange method he calls "rhematic" analysis to make the crucial distinctions among styles of political and philosophic discourse. What the eighteenth century knew as a struggle between social modes of taste, Coleridge transforms into the struggle over interpretations, crucially shifting the terms of cultural criticism itself.

In a speculative postscript, I ask how the Romantics' search for audiences in the early nineteenth century becomes a subject of the late twentieth century's wide-ranging quest for contemporary "response" in both narrow and large senses of the term. Such notions as Jean Baudrillard's "death of the social," Jürgen Habermas's "legitimation crisis," or Jean-François Lyotard's "postmodern condition" speak to a generalized crisis of response and representation in which the term *audience* itself becomes profoundly problematic. At the same time, as the human sciences increasingly transform history and social structure into semiotic modes, I ask what is won and what is lost in this effort to find in the historical what nowhere appears legible in the here and now.

One

Cultural Conflict, Ideology, and the Reading Habit in the 1790s

Aristotle does not discuss varieties of audience with the systematic thoroughness which he brings to the classification of opinion in general. And both Aristotle and Cicero consider audiences purely as something *given*. The extreme heterogeneity of modern life, however, combined with the nature of modern postal agencies, brings up another kind of possibility: the systematic attempt to *carve out* an audience.

—Kenneth Burke, A *Rhetoric of Motives*

IN "For Whom Does One Write?" Sartre recalls a moment, now vanished, when readers and writers of seventeenth-century France could exchange their roles: "The reader, if not strictly identical with the writer, was a potential writer. . . . One read because he could write; with a little luck he might have been able to write what he read. The public was active; productions of the mind were really *submitted* to it." Sartre's lost world of writing and reading is glimpsed once again, this time at the end of history, by Walter Benjamin, who imagines in "The Author as Producer" that the newspaper reader will become once again, at the end of the separation of writers and readers in the capitalist era, its self-active writer as well.[1] For these Marxists, the potential exchange of reading and writing forms both the prehistory and postrevolutionary future of that epoch in between we all inhabit—a period assumed to have begun with the commercializing of reading in the early eighteenth century and now only too familiar in the late twentieth. The eighteenth-century English public has always seemed distinctly modern in contrast to an older, more homogeneous public fostered

18

by patronage and bound together by the common code of classical rhetoric. Entering new economic relationships, the new middle-class public demanded and read new modes of writing. "The publication of books for a general public, completely unknown to the author," Arnold Hauser put it, became "the first form of the relationship to correspond to the structure of middle-class society based on the anonymous circulation of goods." In this cultural boom, eighteenth-century book merchants like James Lackington claimed, "all ranks and degrees now *read*."[2] But neither the breathless bookseller nor the cultural historian admits the difficulty of this epochal transition to a market economy of the text. In this anonymous marketplace, a whole cultural machinery had to be formed to channel books to their readers: the bookclubs, the reading societies, the carefully prepared subscription lists, the circulating libraries, and, not least, the periodical reviews. But of all such mechanisms, the eighteenth-century periodical—what Leo Lowenthal rightly called "the newest and most characteristic medium of the age"[3]—was perhaps the most paradoxical.

First formed in the second half of the seventeenth century, the periodical was the cultural contemporary of the English postal service and the London coffeehouse. This is why the periodical seems to have formed the textual institution of what Peter Hohendahl and Terry Eagleton, following Jürgen Habermas, have called England's "public sphere" in the eighteenth century.[4] Like the coffeehouse, the periodical assembled men from disparate social "ranks," writers with their patrons and potential readers, publishers with their suppliers, politicians with their critics. Social practices of gathering, reading, and writing as "discoursing subjects" allowed these subjects to pursue the rational consensus called the Enlightenment. But, as Hohendahl points out, "this literary public sphere, which evolved into a basis for the political emancipation of the middle class, was not bourgeois in its origins. It was rooted in aristocratic court circles and only gradually freed itself of their domination."[5] In fact, it helped preserve the most characteristic experience of the older aristocratic "literary public" and its shared rhetorical architecture, as Erich Auerbach portrayed it in "La Cour et la ville" and *Literary Language and Its Public in Late Latin Antiquity and the Middle Ages*.[6] Classical rhetoric and its trivium of high, middle, and low styles depended upon the homogeneity of its public, the very possibility of the reader's making himself Sartre's "potential writer." The eighteenth-century periodical now seems most remarkable for having extended into the new cultural marketplace such older relationships between readers and writers. Only now, these face-to-face relations would regulate an expanding cultural economy whose sense of order they must somehow provide.

The periodicals played contradictory tendencies of cultural development against one another. From the *Tatler* and the *Spectator* to the *Gentleman's Magazine* and its countless progeny, a periodical bound a group of writers to a certain set of readers. Published at regular intervals, periodicals formed a serial, continuous relationship between mutually identifiable readers and writers over time. (Women, for instance, were addressed as audiences separately from men.[7]) This way of preserving a more traditional rhetorical contact between readers and writers constructed a knowable community of discourse that united its members and distinguished their social language from that of other audiences. The timed interval, later codified as weekly, monthly, or quarterly, also required strategy—for as the eighteenth-century journal invited its readers to become its writers, its text would become the counter in a serious game of symbolic reciprocity.

Binding together these small communities of readers and writers, the periodicals also, by the same gesture, diversified the larger public by organizing new audiences and introducing them into the widening cultural economy as paying readers. The sheer array of journals at a bookstall or a coffeehouse afforded the Englishman a veritable map of national reading. Such audience-building expanded that middle-class public whose very scope and diversity would, finally, work against the more traditional intimacy of reader and writer. As the journals multiplied, they registered the increasingly heterogeneous play of sociolects—the discourses of emerging professions, conflicting social spheres, men and women, the cultivated middle-class audience, and less sophisticated readerships. This contradictory role—cementing the small audience while subdividing the larger public—made the periodical a singular but socially unstable institution for defining, individualizing, and expanding the audiences who inhabited the greater cultural landscape.

We will see why such relations of reading and writing had to be largely swept away in the 1790s. Eighteenth-century journals had organized English audiences by forming the "reading habit," but after 1790 that habit became the scene of a cultural struggle demanding a new mental map of the complex public and its textual desires, a new way to organize audiences according to their ideological dispositions, their social distances, and the paradoxically intense pressure of their proximity as audiences. But it is also important to see that earlier-eighteenth-century relations of reading and writing were not—as theorists of the "public sphere" require—stable or fixed. They had to be worked out strategically according to the cultural dynamics they formed.

I

Today the "letters to the editor" page remains a faint vestige of what once constituted a periodical's whole mode of public discourse. Peter Motteux combined letters from "correspondents" with his own essays in *The Gentleman's Journal* (1692–94); John Dunton made the *Athenian Mercury* (1691–97) a forum of readers' questions and his answers. Addison and Steele invited letters in the opening issue of the *Spectator*, printing twenty-one readers' letters within the first month. This practice invited as much reader skepticism as participation, since readers wished to know if editors were not really fictionalizing the letters to create the effect of an enjoined public discourse. Defoe flatly denied that his *Review* invented its readers' letters, but Addison's much more equivocal response in *Spectator* 271 implies an intricately knotted relationship between reader and writer:

> I receive a double Advantage from the Letters of my Correspondents; first, as they shew me which of my Papers are most acceptable to them, and in the next place, as they furnish me with Materials for new Speculations. Sometimes indeed I do not make use of the Letter itself, but form the Hints of it into Plans of my own Invention, sometimes I take the Liberty to change the Language or Thought into my own way of speaking and thinking, and always (if it can be done without prejudice to the Sense) omit the many Compliments and Applauses which are usually bestowed upon me.[8]

This writer uses his "correspondents" to calculate his audience, to regenerate his own discourse, and, in a moment of extraordinary license, to absorb the reader's language into his own to produce a dialogic "way of speaking and thinking" in which "Addison" can no longer be confidently sorted out from his interlocutors. In this surprising reversal, the writer not only does not fictionalize his audience; he "speaks" it. The reciprocity of reader and writer becomes so fundamental to the discourse that it must be suspected even where the style is apparently the monological signature of the writer himself.

Just before printing three more correspondents' letters in *Spectator* 271, Addison struggles to distinguish this peculiar nexus between writer and audience from what anyone might suspect, the invention of an "ideal" reader in whom the writer projects his best self: "Some will have it, that I often write to my self, and am the only punctual Correspondent I have. This Objection would indeed be material, were the Letters I communicate to the

Publick stuffed with my own Commendations." The absence of rhetorical praise guarantees an *enjoined* rather than self-confirming discourse, a community of reading and writing and not a projection upon the public. What the "spectator" views and writes about is confirmed by a return of his discourse and a reassuringly slight shift of optical stance.

That readers might exchange roles with writers is not merely an underlying faith of eighteenth-century periodical writing, but an arrangement that must be constantly tested. The monthly "miscellany" journals—from Edward Cave's *Gentleman's Magazine* (1731) and Percival Stockdale's *Universal Magazine* (1747) to Richard Phillips' *Monthly Magazine* (1796)— appeared to be written by their own readers, who signed articles with mock-Roman pseudonyms as though they were personal letters. This letter format lent the magazines a peculiar resemblance to the epistolary novel, perhaps one of those links between journalism and prose fiction Lennard Davis has described as the "news/novel" discourse out of which fiction only fitfully distinguished itself from fact.[9] The purposive confusion between the fictive and the actual extended to audiences as well as the to epistemological status of writing. Each journal offered itself as a tightly knit community of readers and writers who revolve between reading roles and writing roles, the very image of Sartre's seventeenth-century France.

In 1790, at the brink of a cultural shift that would follow upon the "moral earthquake" of the French Revolution, James Anderson published, in his new journal the Edinburgh *Bee*, an interpretation of eighteenth-century periodical reading and writing at the moment such practices were to become obsolete. When Anderson calls this kind of reading and writing "periodical performance," he accentuates its theatricality. But his main point is that in this performance, the audience exchanges places with the performers. Mere reading is incomplete, like observing life passively from a window; but to write is to participate in the life of the street.[10] Reading and writing are not fixed functions but performing roles to be exchanged. Because periodicals are published at timed intervals, "full liberty is given for every individual to become a writer when he feels a propensity to it, without any farther limitation than good manners and becoming politeness requires" (170). Thus the fundamentally creative rather than passive eighteenth-century reader can claim with Corregio, "*ed io anche son pittore*: and I also am a painter" (169). Here, where there is "liberty given for every individual to become a writer" (170), freedom of access to writing gives periodical writing the aura of the democratic and communal—the very opposite, the *Bee* argues, of clerical language, that dictatorial discourse cast down from the pulpit (171). Periodical writing is antithetical to the sermonic; it is a mode of *interdiscourse*, a text of "equality" where "men of all ranks" leave their social identities at the door of what the *Bee* calls the "masquerade" of periodical performance (14).

Yet this democratic "exchange" of reading and writing depends on a hierarchical notion of the public, implying an intricate social chain of "ranks," "gradations," and "degrees." The social text of periodical writing thus joins two dissonant orders: inside the text, a communal, democratic exchange; outside the text, a hierarchically ranked world. The *Bee*'s "unbounded equality" of periodical writing divides the lives men lead in print from their lives in the real, finely blended social order that this writing momentarily displaces. Effacing social differences, the pages of a journal become a phantom social world—an alternative society of the text.

It is not hard to see why the *Bee* would insist on this purely textual community in the late eighteenth century. Peter Hohendahl makes face-to-face contact central to England's earlier-eighteenth-century "public sphere": "In principle, social privileges were not acknowledged whenever private citizens gathered together as a public body. In the reading societies and clubs, status was suspended so that a discussion among equals could take place." Eagleton puts this point more theoretically: "The sphere of cultural discourse and the realm of social power are closely related but not homologous: the former cuts across the latter and suspends the distinctions of the latter, deconstructing and reconstituting it in a new form, temporarily transposing its 'vertical' gradations onto a 'horizontal' plane."[11] But by 1790, the public sphere had itself become an image to be consumed by readers who did not frequent it. The journal displaces the public gathering place: the *Bee* offers itself to the late-eighteenth-century reader as a *portable* coffeehouse:

Men of all ranks, and of all nations, however widely disjoined from each other, may be said to be brought together here to converse at their ease, without ceremony or restraint, as at a masquerade, where, if a propriety of dress and expression be observed, nothing else is required. A man, after the fatigues of the day are over, may thus sit down in his elbow chair, and together with his wife and family, be introduced, as it were, into a spacious coffee house, which is frequented by men of all

nations, who meet together for their mutual entertainment and improvement. (14)

This "society of the text" brings into the after-hours realm of familial pri-
vacy the wider discourse of a public sphere. But if the public sphere now
seems more "public" than ever, it has become a representation instead of a
practice and, as the 1790s will reveal, an image losing much of its force.

By representing the public sphere as a space without social differences,
the periodical projects its audience as that collective formation which has
momentarily displaced its own social origins—a figure which either does
not actually exist or does not *yet* exist in society as presently ordered. This
means the periodical text can be a space for imagining social formations
still inchoate, and a means to give them shape. One of the *Gentleman's
Magazine's* most important functions was to form as an audience, not "gentlemen" in the traditional sense of the landed gentry, but gentlemen in
what Robert Mayo calls the "enlarged Augustan sense," which included the
upper clergy, professionals, well-educated manufacturers and merchants, as
well as gentlemen themselves. This "informed minority" constituted an
emerging alliance between the gentry and the *haute bourgeoisie* which, as
the English liked to remind themselves, contrasted—to the Englishman's
credit—with the Continent's inflexible class boundaries. Cave's magazine
carved its audience among the landed gentry and the upper middle class
and, as Crane Brinton remarked a half-century ago, helped achieve "the
conversion of a large part of the gentry to a culture which was certainly not
'gentle.'[12] Traffic between the gentry and bourgeoisie flowed as wealthy entrepreneurs bought into country houses and gentlemen learned the modes
of profit, but the *Gentleman's Magazine* galvanized this traffic as an audience with articles that valorize work and industry for landed readers still
learning the ways of the capitalist. Stylistically, the journal deploys the personal pronouns of power, the "I" and "you" pronominal forms of address
characteristic not only of politesse but of textual community. Readers exchanged roles with writers as Cave devoted more and more of his journal to
"original correspondence." He was to find that the resulting "society of the
text" could both acculturate and solidify a social stratum still coming into
being.

Thus the twofold function of the "society of the text": to cement an
audience of divergent social ranks as equal interlocutors, and to galvanize a
new audience previously unrepresented in the universe of public discourse.
In 1790, James Anderson's *Bee* could present this universe as incomplete,

still taking shape as periodicals acquired new sectors of the greater English public. As the public journals reached across the ranks and orders of society, they seemed to form "one great society" of readers. Perhaps irresistibly, Anderson could not avoid making comparisons between this reach across the social network and the British trader's reach across the greater globe. As another expanding order that drew social groups within its grasp, colonialism offered an almost inevitable metaphor for the universalizing of public discourse in the periodicals. The journal, one might say, built the greater reading public by colonizing social groups previously excluded from it:

> Nor does the editor confine his views to Britain alone. The world *at large* he considers as the proper theatre for literary improvements, and the whole human race, as constituting but one great society, whose general advancement in knowledge must tend to augment the prosperity of all its parts. . . . British traders are now to be found in all nations on the globe; and the English language begins to be studied as highly useful in every country. By means of the universal intercourse which that trade occasions, and the general utility of this language, he hopes to be able to establish a mutual exchange of knowledge, and to effect a friendly literary intercourse among all nations. . . till it shall comprehend every individual of the human race. (viii–ix)

A vast ambition for a small Edinburgh weekly journal, but Anderson proposes to begin with his own expected audience: "those classes of men who are engaged in the active pursuits of business. . . being at present in a great measure excluded from the circle of literary intelligence," among them the possible readers of "agriculture, manufactures, and commerce" as well as clergy not "possessed of affluence" (viii). For such readers the *Bee* carefully adapts "the particular form of this work, the mode of its publication, and the price at which it is offered." Hence the periodical writer both names and colonizes the social group to whom he writes, drawing into the public those still unincorporated into the universe of public discourse. Every decision of style, topics, print size, page format, and above all the particular frame of its textual community is geared toward that discursive colonialism. That the periodical text can be both a discourse among equals *and* a colonizer of audiences presents no contradiction to Anderson's *Bee*. Such a contradiction appears plain enough to us: "Far from being a type of conversation among equals," Edward Said writes, "the discursive situation is usually like the unequal relation between colonizer and colonized."[13] But the eighteenth-century periodical writer must have it both ways. He cannot imagine his own audience without conceiving its place, often quite precisely, in the greater, well-nigh international and thus universal public through which it reveals its own particular shape.

The paradox in this strategy for defining a readership is that the more specific the audience sought, the more one at the same time constructs the vast, totalized audience in which all readerships find their place. Hence the differences between particular audiences do not imply discontinuous discourses. In the *Bee's* grandly colonial vision of popular writing, journals as different as the *Gentleman's* and the *Bee* articulate a single, continuous, and expanding public speech act. They structure readerships as rough parallels to English social ranks. The idea of a wide audience excites the eighteenth-century periodical writer because he still sees it framed within a general public style (however modified for a particular audience), through which he may organize an infinite number of readers. This stylistic idea resembles the ideal language Defoe envisions for a popular audience: "If any man were to ask me, what I would suppose to be a perfect style, or language, I would answer, that in which a man speaking to five hundred people, all of common and various capacities, should be understood by them all, in the same sense in which the speaker intended to be understood."[14] Defoe imagines an audience of tradesmen; Cave projects an audience of gentlemen and rich manufacturers; Anderson, a readership of businessmen and lesser clergy. The language and format of each journal must first be "adapted" to the specific readership being solicited. But beneath these evident differences lies another, ideally transparent, univocal language that encourages the periodical writer to form audiences as a stone makes ripples in a lake: in a "widening circle." Those concentric circles of reading describe both the "unbounded equality" of exchange within each circle and the distinctions between circles—the way all ranks are intricately connected, yet also distinct. If eighteenth-century England knew a "public sphere," it was in this qualified, dualistic sense. But in the 1790s, when such a sphere could no longer be assumed, writers renounced the "widening circle" and everything it implied.

II

While the French Revolution prepared the way for a new capitalist mode of production in France, for nineteenth-century English writers it inaugurated a new mode of cultural production. "Since the interesting era of the French Revolution," remarked a study of periodical writing published in 1824, "the people of these Kingdoms have been an inquisitive, prying, doubting and reading people. . . . Their feelings received then an extraordinary impetus." In 1852, William Chambers reminded his readers of "the manner in which the French Revolution operated in directly changing the form of English literature . . . in giving a new shape, style, and character to the productions of our periodical press."[15] The fierceness of political conflict would be sublated into an extraordinary mental energy, accomplished and recognized in the periodicals themselves. The volcanic "moral earthquake" of the revolution, as *Blackwood's* put it, converted the moribund public discourse of the later eighteenth century into the "fertile soil" of the nineteenth-century discursive field.[16] In such cultural soil, the widening circle of audiences and its ideal exchange of reader and writer could not cushion the revolution's dislocating shocks against traditional English social arrangements and their structured reading public.

By the 1690s, the English postal service, the London coffeehouses, and the new periodicals had combined to form a widening network of public discourse. But in the 1790s, the radical "corresponding societies," the London taverns where they held meetings, and the radical pamphlets and periodicals they read composed another network, instantly notorious. Thomas Paine's *The Rights of Man* could not have reached its 50,000 readers (for Part I) and eventually 200,000 readers (Parts I and II combined) without this ad-hoc distribution. Alehouses displaced coffeehouses as centers of this insurgent public discourse, where artisan radicals gathered, as the shoemaker Thomas Hardy put it, "on the principle of the representative system."[17] Radical journals—Thomas Spence's *Pig's Meat; or, Salmagundy for Swine* (1793), Daniel Eaton's *Hog's Wash; or, Politics for the People* (1793); William Taylor's Norwich *Cabinet* (1794)—collected an artisan's "great tradition," composed of Old Testament prophets, Swift's and Pope's satires, Shakespeare, and the translated *philosophes*, particularly Rousseau and Volney. But if Addison imagined each of his *Spectator* copies was read by twenty coffeehouse readers (60,000 per issue), English ministers imagined much larger assemblies reading and quoting *The Rights of Man*, making its potent epigrammatical language the mode, in Paine's phrase, of a political "style of thinking and expression different to what had been customary in England."[18]

Different to be sure: Paine's language introduced a symbolic violence into English political discourse, outvoicing even Burke's high hyperbole: "Aristocracy has never more than one child. The rest are begotten to be devoured. They are thrown to the cannibal for prey, and the natural parent prepares the unnatural repast" (*Rights of Man*, 63). Radical language, as we will see in Chapter 4, did not abandon classical rhetorical discourse for a "plain" language of the English common man, as is often argued. It transformed rhetoric into new terms, confronting the radical audience rhetorically rather than, as so many middle-class writers were learning to do, using language to incorporate readers into the very texture of discourse. Like the classical rhetorician, the radical writer assumes an explicit, collectively acknowledged set of conventions and tropes to govern the discursive occasion. Politically egalitarian, the radical rhetorician nevertheless maintains the distance between speaking or writing, on the one hand, and listening or reading on the other. This refusal of authorial intimacy, which the middle-class writer hoped to achieve with his own reader, may be seen as simply an authoritarian stance, lording the privilege of writing over the passivity of reading. But the middle-class writers' desire to merge writing and reading in the same act—with its hope of an ultimate textual intimacy—is also the desire to efface what Pierre Bourdieu calls the "economy of linguistic exchanges": the power relations that enforce the bonds between readers and writers themselves. When radical writers question the right of their antagonists to represent all England, they also interrogate the economy of linguistic exchanges which allows them to speak.[19]

Still, the greatest impact of radical writing could not be measured by its published works. Paine, Thelwall, Spence, and others not only created an audience in the 1790s; they opened up a disturbing darkness in the middle-class mind. The radicals' middle-class and aristocratic antagonists, despite their rhetoric of exclusion, failed to expel radical discourse wholly onto cultural margins or into public jails. Often middle-class writers like Arthur Young came to form their own readerships around a shadowy, antithetical figure—the radical in the text.

Young has been mostly overlooked in the polemical spectacle that engaged Paine, Burke, and other interlocutors of the "Revolution debate." He did not belong to that left-liberal circle—Horne Tooke, Joseph Priestley, John Thelwall, Daniel Eaton, William Godwin, William Blake, Joseph Johnson, Paine, Mary Wollstonecraft, and others—who composed what Marilyn Butler calls "a community of writers, personally known to one another, at first, especially, the writer-readers of a shared project."[20] By 1792 Young—a famed exponent of advanced capitalist agricultural methods in his technical periodical, *Annals of Agriculture*—stood oddly alone, a kind of botched Addison.[21] Success and failure in a range of periodical publishing and writing ventures made him a proleptic sociologist of culture, and in that sense his *Travels in France* (1792) encloses rather than joins the revolution debate.

Young collided with the revolution almost by accident. His *Travels in France*, published three months after Part II of *The Rights of Man*, accounts for three years' travel, in a two-part work whose diary follows the form of his earlier *Tours* of England, Wales, and Ireland (1768, 1769, 1780), while its economic analysis of agriculture follows the main lines of his *Political Arithmetic* of 1774. When *Travels in France* was translated into French in 1793, the Convention ordered some 20,000 copies for distribution to each of the communes.[22] No doubt the Convention had less interest in English tourism or farming than in Young's reluctant but firm conviction that ancien régime France demanded revolutionary change. This persuasion Young documented with daily, detailed accounts of agricultural waste, aristocratic indifference to social decay, and the hot struggles of the poor. Like Wordsworth, Young diligently tried to understand the revolution's complicated theories and bafflingly abrupt shifts of political temperature. Like the poet he also searched through the revolutionary pamphlets and newspapers, hoping for texts to give apparently chaotic events "a form and body" (*Prelude*, 1850, 9.105).[23] No French text could provide him one, but as Young registered the revolution's daily jolts, another, absent order seemed to form an alternative to prerevolutionary decay and the revolutionary energy it invited. Arthur Young would call this form "circulation," an elastic notion of an order that may be at once physiological, economic, cultural, psychological, and even textual. As a cultural metaphor "circulation" becomes in Young's *Travels* a powerful diviner of cultural practices like reading and writing, for an England in which a French-inspired radical discourse now seemed, in mid–1792, to disseminate everywhere.

As he first encounters it, the Gallic landscape is a ruin, a massive wasteland punctuated by hoarded wealth, a nation of fragments. Habituated at home to circumstances that "lead the mind by some gradation to a change," the English traveler's mind boggles when he oscillates violently between French hovels and palaces, or the rutted roads and "noble causeways of Louis XIV's *ancien regime*" (*Travels in France*, 36). "There are no gentle transitions from ease to comfort, from comfort to wealth," Young complains in 1787. "You pass at once from beggary to profusion" (96). Without any mediating social forms, Young finds no degrees or gradations that connect all "orders" one to another in a ceaseless connecting chain. There is no middle in this social hierarchy, and the loss of a middle, rather than any particular indignation at beggary itself, unsettles the Englishman's sense of order and completion. "Circulation is stagnant in France" (47).

The abyss between country and city, or between class and class, appeared to him most symptomatically in French modes of reading and writing themselves. With some authority Young notes that French agricultural societies of 1787 "meet, converse, offer premiums and publish nonsense. This is not of much consequence," he pointedly adds, "for the people, instead of reading their memoirs, are not able to read at all" (21). Provincial towns go without newspapers, and at Château-Thierry, the traveler asks in vain after a coffeehouse, that privileged site of eighteenth-century English reading. Young's reaction is typical: "What stupidity, and poverty, and want of circulation! This people hardly deserve to be free." No pattern of reading and writing binds the French together, and thus they remain enveloped in their own distinctive class languages. Here Young records, in a famous encounter that would become emblematic of the ancien régime for both English and French readers, the language of the poor: "She had seven children, and the cow's milk helped to make the soup. But why, instead of a horse, do you not keep another cow? Oh, her husband could not carry his produce so well without a horse; and asses are little used in the country. It was said, at present, that *something was to be done by some great folks for such poor ones, but she did not know who nor how, but God send us better, car les tailles & les droits nous écrasent*" (144). Against the faltering syntax of the poor, Young counterposes the overrefined conversation of French gentlemen, which leaves no distinguishing marks of individual minds: "The mingled mass of communicated ideas has powers neither to offend nor instruct . . . conversation is like a journey on an endless flat." (34).

Too strongly marked, or blandly unmarked, these oral styles both deindividualize and classify their speakers, collapsing all differentiation of the "degrees" that Young finds the only guarantee of social and cultural order. Thus the Englishman reads French society in terms of language metaphors that bend his perceptions away from chains of connection toward ominous marks of opposition. Earlier such contrasts appeared in the stilted sentences of the poor or the chatter of the polite. But in the political crisis of 1789, they appear to Young as hieroglyphics, a kind of writing on the body:

This was one of the most striking instances of the impression made on men of different ranks by great events. In the streets, and in the church of St. Louis, such anxiety was in every face, that the importance of the moment was written on the physiognomy; and all the common forms and salutations of habitual civility lost in attention: but amongst a class so much higher as those I dined with, I was struck with the difference. There were not, in thirty persons, five in whose countenances you could guess that any extraordinary event was going forward: more of the conversation was indifferent than I would have expected. (122)

In a moment of crisis, social classes now seem to confront each other as the marked and the unmarked, their conflict unblurred by any mediations ("common forms and salutations of habitual civility"). French social order momentarily appears as a sheet of paper, written upon on one side, blank on the other—a paper upon which historical crisis itself "writes." In this perspective by incongruity, the metaphor of writing renders the revolutionary instant—which Young otherwise finds mysteriously opaque—suddenly meaningful. The written-upon page becomes a trope of class conflict. But class conflict also appears as though it can be textually mastered, as nothing finally more or less complex than what happens with pen and paper.

For Arthur Young, the revolution hinges precisely upon reading and writing. He explains the ancien régime's failure to prevent the revolution as an absence of those circulatory habits of reading and writing that preserve a saving class consciousness:

[They have] no meetings, no associations among them; no union with military men; no taking of refuge in the ranks of regiments to defend or avenge their cause; fortunately for France, they fall without a struggle and die without a blow. That universal circulation of intelligence, which in England transmits the least vibration of feeling or alarm, with electric sensibility, from one end of the kingdom to another, and which unites in bands of connection men of similar interests and situations, has no existence in France. Thus it may be said, perhaps with truth, that the fall of King, court, lords, nobles, army, church, and parliaments proceeds from a want of intelligence being quickly circulated, consequently from the very effects of that thraldom in which they held the people: it is therefore a retribution rather than a punishment. (160)

Like hoarded wealth and unenclosed wastelands, like the facial responses of different classes to political crisis, the absence of a network of newspapers and periodicals and the national nervous system they create can be comprehended as a failure to "circulate." England's own circulatory system, now a century old, unites in "bands of connection" that class of Englishmen whose habit is to read.

Young's language, however, suggests a power of circulatory form more complex than the availability of newspapers. Long before Young's insistent use of this term in *Travels in France*, "circulation" had acquired metaphorical resonances as a symptom of national growth. Defoe's paean to commerce traces England's powerful growth to the home trade and its "circulation of trade within ourselves, where all the several manufactures move in a just rotation from the several countries where they are made, to the city of *London*, as the blood in the body to the Heart." That physico-economic metaphor could be infinitely expansive. In Blake's "body of Albion," circulatory form energizes the visionary national form by connecting and vitalistically transforming all the discrete activities isolated by a deadening empiricism; and in the nineteenth century De Quincey would draw on the same metaphor to describe the English mail coach system: "the conscious presence of a central intellect, that, in the midst of vast distances—of storms, of darkness, of danger—overruled all obstacles into one steady cooperation to a national result." Such is the "systole and diastole of the national intercourse."[24]

In his *Political Arithmetic* Young himself joined the tradition of economic thinking, from Aristotle to Condillac, Hume, and Adam Smith, that locates surplus wealth in the circulation of money, the tradition Marx sought laboriously to refute in the "Money" chapter of *Capital*.[25] Arthur Young apprehends the power of circulation as literally in the cultural realm as he did in the economic. Cultural circulation means for Young an intricately prepared system of channels through which people, things, or writings connect and move. Its economic and physiological senses always adhere to its use to describe patterns of reading and writing. Nor can its intricate movements be limited to the cardiovascular system of the social body: circulation also means the synaptic firings of the political ganglia. "London," argues a panoramic description of the great metropolis in 1804, "is, in no point of view, more remarkable than as a center of publication and of intelligence for the whole empire. In the incessant reception and diffusion of all the fugitive history of the time, it seems to discharge a part not unlike that of the heart in the circulation of the blood, or that by which the brain performs the chief functions in the nervous system."[26]

Thus this infinitely adaptable metaphor represents not only the channels through which newspapers and other texts move among their readers, but also those channels of the *mind* prepared by particular acts of writing. This is a moment in *Travels in France* when Young's revulsion at the possibility of revolution in England bursts through his usual reserve. As the orators of the Estates-General quarrel about the definition of "the people," Young retorts:

> So the mob plunder, burn, and destroy, in complete ignorance: and yet, with all these shades of darkness, this universal mass of ignorance, there are men every day in the States [Estates-General], who are puffing themselves off for the First Nation in Europe! the Greatest People in the Universe! as if the political juntos, or literary circles of a capital constituted a people; instead of the universal illumination of knowledge, acting by rapid intelligence on minds prepared by habitual energy of reasoning to receive, combine, and comprehend it. (159)

What ultimately must circulate is a discourse that can create patterns of reception in the minds of its social readers. Here circulating seems to involve both the way writing is distributed within an intricate, systematic social network *and* the way it is produced by the writer. By such special acts of circulating—repeated acts of certain kinds of writing and reading—a public is shaped to read discourses in deliberate, directed ways.

For readers are *made*, created as a public through a network of circulatory channels and the writer who consciously directs the reader's "habitual energy of reasoning." This is the "reading habit," cultural dispositions formed by a circulatory network of texts and a purposive act of audience-making. From the rhetorical turns of a writer's sentences to the network of channels that circulate writings among readers, Young's "circulation" becomes a crucial investment of what Pierre Bourdieu calls "cultural capital."[27] Such capital is not a stock of particular ideological positions, nor even a particular content. (As Young's subsequent texts would show, he could take up and discard such positions as the political winds veered.) It is, rather, a framework of reading, a habitual energy, a mode of reception and comprehension. That mode must be inscribed in language as well as in social relations, in prose style as well as in publishing institutions. For if readers are not thus *made*, Young will insist, they can be spontaneously called forth by "visionaries," purveyors of "theoretic" systems, and others who stand outside the circulatory system and threaten its unifying order.

This half-articulated notion of circulation guides Arthur Young's sense of what his own writing accomplishes. For even if circulation mediates all oppositions and social contrasts, setting into motion various kinds of wealth in a complex national exchange, Young nevertheless envisions its opposite and, in 1792, a particular English text that represents the very antithesis of circulation. In France, the revolution generates a discourse that threatens a circulatory order and engulfs the primitive French pattern of reading and writing. Even as he denounced it, Young grew fascinated with the effusion of French radical literature and later brought back to England satchels full of Jacobin revolutionary writings.[28] Yet Young scolds the ancien régime for allowing seditious reading matter to spread among the people, for the most remarkable sign of the new historical dawn is that "a spirit of reading political tracts, they say, spreads into provinces, so that all the presses of France are equally employed" (104). Where London forms the circulatory heart but not the absolute center of British writing and reading, Paris tells the provinces what and how to read. There are no Edinburghs, Sheffields, Bristols, Manchesters, or Norwiches that prevent the capital's domination of discourse. Radical writing, Young suspects, radiates outward from an authoritarian center, constructed and now forsaken by the ancien régime itself.

For Young this radical writing constitutes a kind of negative circulation—in fact, it does not circulate at all, but "disseminates": "I am all amazement at the ministry permitting such nests and hot-beds of sedition and revolt, which disseminate amongst the people, every hour, principles that by and by must be opposed with vigour, and therefore it seems little short of madness to allow the propagation at present" (105). To circulate is to follow a path, however circuitous or labyrinthine its windings, along an ordered itinerary; in this motion, a cultural profit accrues. Circulation, to paraphrase Marx's remark about money, secretes the reading habit from every pore. But to "disseminate" is to flood through interstices of the social network, into the social cracks of the ancien régime. Dissemination takes place where there is no circulation, where there are no preformed patterns to guide the flow of language or ideas. What is disseminated "propagates" or reproduces itself without the orderly expansion of circulation.[29] For Young, such "propagating" is *propaganda*, a form of language where readers are not (as for example in Young's own style) led to be persuaded through a highly qualified process of common reasoning between reader and writer. "Principles" disseminate, and Young—who rejects "theoretic systems" and embraces "perfect examples"—exclaims that "in revolutions, one rascal writes and an hundred thousand fools believe" (154). Nothing is more anathema to Young's own style than the style of radical discourse, with its unvarnished assertion of principle, its firm oppositional structuring, and its explicit rhetoric. The style of circulation conflates the distance between reader and writer; the radical writer accentuates it. Through this play of metaphors, Young thus sketches the problematic of the middle-class writer and the emerging radical public of writers like Thomas Paine.

For it is Paine that Young has uppermost in mind. While Young was completing *Travels in France* in 1791 and 1792, Paine's work was finding its artisan public among members of the corresponding societies who met and read in British taverns. That fact was not lost on Arthur Young, for whom a topography of reading can distinguish the qualities and implications of the ways people read. In an early *Spectator*, Addison had located his readers at the tea table and the coffeehouse, and when Coleridge in 1795 tried to find the line to be drawn between "ranks possessing intercourse with each other" and the lower orders whom the philosopher should "teach their Duties in order that he may render them susceptible of their rights," he found that line "between the Parlour and the Kitchen, the Tap and the Coffee-Room—there is a gulph that may not be passed."[30] Arthur Young imagines that social sites of reading also distinguish the languages of circulation and dissemination. The middle-class reader gravitates to sunlit coffeehouses and breathes their air of freely ventilated opinions. But radical writing festers in dark, moist places—among "assemblies in alehouse kitchens, clubbing their pence to have the *Rights of Man* read to them" (*Travels in France*, 465). Alehouse kitchens become hidden, dangerous folds in the social fabric, the site of illegitimate reading, as though a radical disseminating discourse itself were intoxicating, bypassing the carefully prepared channels of middle-class circulatory patterns to put in their place the fermenting of radical subculture.

For his own readers, who had more probably heard about Paine's writing than read it, Arthur Young represents radical writing as a shadowy presence that forces middle-class readers and writers to define their own ethos of reading and writing against it. Circulation no longer can embrace the harmonies of a "public sphere" where reading and writing may be exchanged. Such acts cannot be the practices of a middle class whose ordered hierarchy of ranks will now be cast in doubt, a class that cannot be sure it is still the "middle." In the older world Joseph Addison had plunged into the Royal Exchange, where he discovered an ordered center that confirmed the middle-class reader's topographical place. London marked the center of the world, the stock exchange the center of London, and at the heart of the Exchange stood the merchant who would "find work for the Poor" and "add Wealth to the Rich."[31] No such confidence in the middle-class reader's place between rich and poor is visible in writers like Arthur Young, who sees in French class conflict the spectre of imminent English class rupture. Thus the notion of circulation defines a middle-class movement *outward* into the social world, incorporating all social and mental activities within it. Yet at the same time, this extension outward needs some resistance against which to define its own movement: circulation must have an antagonist, a dissemination which constitutes the writing and reading of the "lower orders." To the extent that an orderly structure of ranks no longer defines the function of being middle class, the latter must find another social force against which its own activity assumes definitive shape.

In the eighteenth century, the "reading habit" had been formed by writers in the very texture of prose, organized by publishers and distributors, located at preferred sites of reading, engraved in repeated neurophysiological acts of an audience. Yet as Arthur Young's and Coleridge's sense of that habit show, it cannot be a universal habit. It must always be politically and socially defined. Coleridge echoes both William Godwin and Arthur Young when he writes, in 1795, "Truth, I doubt not, is omnipotent to a mind already disciplined for its reception; but assuredly the overworked laborer, skulking into an alehouse, is not likely to exemplify the one or prove the other."[32] Such a claim for truth is profoundly tautological, the logic of habit itself. The Truth will always already be recognized as the Truth by a mind habituated to receive it. To thus habituate readers will be the most profound task of nineteenth-century writers, as Wordsworth announces in his paradoxical desideratum, the necessity of "*creating* the taste by which [the writer] is to be enjoyed." For the classical aristocracy, "taste" was precisely that quality which could not be created, the natural expressivity of the class whose destiny was its cultural inheritance. Only the middle class would need to determine consciously the nature of its tastes, and the act of writing for a middle-class public in the eighteenth century could be the perpetual making of a consensual taste only as long as that public remained middle class and firmly convinced of its place in the great hierarchy of ranks. The cultural jolt of the 1790s cast that place deeply in doubt.

The "reading habit" becomes a textual domain of all cultural habits. But this is a habit that must be deliberately formed, and it can be formed only by texts and by the conscious acts of writing that produce them. The special demands of the reading habit may be glimpsed in Wordsworth's struggle to define it in the *Preface* of 1800, where he locates two realms of the habitual—the rustic's natural habits uncorrupted by history, and the middle-class audience's habits formed by unprecedented historical change and debased by popular cultural production. That this audience "craves" the "stupid German tragedies" it consumes betrays its absorption in a particular habitus, which Wordsworth attributes to war, economic crisis, overpopulation in cities, and the degrading "uniformity of their occupations." Since a properly functioning taste would express its preferences rather than its cravings, "creating taste" means overcoming the stranglehold of the urban middle-class habitus by transforming the reading habit. Such a task can be accomplished only in that very medium of the habitual, language itself. Whether what both Wordsworth and Coleridge call "the best part of language" derives from deeply rooted habit, or from the mind's reflections on its own acts, would remain for Coleridge to argue vigorously in the *Biographia Literaria*.[33] But for Wordsworth, language allows the writer to transform the effects of the habitus by means of remaking the reading habit. Its reformation will in turn *rehabilitate* the mind made dull and torpid by the material conditions of the late eighteenth century which produced the middle-class habitus in the first place. In other words, a certain reading habit *must* be formed if Wordsworth's audience is to escape the material impact of the destructive urban habitus itself.

It is no accident that Coleridge and Wordsworth, increasingly committed to redefining the political realm in terms of cultural practices, both planned periodicals, the very locale of the reading habit. Wordsworth dropped his proposal to William Mathews to publish jointly a weekly journal, but Coleridge plunged ahead with the *Watchman*, which he headlined with the motto "That All may know the TRUTH; And that the TRUTH may make us FREE!" As he had written in 1795, however, Truth was not for everyone. The "All" of his motto had to be rigorously selected during personal tours of Bristol and the Midlands to secure subscribers. That careful selection of his audience owed something, no doubt, to Arthur Young, whose *Travels in France* Coleridge quotes generously in the Prospectus he used to enlist his readers. These readers would be inventors, members of the Bristol Lunar Society, amateur engineers, venture-capital entrepreneurs, and other middle-class Dissenters, mounting up to an audience of nearly a thousand.[34] But within the liberal middle-class limits of his intended public, Coleridge imagined an "all" whose response would be as consensual in its recognition of Truth as those "societies of the text" envisioned in the older monthly and weekly journals of Cave and Anderson. Who would not be surprised then, when, with each issue of the *Watchman*, large parts of this audience peeled away like the layers of an ideological onion? An essay against fast days lost him "nearly five hundred subscribers at one blow," and a blast against "French *psilosophy*" turned away the paper's "Jacobin and Democratic Patrons."[35] Nor could Coleridge elicit enough correspondents to even imagine turning the journal into a place where readers and writers regularly exchanged roles. No society of the text for this periodical audience! Public discourse had become an ideological minefield, and the passively "spectating," "idling," or "rambling" eighteenth-century periodical writer had now, in the new discursive field, become a vigilant, censorious "watchman." In such conditions it was no longer enough to "*know* the Truth that it will make us Free!" For Coleridge had assumed in the *Watchman* a prior state of habituation, a set of minds already disciplined for his truth, that had now proven to be a mirage. The mind of the middle-class audience would now have to be *formed* to know the Truth, shaped in those deliberate ways he would begin to essay in *The Friend* and not complete until *On the Constitution of Church and State*. That effort still lay on the other side of his encounter with German philosophy, but its necessity seems to have been already clear when Coleridge wearily resigned his *Watchman* for having "watched in vain!"[36] Contrary to James Anderson's and the young Coleridge's hopes, readerships were no longer waiting to be discovered and acculturated; they could not be colonized. They must, as Coleridge would come to understand in the most profound way, be *produced*, in the syntax of a sentence and the interpretive mode of a discourse.

III

New periodicals in the 1790s suggest the directions this making of audiences would take in the early nineteenth century. For what Voloshinov and Bakhtin called the struggle over the sign will also become, in this confusing historical moment, a struggle over the kind of reading habits needed to activate those signs. Audiences will be formed that learn their identity as audiences only by becoming aware of the pressure of other audiences, interpretively and socially competing for position in cultural and social space. For Coleridge the most important of these publics were the radical audience and the fissuring of a middle-class public into cultivated and what we should now call "mass" readerships. Those boundaries already became faintly visible in the 1790s, where the political and economic dislocations that led Wordsworth toward his own taste-making act of writing also generated experiments in periodical writing that nineteenth-century writers would take up with the most telling effect.

As Richard Phillips and Joseph Johnson published the first *Monthly Magazine* in February 1796, they did not classify its readers as gentlemen, merchants, tradesmen, or any other familiar eighteenth-century social group. Rather, their journal held out for readers "the propagation of those liberal principles. . . which have been either deserted or virulently opposed by other Periodical Miscellanies."[37] Its ideal reader did not belong to a rigidly defined social category but rather responded to that loose collection of ideas called philosophical radicalism. For young English intellectuals who were fascinated and disturbed by revolutionary politics, utopian rationalism, psychological materialism, Unitarianism, and Dissent, the *Monthly Magazine* represented a new kind of ideologically cohesive discursive community. Like the miscellany journals, whose "original correspondence" format it followed, the *Monthly* collected readers and writers as interchangeable participants. But the political quality of their discourse made them, not a "society of the text" in the eighteenth-century sense, but a "polity" of the text which presupposed other, competing polities. To be sure, it was not a Jacobin, much less a party journal. Its cohesion lay at another level, what *Blackwood's Magazine*, paying tribute some thirty years later to this great precursor of its own public discourse, called with studied ambiguity "the serious." Not only did its lofty tone and chosen issues make older journals seem trivial, and the *Gentleman's Magazine* in particular uselessly antiquarian, but it also demanded those "serious" readers—book readers and self-styled intellectuals—who had earlier scorned periodical writing itself.[38] Later writers saw the *Monthly* as the first to form an audience for such journals as *Blackwood's*, *Fraser's*, the *London*, and the *Metropolitan* magazines of the early nineteenth century. In such journals a kind of "intelligentsia" would discover itself in contact (and contrast) with wider readerships. *Blackwood's* pointed to a curious cultural mutation in which readers first joined by the *Monthly* would later regroup according to a new division of intellectual labor. Professionals came to demand writings and journals devoted to their own specialties, while a purer, more free-floating intelligentsia would demand a periodical writing (like *Blackwood's*) which exercised its fecund capacity for self-reflection. Like the *Monthly Magazine* those periodicals would not simply "represent" a given social group or reflect it back to itself; now they would embody a principle, become actively ideological, and reshape the very contours and self-definitions of the readerships they addressed.

For the *Monthly Magazine* itself, liberal or radical principles were situational, useful at a time when the making and cultivating of "mind" was being fettered by a sclerotic English ancien régime. In one essay, for instance, "Are Mental Talents Productive of Happiness?" the writer first portrays "pleasures of intellect" which "give dignity and independence of character" as "incalculably more varied, more constant, more in the power of the individual, and less dependent upon local circumstances and external event." He describes the psychological ideal types of intellectual man and the self-indulgent, aristocratic "man of sense." But at the end, the writer turns this conventional contrast of character types toward contemporary politics, expanding his ideal intellectual man into a more specific middle-class intellectual facing intolerable contraints:

> The pains of intellect have hitherto, in many, or in most instances, overbalanced the pleasures; may not this have arisen from the peculiar and disordered states of society, rather than from the natural tendency of cultivation and refinement? A commercial country, the sole moving spring of which is pecuniary interest, must necessarily be unfavourable to those who, intent on mental improvement, require for their pursuit abstraction and leisure, by involving them in external difficulties. Honour, fame, and the pleasure which is found in the pursuit, rather than pecuniary gain, are supposed to constitute the recompence of literary eminence. Aristocratical and feudal institutions, by factious privileges and artificial distinctions, deprive merit of its encouragement, and talents of their just and natural reward. Talents, therefore, to adopt the commercial style, are not free to find their level. Monarchical and despotic governments, by their splendour, their allurements, and their terrors, have a tendency to debauch the taste, corrupt the heart, and fetter the mind, and afford a temptation to the prostitution of talents. These appear to be among the difficulties, the nature of which is to suppress, pervert, or impede, rather than awaken and stimulate, the intellectual powers. Whether republics may be less inimical to the production, the encouragement, and the reward of mental excellence, has not yet, perhaps, been sufficiently ascertained by experiment.[39]

Hemmed in on both sides, intellectual man escapes both mercantile and aristocratic fetters by embracing liberalism and its meritocracy of mental energy. After 1800, the *Monthly Magazine* would shed its "republicanism" like a fustian coat, but it remained the celebrant of intellectual man even while that ideology would be given a ringing new form in the prose of *Blackwood's*. Coleridge referred his few remaining readers of the *Watchman* to the *Monthly* in the same terms: "Long may it continue to deserve the support of the Patriot and the Philanthropist, and while it teaches Rational Liberty, prepare its readers for the enjoyment of it, strengthening the intellect by Science, and softening our affections by the Graces!"[40] That strengthening and softening was the action of a particular reading habit. For its early forming, writers of the early nineteenth century credited the *Monthly Magazine*, first organ of a newly self-conscious English middle-class reading audience.

If middle-class intellectuals found common cause with Jacobin artisans and the "useful and productive classes" between 1791 and 1795, their "apostasy" after 1795, for which Coleridge and Wordsworth have long stood as the most complex examples, followed what E. P. Thompson calls the "state of apartheid" between radical and working-class interests on the one hand and those properly bourgeois manufacturing and commercial interests on the other.[41] The *Monthly Magazine* reveals both the early radical/middle-class alliance and the later estrangement But the difference between radical artisan and radical middle-class audiences could already be glimpsed in the frenzy of radical publishing from 1792 to 1794. Daniel Eaton's *Politics for the People* (1794), for example, combines quotations from a long high-culture tradition of political dissent and its own gestures of defiance drawn from artisan culture's visceral politics of popular resistance. Eaton anthologized such essays as "The Origin of the Nobility" and "The History of England," passages from Godwin's *Enquiry into Political Justice*, and frequent passages from public speeches. These texts combine to form a curious code of the avowedly cultural and the very antithesis of cultural discourse, the body's resistance. Between passages from Shakespeare and Rousseau one could read "The Honest Cobbler":

Not many years ago an honest cobbler, who had a vote for a certain borough, being accosted by a court candidate for his vote, declared he would reserve it to the last; when being again applied to, to name his terms, why then, says honest Crispin, "kiss my arse are mine." The polite courtier, offended at such indelicacy, offered any sum, etc., but still Crispin was resolved, and "kiss my arse or no vote from me" was the resolution. The fate of the election depended on his single voice. The polite courtier complied, and the cobbler voted for *t'other side*, as his conscience directed; declaring that a scoundrel that could be mean enough to "kiss his arse" was unworthy of a seat in Parliament. May the nation never be without such like honest Crispins; and may all such, or other bribing scoundrels, be alike served at every election, and then the house will be without knaves, and the people with grievances.[42]

Confused by the slipperiness of the politician's cultural codes, the artisan employs his body to subvert them, the only move in the absence of a textual countercode of political discourse.

Paine had begun to produce one, but in the 1790s this language could only be elaborated in the systematic and theoretical prose of the Norwich *Cabinet*, whose neo-*philosophes* blended the thought of Rousseau, Godwin, and Paine in its arguments for political and natural rights. But where Paine could compress a social contradiction in a spare, resonant antithetical clause, *The Cabinet*'s writers belabored it in prolix, heavy-going prose:

> To convey to the rude minds of savages the tendencies of an evil deduced from historic experience was beyond the power of man: even in a more advanced state of society, if there were men whose genius was equal to the task, and patience to the toil, of collecting from monkish annals, or traditionary information, the requisite knowledge, there were no means of disseminating and diffusing it among their fellow men: besides men have, in all ages, been prone to content themselves with the remedy that first offers against any calamity, little anxious as to remote consequences and distant probabilities.[43]

Sentences like these went largely unread outside the Norwich circle itself. The *Cabinet*'s language submerges the priorities of "intellectual man" within the politics they share with the plebeian movement. But the two would not take very long to sort themselves out. Among the *Cabinet*'s chief architects, William Taylor soon became a major contributor to the *Monthly Magazine*.

The difference between modes of writing in *Politics for the People* and the *Cabinet* suggests that radical discourse can only be a new mode of *inter-*

discourse, a language of countermand and critique, a dialogue in the most explicit sense. But this cannot be the dialogue of a "society of a text," whose readers and writers strategically exchange roles within strictly defined assumptions about what can and cannot be said. Radical writers quote, parody, compile, ridicule in a politics of warring contexts, the "arse" with the "vote." This riotousness of the radical text becomes its defining mark in the early nineteenth century, when the lines between the cultures of intellectual man and artisan radicals have become more clear-cut. The *Cabinet*'s language finds its more tenable form in the discourse of the *Monthly Magazine* and its progeny. Meanwhile, the radicalism of Eaton's and Spence's journals reappears, more richly textualized, in the radical journals of Cobbett, Wooler, Carlile, and others in the years 1816 to 1820.

But middle-class radicals could also gravitate away from intellectual man, toward what would in the nineteenth century ultimately become "mass" man. No mass audience would clearly appear in England before the 1820s, but in the troubled 1790s, a third kind of periodical writing, directed neither to middle-class intellectuals nor to radical artisans, was beginning to emerge. In Newcastle-upon-Tyne, James Losh began the *Oeconomist* (1798–99), which conceived its northern, mainly rural readership in the eighteenth-century sense of *oeconomy* as domestic economy, "a society ordered after the manner of a family" *(OED)*. Losh had shared Wordsworth's and Coleridge's idealist republicanism during the revolution, but by the later 1790s Coleridge could point to him as an apostate who sought domestic comforts as balm to political pain.[44] Subtitled "The Englishman's Magazine," the *Oeconomist* assembled its writings—"On Tyranny," "Anecdote of Charles Duke of Burgundy," "The Cottage," "Directions to the Poor"—for the price of one and a half pence, a fraction of the average magazine's cost. It was appropriately cheap, speaking to its freeholding and small-proprietor readers a somber language of "improvability" and self-cultivation as defenses against "the political difficulties of this awful moment" and the "astonishing crisis" for which "there is no analogy . . . in the history of the world."[45] Not only the Continental wars but the first serious depression in England's Industrial Revolution had put a stranglehold on freeholders and small proprietors in the late 1790s. The only hope held out to the *Oeconomist*'s readers in this literally unprecedented situation is to gain knowledge, cultivate domestic virtue and economy, or announce, in a typical *Oeconomist* verse, "I envy not your splendid lot / But smile content within my cot." Thus what Raymond Williams describes as a key function of many eighteenth-century novels—to frame "the long process of choice between economic advantage and other ideas of value" in the English countryside—appears more abjectly in the *Oeconomist* as a counsel of stoic despair.[46]

When it substitutes domestic economy for national issues, or self-improvement for political activity—"Bear free and patient thoughts," it quotes Shakespeare—the *Oeconomist* anticipates the social pedagogy practiced on a much wider basis by the *Penny Magazine*, the *Mirror of Literature*, and *Chambers' Edinburgh Journal* in the 1820s and '30s. To audiences overwhelmed by the uncontrollable economic forces and baffling technological transformations of the nineteenth century, such journals would also counsel the "diffusion of knowledge" and self-improvement, but in ways that offer far more imaginative and various symbolic escape routes from it. Their readers will be urban rather than rural, but will occupy a similar position between what the *Oeconomist* had earlier called the "numerous, wealthy, and well-informed middle class" and the "indigence and slavery" toward which the "lower orders" seemed to be driven by the rapacious rich. It will be clearer in the 1820s and 1830s than in the 1790s that the making of a "mass" audience presumed the prior conflict between middle-class and radical audiences and the writers who gave them shape.

The new periodical writing of the 1790s foregrounds the discontinuity of publics, and it is the division among public discourses that makes essential the reformation of the reading habit. The *Monthly Magazine*'s incipient middle-class intelligentsia, the radical journals' activist artisan public, the *Oeconomist*'s threatened rural readers—such publics cannot easily be assimilated to that older colonizing activity of eighteenth-century periodical writing. It remains in the next three chapters, then, to reconstruct what new relationships bind readers together or mark their differences. At the same time, the object of our focus will shift from the journals' discursive stances toward readers, as we have briefly surveyed them here, to the language with which they form publics, interpreting in their rhetoric and style Sartre's remark that "all works of the mind contain within themselves the image of the readers for whom they are intended."[47] But that image is no more than a projection, which in historical practice often misfires. The audiences that writers struggled to make, and those that actually came into being, were not always the same. Historically, readers acquired the reading habit by acquiring self-consciousness as members of a particular audience, and after 1790 in England that knowledge could only come from the pressure of adjacent social audiences. Such cultural boundaries were imagined first of all in texts, and at the end of this period of intense audience-making, writers in the 1830s could begin to visualize the world of reading and writing that had come largely into form.

In 1831, for instance, the *Metropolitan* portrays the English middle-class audience in terms hardly thinkable only forty years before. The *Bee's* rhetorical sense of community has not survived in the new world of reading and writing. "The age of things is arrived," intones the *Metropolitan*, "and we no longer have time to throw away upon words." The new periodical writing is a portable property "better adapted to the wants and habits of the consumer," the proper form for an emerging *société de consommation*. With readers who are no longer potential writers but now consumers, the *Bee's* communal exchange of reading and writing in the text's alternate society has vanished. The *Metropolitan* acknowledges the now distanced reader as an embodied historical pressure: "The world suffers too keenly, not to think intensely: and while kingdoms are revolving into their first elements, and governments crumbling to pieces on all sides, the most graceful trifling will no longer catch the attention even of waiting-maids, and the dandies of the second table. If Nero fiddled while Rome was burning, he was not dependent for his bread on the voluntary payment of his music by an audience of subscribers."[48] In an inescapably historical world subject to the creation and destruction nineteenth-century readers were learning to appreciate in the most quotidian way, popular writing must be constructed on the wreckage of the past for a modern, harshly demanding, commodity-buying public.

Moreover, the language basis for a community of reading and writing has disappeared with that "hotbed growth and rapid succession of authors [that] allow no time for any one of them to be erected into an infallible standard. . . . Each age, hereafter, will choose its own manner of writing, as it will the fashion of its clothes, or the cut of its political constitutions."[49] In the *Metropolitan*, "style" becomes a pliable concept with which to negotiate modern discontinuities; so there can be a style of the age, a style of a group of writings, a style of a single journal, or finally, the signature of an individual writer. In this way, the *Metropolitan* can abandon the rhetorical ideal of public language to anticipate John Stuart Mill's poet who talks to himself. It criticizes from this stance those contemporary writings of *Blackwood's*, *Fraser's*, the *New Monthly* and other magazines for middle-class readers for being, in essence, too much a part of the old rhetorical framework. Such writings are "positive experiments upon the minds of the readers—not the unburdening of the minds of the writers themselves. . . . Authors write best for the public when they write for themselves."[50] This familiar figure for stylistic individualism erases any "exchange" between writer and reader and puts in its place some mechanism for *substituting* one for the other; writing for himself, the writer more or less automatically writes for the public. Thus the distance between audience and writer becomes the paradoxical condition of their closeness. The singular writer unburdening his mind touches the singular reader who, by a mysterious quality of style itself, becomes so intimate with the writer as momentarily to merge with him. Hence the individual writer's pursuit of a certain perfection also guarantees, by the multiplication of innumerable solitary reading acts, the greater good of the collective public.

Early nineteenth-century journals, as their writers attempt to define the intellectual contours of rapidly forming readerships, often strain toward this metaphysical sense of style. For a certain middle-class audience, style becomes one of the crucial modes of the reading habit that writers must forge in the new world of class-divided publics. But they also can subordinate the role of style itself to a wider play of signs—a field in which, as Fredric Jameson has remarked, style is only one of the more privileged of possible textual signs.[51] Writers in the great public journals will lead their readers from verbal and cultural to social and economic signs, the written text an unparalleled map of the social text. Audiences will come to define themselves according to the interpretive mode they possess and the interpretive strategies through which that mode somehow allows them to "read" other audiences whose pressure, in the early nineteenth century, cannot be escaped.

Two

Reading the Social Text

> Now while the common multitude strips bare,
> feels pleasure's cat o'nine tails on its back,
> and fights off anguish at the great bazaar,
> give me your hand, my Sorrow, Let's stand back;
>
> back from these people! Look, the dead years dressed
> in old clothes crowd the balconies of the sky.
>
> —Baudelaire, *Recueillement* (trans. Robert Lowell)

IN *The Statesman's Manual* Coleridge decried the "luxuriant misgrowth" of a middle-class reading audience, but his diagnosis was by no means clear to even his most attentive readers. When Hazlitt, writing for the *Edinburgh Review*, read Coleridge's complaint—"I would that the greater part of our publications could be thus *directed*, each to its appropriate class of readers"—he queried in a footnote: "Do not publications generally find their way there, without a *direction?*"[1] The *Edinburgh's* reviewer can scarcely imagine the phantasm of a mass, chaotic, alien public Coleridge called the "promiscuous audience." Coleridge directed his own sermons *ad populum* or *ad clerum*, but between the populace and the learned, an amorphous middle class had become readers of the great public journals—the *Edinburgh* and *Quarterly* reviews, the *Monthly* and *New Monthly* magazines—and they would soon read *Blackwood's Edinburgh Magazine*, the *London Magazine*, the *Westminster Review*, *Fraser's Magazine*, the *Metropolitan Magazine*, and the *Athenaeum*. In such journals, Hazlitt assumed, texts would find their appropriate readers. But *A Lay Sermon* (1817) portrays a far more volatile universe of public discourse, troubled on the left by an insurgent radical audience, on the right by an "Overbalance of the Commercial Spirit" that threatens the very "foundationless" being of the "upper and middle classes" Coleridge was now addressing. Such classes must, Coleridge pleaded, acquire "an habitual consciousness of the ultimate principles, to which your opinions are traceable." This strange kind of habituation is not "the skirts of Custom" to which the masses cling, but the redoubled self-consciousness that means "to walk in the Light of your own knowledge."[2] So intellectual a habit must be conditioned by cultural practices, a new reading habit to be formed against all existing modes of reading.

The twelve months between November 1816 and October 1817 crystallized the tension between modes of reading prefigured in the 1790s. Coleridge published the *Statesman's Manual* in December, *A Lay Sermon* in March, the *Biographia Literaria* in July; William Cobbett brought out the two-pence version of the *Political Register* for a wide radical audience in November 1816; William Blackwood began the *Edinburgh Monthly Magazine* in April 1817 and replaced it with *Blackwood's Edinburgh Magazine* in October. In the *Biographia* Coleridge called attention to a far-reaching transformation of cultural practice: the age of self-publishing was now over. His own failure as writer-publisher of the *Watchman* and the *Friend* meant to him that writers could no longer combine the act of writing with the institution of publishing.[3] Yet in the same year, William Cobbett, the most powerful single writer-publisher of the nineteenth century, was demonstrating how effectively an older and now discredited cultural practice could be taken over and reworked for a new audience. The self-publishing periodical essayist had become the self-publishing radical writer forming an artisan public. Here, as elsewhere, the middle-class cultural critic mistakes for a historical end—the loss of the periodical essay—what is in fact a shift in cultural practice from one social class to another. But Coleridge was not wrong to see how the middle-class writer now had to become institutional to survive. The monthly and quarterly journals had begun to absorb their writers into the discursive mode of each journal, often merging writer, editor, and publisher into a corporate, collective "author" institutionally set apart from its readers. Gazing unhappily at this emerging discursive event, Coleridge reverts to the stance of preacher, sermonizing against the world of reading and writing coming into visible form.

But the journal writers were also beginning to recognize what Coleridge already knew: the middle-class audience must be redirected to become fully conscious of its hegemonic cultural power. The *Edinburgh*

Review's own confidence in the English audience seemed shaken when Francis Jeffrey warned in October 1819: "We take the most alarming signs of the times to be, that separation of the upper and middle classes of the community from the lower, which is now daily and visibly increasing. The conduct of all parties, and of every branch of society, has contributed more or less to produce this unhappy estrangement between the two grand divisions of which the population consists."[4] The Whig quarterly feared most the ominous language of class revolt among those artisan and working-class readers who were reading the "mischievous, profligate, insane" radical writers Cobbett, Thomas Wooler, and Richard Carlile. In *A Lay Sermon* Coleridge absurdly classed Francis Jeffrey with Cobbett and Henry Hunt, but Jeffrey knew better his mediating position between the real radicals and middle-class readers learning to define themselves by opposition to that insurgent audience. Where the boundaries were to be drawn was crucial; a new French Revolution in England would take place if "the classes of small proprietors" unite "with those who have no possessions at all, and...produce a most alarming separation, not of the labouring poor from the rest of the community, but of all the rest of the community from the rich" ("State of the Country," 297). Radical discourse testified to that unsettling alliance, and it could only be deconstructed by some newer, more powerful conception of what binds the middling classes to one another—a representation in which the British middle class could become acutely conscious of itself.

The adventures of the commodity—an "Overbalance of the Commercial Spirit" in *A Lay Sermon*'s phrase—also threatened the middle-class from within. By the early 1820s cheap periodicals like the *Mirror of Literature, Amusement, and Instruction* or the *Hive* were to flood British bookstalls and coffeehouses with circulations of fifty thousand or more, dwarfing those of the quarterly reviews and monthly magazines. There, as Marx put it, the social relations between people would assume, in the eyes of its huge audience, the "fantastic form of a relation between things."[5] In 1800 Wordsworth intuited a commodified popular culture emerging to displace the reading of Shakespeare and Milton. He claimed that a new language of poetry could resist the cultural entropy of a "torpid" middle-class mind. But that mind was not merely passive; it could be shaped, as the mass journals would show, to interpret the nineteenth-century world in a peculiar but ultimately powerful way. Forging their own interpretive strategies to counter those emerging all around them, middle-class writers intimated to their readers an unparalleled power of reading itself. To that end, one might say, the middle-class audience would come to see the social relation between people in the fantastic form of a relation between *texts*.

I

The ruthless criticism of poets, warring between Tory and Whig positions, the "puffing" of a publisher's book by the periodical he owned—such well-known practices of the early-nineteenth-century journals were not unimportant, but they were not what was most culturally profound about the journals' role in public discourse. The most significant journals gathered audiences of five to fifteen thousand readers each: the *Edinburgh Review* (1802), the *Examiner* (1808), the *Quarterly Review* (1809), the *New Monthly Magazine* (1814), *Blackwood's Edinburgh Magazine* (1817), the *London Magazine* (1821), the *Westminster Review* (1824), the *Athenaeum* (1828), *Fraser's Magazine* (1830), the *Metropolitan* (1831). Their total readership could only be guessed at, but Francis Jeffrey's estimate still stands: some twenty thousand among what he called "fashionable or public life": upper civil-servants and clergy, the richer merchants and manufacturers, the gentry, and the professionals, all earning more than eight hundred pounds a year. Much more selectively, the journals also reached into the "middling classes" of some two hundred thousand teachers, lesser clergy and civil servants, and shopkeepers, each earning three hundred pounds or less per year.[6] The definition of readers sought by these journals was unavoidably imprecise by contrast to eighteenth-century journals, which mapped their audiences by targeting specific ranks. Nineteenth-century periodicals often deliberately smudged social differences among their readers. It became important, for reasons that will shortly become clear, to make one's intended reader potential, not already well-defined, prior to the journal's own discourse. The intended audience must be defined by its ethos, its framework of educational capacity, ideological stance, economic ability, and cultural dispositions. But the readership must not be assigned a specific rank, nor be localized in a social order that it will become compelled to "read" as though it did not belong to that order. Only at the outer limits of this audience would the essential determinations be made, and these were mainly economic: the quarterlies cost four to six shillings each, monthly magazines two to three shillings. Even if workingmen had joined together to buy a copy at these prices—even if they had been faintly interested in what *Blackwood's* had to insinuate about them—such reading matter would have cost a member of the "lower orders" an unthinkable full day's pay.[7]

Writers enlisted with publishers according to personal connections and political agreements; Hazlitt wrote for Jeffrey's *Edinburgh Review*, Leigh Hunt's *Examiner*, or Henry Colburn's *New Monthly Magazine* (Colburn paid well), but he would not have written for Lockhart's and Wilson's *Blackwood's* or Henry Stebbing's *Athenaeum*. Prolific writers, like John Wilson of *Blackwood's* and Cyrus Redding of the *New Monthly*, became covert editors. This intricate nexus between publisher, editor, and writers made assigning personal responsibility for this decision or that text hard to establish. But one party did not belong to the corporate journal: the audience who in the eighteenth century had been its potential contributors. From the *Edinburgh Review* on, public knowledge of ample payments to contributors signalled the distancing of the audience. No longer a society of readers and writers, the journal represented itself as an institution blending writer, editor, and publisher in what could only appear to be an essentially authorless text. Knowing readers might infer the identity of the writer by his "style," but playing this game of authorship meant that what is at stake is not the author of the discourse, but the position it occupies on a diverse discursive landscape. One can determine authorship only by the text it secretes. The importance "style" itself assumes in the nineteenth century owes partly to this impersonality of the public text. Style becomes a sign, a marker of the (always inferred) relation of the audience to the writer hidden behind the corporate text.

What will finally distinguish the new middle-class audience of the nineteenth century from its radical antagonists and the mass public's fascination with commodities is the activated interpretive mind in its power to reincarnate everyday life: to form a "philosophy" of one's encounter with the street and the city, with fashion, with social class, with intellectual systems and the mind's own unpredictable acts. Generalizing the philosophic, interpreting mind for the active middle class will mean making this audience intensely aware of moving between alternative vocabularies of social and intellectual order, of responding to the most varied, at times extreme exercises of "style," searching for privileged, nodal points at which to anchor a sense of cultural power. Above all, this audience learns to operate those interpretive strategies through which it can "read" a social world, a symbolic universe, a textual field, and to discover its own purpose within them. Manipulating or fabricating signs, this public both learns and asserts what it means to be "middle class" in the nineteenth century. When we look closely at the language of its texts—in such representative journals as *Blackwood's*, the *Athenaeum*, the *New Monthly*, *Fraser's*, and the *Edinburgh*

Review[8]—a powerful transauthorial discourse echoes through its protean collocation of styles, topics, and voices. The readers gathered by this discourse form not only an empirical audience, but a collective interpreter mapping out the cultural physiognomy of Britain.

II

From its first pages in 1817, *Blackwood's Edinburgh Magazine* made its unwavering task the molding of a "reflecting" readership for its Tory politics and High Church, aristocratic ethos. With a lively conservatism directed more toward commercial and professional readers than toward the *Quarterly Review*'s gentrified audience, *Blackwood's* argued economic positions independent of both aristocratic and classical mercantilist doctrine, anticipating distantly the Keynesian and welfare-state economic program of a future age.[9] Notorious for its satires—the "Chaldee Manuscript" of October 1817 the most outrageous among them—*Blackwood's* parodied not only contemporary letters but the eighteenth-century public sphere of the coffeehouses in "Noctes Ambrosianae," a famous series of mock cultural conversations among the literati at Ambrose's. The journal translated German poetry and drama, reviewed literary and historical works, debated Whig writers, and collected popular narratives later anthologized as *Tales of Blackwood's*.[10] But *Blackwood's*' most reflexive, audience-making act was its tireless promotion of "intellect," or what it called "the structure and workings of the human mind, as they are exhibited in its reasoning powers, in its imagination and invention, in its taste, as well as in its mode of expressing them." As an avatar of the "national mind," *Blackwood's* tested its proto-Arnoldian faith that "the ultimate and permanent results of the excitement and workings of the mind must be advantageous" by working to create that reader for whom intellect, "like caloric...expands whatever it enters into [and] must enlarge the capacity of the human mind, creating new intellectual desires and wants, and the means of satisfying them."[11]

An engine that produces intellectual desire—such a writing machine will produce a self-reflexive, desiring reader conscious of the expansive mental power that extrudes through his reading of any particular content. These "experiments on the minds of readers," as the *Metropolitan* would later call them, might either take the form of arguments on the powers of mind themselves or, just as often, become a penchant for trying out prose styles not commonly associated with serious intellectual argument. Shaping the *Blackwood's* reader demands an inexhaustible panoply of stylistic resources so that it can demonstrate a "power of thought" which is doubled and redoubled in an endless intellectual exertion. In this early *Blackwood's* text, for instance, the writer establishes a discourse that foregrounds the *sentence* and its various stylistic turns as the individualizing mark of his intellectual act:

> When a man looks back on his past existence, and endeavours to recall the incidents, events, thoughts, feelings, and passions of which it was composed, he sees something like a glimmering land of dreams, peopled with phantasms and realities indistinguishably confused and intermingled—here illuminated with dazzling splendour, there dim with melancholy mists, —or it may be, shrouded in impenetrable darkness. To bring, visibly and distinctly before our memory, on the one hand, all our hours of mirth and joy, and hope and exultation, —and, on the other, all our perplexities, and fears and sorrows, and despair and agony, —(and who has been so uniformly wretched as not to have been often blest? —who so uniformly blest as not to have been often wretched?)—would be as impossible as to awaken, into separate remembrance, all the changes and varieties which the seasons brought over the material world, —every gleam of sunshine that beautified the Spring, —every cloud and tempest that deformed the Winter. . . . The soul may be repelled from the contemplation of the past as much by the brightness and magnificence of scenes that shifted across the glorious drama of youth, as by the storms that scattered the fair array into disfigured fragments; and the melancholy that breathes from vanished delight is, perhaps, in its utmost intensity, as unendurable as the wretchedness left by the visitation of calamity. . . . It is from such thoughts, and dreams, and reveries, as these, that all men feel how terrible it would be to live over again their agonies and their transports; that the happiest would fear to do so as much as the most miserable; and that to look back to our cradle seems scarcely less awful than to look forward to the grave.[12]

This almost unendurable passage begins John Wilson's assault on the autobiographical writings of Rousseau, Hume, and particularly Coleridge. What is new here is the way *Blackwood's* drives a florid "poetic diction" into the very texture of argumentative prose. In this passage, the writer frames his hyperbolic, overblown language in melodramatic antitheses that mark off experiential boundaries no one can pass beyond ("all our hours of mirth and joy, and hope and exultation...all our perplexities, and fears, and sorrows, and despair and agony"). Yet, at the same time that he names these antithetical opposites, the writer also denies them. He makes remembering distinctly our tumultuous personal emotions "as impossible as" clearly recalling the wildest extremes of nature itself; in the same way, nostalgic melancholy is "as unendurable as" reexperiencing old pain. At last, even the finalities of beginnings and ends—cradle and grave—cancel each other out.

But even as the writer recoils from them, such pairings of opposites signify a suggestive realm in between, its implicit richness defined by the "unendurable" extremity of these outer limits. Opposites must be named in the most drastic language so that we can withdraw from them, yet still feel their experiential resonance. Declaring everything to be neither this nor that, the writer invites the reader to step outside the circle of opposites— often layered upon other opposites—into a sense of ineffable but ubiquitous "meaning."

This rhetorical power of suggestion also appears in the tautological doublets ("visibly and distinctly") or the catalogs ("incidents, events, thoughts, feelings, and passions") that strain indecisively to name something that eludes language but can be repeatedly gestured toward by piling up words, or loading the page with an inexhaustible metaphoric vocabulary ("disfigured fragments," "glorious drama of youth"). This style—"besotted with words" in Hazlitt's phrase—is calculatedly popular, drawing on that warehouse of clichés and stereotypes that, as Roland Barthes suggested, forms raw material for even the most apparently personal and original stylistic tropes. Yet it also suggests insecurity about what the language of nonfiction discourse means. The *Blackwood's* writer uses words as though they are no longer anchored in things, but now float almost magically free of any particular referent. As Hazlitt complained of the late-eighteenth-century "hieroglyphical" style, "Objects are not linked to feelings, words to things, but images revolve in splendid mockery, words represent themselves in their strange rhapsody."[13] But in the hands of a *Blackwood's* writer like John Wilson, this style has another purpose that Hazlitt overlooks. It forms messages about "reading" itself, which now becomes an "experience" as the crowded metaphors are repeatedly balanced against each other and dismissed. To be sure, not all *Blackwood's* writers try to make such metastatements about the hidden powers of nonfiction discourse; many rehearse a traditionally balanced, rhetorical, representational style.[14] But there is a strong stylistic tendency in this most influential of middle-class journals to experiment with turning the form of a discourse into a layer of its content, forcing the sentence to signify more than it can possibly say.

For underwriting *Blackwood's'* adventure in nonfiction style is a full-blown ideology of the power of mind itself. At its most ambitious, this discourse could explore an analogical space linking mental and social laws. If the individual reader experiences his own mental power in the act of reading such texts, they may also lead him to generalize such powers to those of the nation in which he participates as a reader—as a member of a certain audience. The following text, for instance, asks how an empirical individual's ultimate form of self—"genius"—can form both the model and the foundation for realizing a greater collective self. Few questions could be so central to *Blackwood's'* project of imperializing mental energy.:

> [There] is a just and true sympathy in common men, with that condition of the mind in which its highest faculties are best exerted—a sympathy of no ordinary moment. If we consider what the high exertion of those faculties must be, we shall perceive that the subject of our regard is nothing less than a spiritual agent in freedom of its power, satisfying its own native desires out of the means which its union with life may yield it; for life is different to every mind, according to its own constitution—to that of the bodily frame in which it breathes and feels, and to the thousand-fold contingencies which make up to it the circumstances and course of the individual being. But whatever is thus brought into the soul of pleasure and of pain; —whatever the affections of the mind, modified, as they thus are, into peculiar character; — whatever the sense and the intelligence, thus moulded or endowed for peculiar discernment, may gather up from the world of life, for joy or sorrow—for delight and awe—for knowledge infinitely diversified—for self-springing conceptions of unsleeping thought; —whatever life itself, by its beauty, powers, destinies—its passions, hopes, privileges—its multiplied relations and ceaseless change—can yield to the intellectual and sensitive soul for feeling and thought, —these are the materials, the means, which its union with being brings before it for the exercise of its faculties, according to the tendencies, the impulses, the desires of its own peculiar nature.[15]

Like the first passage on memory, these sentences use antithesis ("for knowledge infinitely diversified—for self-springing conceptions of unsleeping thought") and catalogs ("by its beauty, powers, destinies—its passions, hopes, privileges") to draw from a bottomless well of apparent meanings. The sentence not only alludes to so many realms of experience, but could also *go on* alluding to them indefinitely. Relentlessly abstract, each sentence cannot descend to any particularity. It cannot name some concrete empirical thing, but must, rather, glide through abstracted categories that can be called up one after another:

> If that mind, then, has but lived in freedom of its powers—if the act of its faculties, in the continual progress of life, has been impelled from within—if it has trusted itself to feel, and rejoiced to know, as its nature led—if it has been true to itself, and cherishing its own inward discernment, and guarding the fountain of light within itself—has been able to shed from that source a pure unfailing light upon its own thought and its own motion, —if it has used intelligence and feeling as gifts made immediately to itself, for its own strength and guidance—it will, in its maturity of thought and power, and in the season of productive genius, perform the works of its great conception in the spirit in which it has lived—it will bring into being, by its operative art, substantial expression and likeness of those peculiar and individual forms of feeling and thought which it has entertained and cherished within itself in its long communion with being; and that peculiar impress on its works, may be regarded as the symbol of an individual nature unfolded in the mind—as evidence of an unoppressed spirit of life in the soul—of a mind maintaining its endowed powers entire in their native liberty. ("Analogy," 375-76)

Almost endlessly expansive, these sentences gain their shape from the framing anaphora: "whatever...," "for...," and "if..." clauses. Prefacing the main propositions, which appear almost mutely after the masses of qualifying clauses, the anaphoras arrange the various perspectives through which these statements should at last be understood. Such anaphoric motions mark the limits of the phrases they govern. For each sentence can only go so far in imitating or alluding to some energy that either comes before or falls outside language itself. Anaphora in these sentences repeatedly gestures toward this energetic yet unnameable activity.[16] Deferred from closing decisively around its unit of thought, the declarative sentence verifies its signifying power at the same time that it refuses to name it.

These passages cannot describe mental process without trying to reenact it. The gestural motions of their language redound back to something analogous to the "deep and exhaustless source" upon which the individual mind finally draws "the elements of its ceaseless creations" (377). With this description of the mind's act, the writer then turns to another, analogous "self-communion in the spirit of the people" promised in his title, "On the Analogy between the Growth of Individual and National Genius." He must make an exact homology between the empirical individual and what Carlyle in "Characteristics" would call the "new collective individual."[17] The great man and the English collective individual share identical "unfoldings, as it were, of their own spirit in their own life—shewings forth of their mind in realized act" (377). So, acting and reacting upon each other until cause and effect blur in a continuous circle of influence, the great individuals thrown up by history and the collective individual of Britain itself appear as a singular form.

Hence, the reader is now prepared to see both the nation and the individual anchored in the same self-consciousness:

> The objects which present themselves to the mind are continually varying their aspect, and so far tending to perplex their own impressions. The weaker mind is overcome by this variableness of impression, and loses its self-consistency; but the spirit of stronger quality is able to maintain its own uniformity of feeling and belief in the midst of much variation, and by that means forms its own strength, making its inherent qualities more and more predominant over the impressions, by which they are continually called into play. But that continual recollection and recovery upon itself of former emotion, affection, and sensation, by which alone this superiority to present impression can be maintained, is of the nature of a self-communion; it is a reflection of the mind upon itself; it is a self-consciousness prolonged or reproduced; it is an internal repetition, with consciousness of its own emotion, to which it attaches itself more and more. (378)

The psychological and the social merge in this description. The "variableness of impression" to the mind's eye is also that congeries of empirical individuals swarming in a nation, and both must be somehow essentialized by an extreme, abstracting power of will. This victory over dispersion comes in the mental act that is again and again rehearsed in language. Like the anaphoric repetition in the previous passage, here the mind returns, repeats, and deepens its own acts. Each repetition incrementally increases self-consciousness, creating a "personal identity begun and carried on in

these uniform recurrences" (377). Through such acts of repetition and return, something emerges against which a present dispersion—the overwhelming impact of empirical "impressions," or the baffling swarm of
different people or social classes—can now be read for its latent *unity*.

Redeeming social and psychological fragmentation by recollectively
bouncing back toward a fusion with the self's own ultimate ground was
something writers had to describe quite differently for different audiences.
In *Chambers' Edinburgh Journal* (1832), written for an emerging mass audience, the writer would confer on the "common" man of the street that
power to repeat and return to a primal collective scene whose repossession
allows one to see, through the aimless social atoms of the crowd, a common
core of the recognizably human within.[18] For the self-conscious middle-
class reader of *Blackwood's Magazine*, such redemptive powers are reserved
for the representative "man of genius." But the language *Blackwood's* uses
to describe these powers also labors hard to give its readers the *sense* of this
mental activity by approximating its movements. In this way, the elaborate
anaphora, antitheses, and catalogs in these texts become so many marks of
an activity already meaningful in itself, regardless of any emotion or idea
"to which it attaches itself more and more." Such sentences are signs for
the middle-class reader's growing capacity to turn the form of a discourse
into its own content. An older balanced rhetorical style had attempted to
equate the form of a sentence with its concept, to render the shape of a
completed thought. But as nineteenth-century writers begin to posit realms
of meaning beyond the grasp of verbal signs, the extravagant formal gestur-
ing of their sentences both displaces such content and becomes a content
in its own right.

Blackwood's Magazine thus acts as a force field for the power of
thought, miming in its stylistic turns the feeling that "the *Human Mind* is
extending its empire."[19] Page after page in *Blackwood's* promotes this ideology, so that inevitably, in "Thoughts on the Advancement and Diffusion of
Knowledge," a *Blackwood's* writer will at last demand a revaluation of a
whole *episteme* and its privileged symbol, the encyclopedia. If eighteenth-
century knowledge could be totalized in a mind, in a book, in the encyclopedic, that totality can no longer be imagined to assume a visible shape:
"The Mind is no where, the single mind is not, cannot be, in which that
collected wisdom and power of all, contemplated by us, has its seat: but by
the fancied inter-communion among all of rights, and interchange of
powers, by the felt union of desires to the same great common ends, the innumerable associated multitude of minds appear to us as one" ("Thoughts,"

26). Omnipresent yet unrepresentable: this is how Alexander Blair conceives "knowing" in the early nineteenth century. Here, in a popular journal for "reflecting" middle-class readers, we find a critique of the cardinal points of eighteenth-century knowledge to which Michel Foucault gave the name "representation." In his essay Blair arraigns the encyclopedists' errors:

> a conception of knowledge which may perhaps be expressed by saying, that it is viewed, or reasoned of, as if it consisted solely *in the perception of relations*. —Secondly, a conception of it, as being a species of *definite possession* to the mind, not a *power* of thought, necessarily indefinite: —as something, thirdly, in itself *limited*, and already *completed*: —In the fourth place, a fallacious idea of the participation of any one in the light and progress of his age as requiring, and consisting in, the *knowledge by him* of what is known to his age: Fifthly, to go no further, misconceptions, to which we have more than once adverted, of the unity of knowledge. (29)

By this account, the eighteenth century's attempt to make encyclopedic knowledge comprehensible to one mind revealed a misplaced faith in the power of signs to represent things. Signs do not represent things, the *Blackwood's* writer argues, but rather "the power of thought, necessarily indefinite." Belief in the transparency of knowledges has led the encyclopedists to mistake "the effective, *practical* connexions of the Sciences" with "*their imaginary conjunction*" (29). But the sciences are separated by their incommensurate internal principles, *Blackwood's* asserts, so that none is readable in terms of another.

Such a thesis unexpectedly confirms Foucault's hypothesis in *The Order of Things* that the "space" of nineteenth-century European knowledge shifted "archaeologically" from the table of representation and its emblematic encyclopedia to another "depth in which what matters is no longer identities, distinctive characters, permanent tables with all their possible paths and routes, but great hidden forces developed on the basis of their primitive and inaccessible nucleus, origin, causality, and history."[20] For *Blackwood's*, the "power of thought"—and the style that confirms it— reveals itself by a repetitive but intensifying reach after that "inaccessible nucleus" of meaning. Elsewhere, *Blackwood's* celebrates a division of intellectual labor into separate professional spheres, and the writing of journals for specific professional audiences, each one devoted to a topical content.[21]

But for its own readers, *Blackwood's* reserves the ultimately contentless activity of the mind's self-discovery.

III

The positive hermeneutic of *Blackwood's Magazine* constitutes the most self-conscious moment of public discourse as the language of intellectual desire, a desire to be acted and reenacted in the moment of reading itself. In the 1820s the middle class read widely about its own intercourse "of mind with mind, the combination of individual thought into one mighty mass of intellect, the gathering of private judgments and experiences in their infinite diversities of forms and colouring, into that vast embodied essence of society called Public Opinion, [which] is but a consequence of the laws and constitution of our moral nature."[22] So argued the neo-Coleridgean "Apostles" of the *Athenaeum* (1828), for whom the discourse of *Blackwood's* has "the strongest hold both upon the mind and heart of its readers" (336). Yet *Blackwood's'* theory of knowledge and its practice of discourse were founded on a disturbing faith, one the *Athenaeum's* writers both shared and publicly doubted. If the encyclopedia or the single voluminous mind no longer encompasses the sphere of knowing, that sphere must now be realized in a collective formation—a collection of texts, a collection of minds: the new middle-class audience and its reading. Innumerable individual acts of reading must produce a centralized intellect, a "vast embodied essence" that will now be capitalized as Mind. But it remains to ask, What mechanism guarantees the production of this Mind from these solitary acts? What prevents the differentials among these textual encounters from yielding up, not an embodied essence, but a confused gabble? At stake is the very identity of the newly aroused middle-class audience, whether it can realize its potential to cohere as a cultural formation or—no less possible—merely disperse among the internal pressures of its differences.

Those myriad differences must always be registered in public discourse. The middle class derives its authority partly by its sheer variousness, its protean capacity to manage the calculus of all the interests and the passions. The institution of public discourse

> can then only fully discharge its office when it is perfectly unrestricted
> in its operations; when its machinery is so free that it will answer to
> the slightest touch, and act as an index to the different variations in
> the social body.... In the fluctuations of society, the mingling to-

gether of pursuits and interests, the varying excitements and recognized principles, and the alternations of passion and their
corresponding prejudices, an almost unlimited scope is given to speculation, and events occur calculated to awaken by turns every feeling of
the human heart. (335)

It could be no accident that the *Athenaeum* explains the periodicals' heterogeneity in the accents of *The Wealth of Nations*. But it also invokes the
necessity of balancing the interests *against* the passions recognized long before Adam Smith's proposal of a harmonizing Invisible Hand.[23] As other
writers of the 1820s insisted, the dominant cultural discourse can no longer
be protected or decreed by the state. William Pitt's government had used
the state's force against the radical writer's passions in order to preserve a
dominant English culture's interests between the French Revolution and
Peterloo. But after 1820 that culture had to become capable of generating
its own principle of protective control. Yet the massive preparation of the
cultural machinery could not by itself guarantee such an end. Arthur
Young's vast network of "circulation" forms a necessary but insufficient
condition of a hegemonic public discourse. The great national Mind fal-
ters, says the *Athenaeum*, when the middle-class audience's texts betray "no
national character, or strong pervading and assimilating element," no
"style which, though varying in its tone, would have the expression of a
common and connecting feeling." Despite the ambitions of *Blackwood's
Magazine*, public discourse of the 1820s has produced "a reading public but
not a thinking people." For the *Athenaeum*'s cultural conservatives the hermeneutics of the public mind generate deep anxiety about its grandest
claims. Yet what Herbert Marcuse would call "the affirmative character of
culture" does not affirm, so to speak, only by affirming: it also affirms by
criticism.[24] If the middle-class public could never be certain what it *was* in
the ever-receding Mind just beyond its grasp, this audience might recognize
itself by interpreting what it was not.

IV

As the language of intellectual desire gestures toward the fullness of
meaning, it also pushes meaning into a realm that cannot be captured in a
sign. This positive hermeneutic, however, must be balanced for middle-
class readers by an opposing, negative hermeneutic that plunges the audience into a welter of signs.[25] These are all the social signs of a world

organized into ranks, degrees, or social classes. No longer obsessively seeking out the immanent presence of meaning, this critique of signs unmasks the absence of meaning. For writers in the *New Monthly Magazine* or the *Edinburgh Review*, this criticism of signs both installs the reader in the social world—for being "middle class" will finally mean being in a position to "read" social signs correctly—and also grasps for both reader and writer a necessary distance from being class-typed themselves. Turning from inner psychological process to a concretely externalized world, this social semiotic makes its middle-class audience the adroit manager of all sign systems in which it might otherwise become ensnared.

Typical of this growing attention to social signs is the *New Monthly Magazine*. Henry Colburn began the journal in 1814 as a neoconservative reply to the earlier Jacobinism of the *Monthly Magazine* (1796), but his legion critics suspected less political than commercial motives for entering the periodical realm: Colburn was the most notorious nineteenth-century practitioner of "puffing," having the books he published promoted and well-reviewed by his periodical.[26] But Colburn's opportunism may have had another, greater impact on his magazine, namely its extraordinarily detailed attention to *le monde*. The *New Monthly* showed great interest in what it called "tokens of the times," widely scattered signposts of social life after Peterloo. Its highly paid writers searched for cultural straws in the wind, taking as signs of the times not national events or political cues but public attendance at Old Bailey executions or popular boxing matches, all symptoms of a national mind grown "callous and deceitful." One of its writers claims that "those who possess a laudable curiosity as to the meaning of things" should look "not to the leading article of the leading journal"—that is, not to political or philosophical discourse—but rather examine "its advertisements, where popular wants and popular desires are best indicated." So in the essay "Advertisements Extraordinary," this writer catalogs "mercantile phraseology" in all its amusing obfuscations and subliminal enticements.[27] Such a text acts as a web to snag the proper nouns of public life, unexpectedly discovering in them "the meaning of things." Philosophy sheds its cloisters to reappear as "The Philosophy of Fashion," a new intellectual necessity when the public world is no longer presided over by the "well-bred gentleman" but now by *haute monde*, the pretentious bourgeois, "him of the bastard breed...in the drawing room, in the theatre, or the street." The bourgeois is to be known by his incessant signifying, that figure whose instability of fashion and form now demand a social semiotics.[28]

To know such a society, one must become a reader of the social text. In the 1820s, the journal's nominal editor Thomas Campbell had much less impact on its social hermeneutic than its guiding editorial hand, Cyrus Redding, whose own essays often query the signs being manufactured in everyday life. Charles Lamb, Leigh Hunt, Stendhal, Bulwer Lytton, Horace Smith, and Hazlitt—who published much of his *Table Talk* and *Spirit of the Age* here—formed a repertory company of social interpreters in what Redding would later claim was the most widely circulated monthly journal at the highest price.[29] Surely the *New Monthly* was at the least the most prolific producer of social and cultural "distinctions," the great classifier of bourgeois life, testifying to what these writers began to describe in the 1820s as an amusing but essentially debased modern middle-class world.

Such debasement comes as a suprise in a journal noted for being "sparkling and elegant" in the 1820s, a monthly textbook of middle-class fashion. But as the writer of "Life in London" relentlessly shows, the fashion system is wracked with pain. T. C. Morgan classifies "metropolitan strugglers" as he ascends paragraph by paragraph up the scale of social ranks, from manual laborer to small tradesman to the professionals, dowagers, would-be gentlemen of the clubs, and finally the disdainful aristocrat, each level redoubling the misery of the rank beneath it.[30] In the older world it took money to produce distinctive signs. But if Morgan's nineteenth-century world is devoted to "making an appearance in the hope of making money," distinctions have to be displayed before one gets what makes one distinctive. Cultural capital does not arise from economic capital but must be, so to speak, borrowed on social credit to make wealth possible. Those in the "middle" suffer this borrowing as a painful pressure:

> Pride and vanity also find frequent sources of mortification in the contrast arising from the close juxtaposition of professional men to the really opulent, with whom their education and habits of life intimately connect them; and their self-love is perpetually wounded by the ostentation of upstart *nouveaux riches* their contemporaries, who in the more money-getting branches of industry have thriven, precisely because they have wanted the higher order of intellect on which professional men found their hopes of success. ("Life in London," 227)

As the nouveaux riches, the professionals, and the "really opulent" all struggle for position in social space, they become self-defeating performers of the social theatre. One's real economic place evaporates into clouds of cultural display. Thus the dowagers, "possessed of an easy fortune, are yet tormented with the itch of living in what they conceive to be good company; and...inflict upon themselves all the ills of poverty and dependence, in order to cultivate those who are above themselves in the hierarchy of fashion" (228). Somewhat higher up, the clubman can "rub his skirts against lords and members of Parliament" without any serious hope to be one of them. The *New Monthly* writer does not portray the club as a space of freely discoursing subjects who have become equals in the camaraderie of a public sphere. No such discursive equality appears possible for this journal, whose social grid accentuates only the rubbing, the semiotic friction of disparate ranks now visibly ajar from their older, tighter fit in the great chain of privilege.

Struggling for pleasure in the metropolis only guarantees its elusiveness. Pleasure must somehow be a by-product, achieved without the effort to reach it.[31] This impossible desideratum appears most tellingly in the revolting figure of the aristocrat, whose inheritance of economic capital would, by any older logic of the social order, make him the "true possessor" of London's cultural wealth. But, infected by an "appalling distaste for all around them," the highest orders fall victim to their own boundless disgust, a stance that in turn should disgust the reader: "Of all forms of human woe, this is the most sickening" (230). What sickens is the paradoxical lack of fit between a social subject and his pleasures. While the poor man's physical hardship leads understandably to his great personal suffering, the aristocrat's suffering arises "out of the plenitude of indulgence," and misery finds itself "seated on the throne of pleasure." At this the *New Monthly* writer recoils: it is "so perverse and so unnatural" that it well-nigh "exasperate[s] the spectator against his species." Among metropolitan strugglers, the demand for pleasure has produced its opposite, and thus dislocated, the social world of the 1820s demands a rereading, a new interpretation of the social text, in which the old social *index*—with its predictable fit between rank and sign—has now been displaced by the profusion of utterly excessive cultural signs.

But the *New Monthly*'s most plaintive, acute readings of social signs are reserved for the rude displacing of a more genteel mode of English living by newly rich merchants and manufacturers. "English Pride," for example, anatomizes the *haut bourgeois* invasion of the country estates, deconstructing those "fantastical shades of difference" which the countryside classes assign to their own emblems and gestures:

There is scarcely a parish in England which is not divided into visiting

classes, kept separate with almost as rigid an inviolability as the castes
of the Hindoos. The squire, the retired manufacturer or merchant, who
inhabits the great mansion, looks around him for all the similar estab-
lishments within the limits of a drive or ride, and confines the honour
of his acquaintance to those whose merits are attested by an unques-
tionable quantity of brick and mortar. He visits the house, not its in-
mates; and his mode of estimating their value, is not a whit less
preposterous than that of the pedant in Hierocles, who, having a house
to sell, used to carry about a brick in his pocket as a specimen. Next
comes the class who, without arriving at the dignity of a park or a domain, have been fortunate enough to lay up a store of gout and ill
health, by keeping their own carriages. They remember the proud exclamation of the Spaniard who fell in crossing his garden—"this comes
of walking upon earth"—and carefully abstain from noticing all such
terrestrial animals. They compose friendships as Sir Richard Black-
more did his poems, to the rumbling of their carriage wheels, and entertain a vague notion of Damon and Pythias, Pylades and Orestes,
Aeneas and Achates, as gentlemen in easy circumstances, who duly
went to call on one another in their own chariots, and scrupulously
left cards if either happened to be out. In the third class are those petty
dignitaries, who, as a line must be drawn somewhere, openly maintain
the double resolution of only visiting where a man-servant *is* kept, and
a shop is *not* kept. The former is the grand desideratum. It was once the
fashion, says the author of the *Tale of a Tub*, for all the world to wear
shoulder-knots. "That fellow has no soul, exclaims one; —where is his
shoulder knot?" Exactly thus do their modern imitators doubt whether
a man can possibly possess a soul fit for their sublime notice, unless
there can be a tag, rag, and bobtail, flapping from his servant's shoulder. That Desdemona should "see the Moor's complexion in his mind,"
and fall in love with a black, they condemn as unnatural, at the very
moment when they are perhaps attaching themselves to a blackguard,
because they see a bit of gold lace upon his footman's collar.[32]

Bricks, chariot-carriages, shoulder knots—each is an absurd, empty sign
whose apparent meanings, as Swift's shoulder knot supposedly signifies a
soul, can be emptied out by showing it as merely a means to demonstrate
"shades of difference." Against these empty signs of false pride and fraudulent superiority, the writer opposes citations from classical myth and literature, or the occasional French phrase. These countersigns to the signs he

demystifies all act as cultural figures of a more genuine, ineluctable meaning. Such signs cannot collapse under criticism, for they are always prior to
the social signs they can be used to unmask. The squire and the petty dig-
nitary are modern imitators, following ridiculously upon the echoes of
mythic figures, repetitions of the fools constructed by Hierocles or Swift, or
farcical shadows of tragic Shakespearean action. These hapless modern pre-
tenders appear as so many afterthoughts of history, caught in a larger signifying chain they cannot comprehend. Within this chain they must always
remain secondary, unconscious of their sources and predetermined in their
codes.

But, as the *New Monthly*'s writer Horace Smith implies to his reader,
"we" are quite consciously inscribed in the greater cultural codes. A merely
partial access to the empire of signs condemns the aspirant to a kind of
eternal recurrence, lost in a maze of gestures which he nevertheless con-
tinues to master in order to rise up the scale of social differences. We can
envelop these aspirants and their signifying system within our own cultural
system, and thus always remind them of their secondariness, their tawdri-
ness. Such outmaneuvering depends upon the warring of two sign systems,
in which one assumes a posture of authenticity as the other is dismantled.

Through such semiological one-upsmanship, the writer of "English
Pride" can then reclassify the English social order according to how its
members manage signs themselves. So there are the "middling classes,"
whose partial, inadequate command of signs falls under the more general
sign of "pride." Opposed to them are the great masses,

> . . . the *oi polloi*—the *canaille*—the rabble—the lower orders, as they are
> termed, whose social intercourse, if not so refined as that of their supe-
> riors, is probably more productive of enjoyment by its freedom, unre-
> serve, and exemption from all heart-burning and rivalry. Knowing that
> "their miseries can never lay them lower," they exemplify the meeting
> of extremes, and prove that the only classes who taste the true comforts
> of fellowship, are the few who are above jealousy, and the many who are
> beneath it. (137)

These masses of Englishmen stand wholly outside the empire of signs and
have hardly a role in it. The writer celebrates the spontaneity of the lower
orders because they remain innocent of the meanings and sign systems of
culture. The poor and laboring can thus be imagined to possess some surplus "fellowship" in a circle of collective plenitude unbroken by the representational, mediating function of signs.

And third, never named except as "the few who are above jealousy" but surely most important of all, is the "cultural" class of which the audience becomes a member in this text. Its cultural sign system has prevailed over the social semiotics of the "middling classes," and so this audience seems to escape classification through the victory of its own codes, which magically allow it to step outside class order altogether. The classifiers have avoided being classified, the penultimate strategy in reading the social text. Yet the classification takes form in another shape, less legible because it is the precondition that makes this reading possible: this classification is no doubt the form of the audience itself.

Under the satirist's knife, a whole intricate anatomy of social distinctions and differentiating signs has been demythologized in this text, only to be replaced by what we would now recognize as a more "modern," three-tiered notion of class. If the elaborate distinctions of "rank" and "degree" no longer function for a *haute bourgeoisie* as they once did for a genuinely aristocratic society, they must now be replaced by another interpretive system. A class will henceforth be defined by how it interprets signs, how it "reads" society as a whole. Even when writers do retain customary vocabularies of "rank" and "degree," they often gravitate to a more dynamic "lower," "middling" and cultural class model. What allows this shift between models of social order is not the idea—common in the eighteenth century—that character is already determined by social class but rather that a "reading" of society permits one to escape being typed or determined by his own social class. "Improvement," a *Fraser's Magazine* writer tells his audience, "can only be attained by men from examples not only striking, but separated and apart from themselves.... [It] must be effected by strongly contrasting one class with another."[33] An eighteenth-century writer might contrast a middle-class "intellectual man" against an aristocratic "man of sense," as the *Monthly Magazine* once described the inevitable difference between character types determined by their class membership. But the nineteenth-century writer presents classes as a medium of pedagogy. Here the learner discovers how to read social classes as instructive, interpretive signs:

> If you wish to hold up a lesson to a nobleman, who is a gambler, for instance, it will not be sufficient to point out as an example another nobleman of his own rank and circle in society, because the lesson loses its force by too close an approximation.... Take two lumps of marble from the quarry, and there is an obvious difference in their respective sizes and forms; but put them into the hands of a workman, and let

him cut them into exact cubes, and give them an equal polish, and
what eye shall distinguish one from the other? It is the same with man
between his rude or lowly state of moral excellence, and his high condition of refinement. The courts of all civilized princes are alike; the
manners of all aristocracies are uniform; in the lower grades of society
only are shades and distinctions made visible. What idea will the view
of a blank brick-wall afford? But a painting, however rude, and however
contrary to the rules of art, will nevertheless leave some scope for the
play of imagination. ("Fashionable Novels," 320)

Wherever "all is openness and nature, because the mind is untutored, and
the conduct inartificial and unsubdued"—that is, in the lower orders—the
social learner finds morally instructive marks of difference. Opposing the
polished, "blank" or nonsignifying class to the "shaded" or signifying class
requires neither deploring nor exalting class order. It merely shows how
necessary class differences become to the essentially middle-class ideal of
"improvement": classes are needed to produce a certain kind of knowledge.
The lower orders or working class may be innocent of signs, as the *New
Monthly Magazine* wanted to show, but only because they embody a signifying field for *other* classes.

From such texts, the middle-class audience can draw several critical
conclusions. If, as so many popular writings show it again and again, this
audience is especially privileged to interpret correctly the mass of signs
thrown forth in daily social intercourse, it is also made acutely aware of the
class below it by reading it as a text. The middle-class reader moves artfully
between a vestigial aristocracy always known by its ostentatious signs (here,
"gambling") and the "lower orders" who—innocent of signs, sometimes
frighteningly violent, at other times the sole repository of goodness and human community—offer a sign by their very crudeness. Thus reading society
as a symbolically instructive text, the middle-class reader edges away from
any class identity of his own, standing outside the order of social classes to
the extent he can textualize it.[34]

V

Yet the reader of the social text need not only manipulate signs; he can
also fabricate them. This reader does not embody a national Mind who can

be led by the hand of style to discover the collective mind fermenting in the recesses of his own psyche. Nor is he absorbed in the welter of public sign systems, learning social criticism by exposing false signs, or reading the signs posted by social order. Rather, the audience shaped by such journals as the *Edinburgh Review* is, in John Clive's phrase, *l'homme moyen intellectuel*, "the reader to whom everything did not always have to be explained."[35] From this stance of implicit knowingness, such a reader loftily reviews the array of social signs without being bound up in them, grasping the whole of society and the entirety of thought all at once.

No discourse was so immediately identified with power in the nineteenth century as that of the great party quarterlies, the *Edinburgh Review* and the *Quarterly Review*. Until 1816, when William Cobbett turned his *Political Register* into a widely read instrument of political education, the two reviews carved between them what seemed to be the universe of political thought. The *Quarterly* followed a narrow, predictable interpretation of Tory principle, but in its early years (1802–) the *Edinburgh* veered unpredictably from right to left, sometimes expounding the conservatism of a balanced constitution, at other times appearing almost radical as it spoke for the more progressive Whigs—as one Tory critic complained, "exalting the mob."[36] On the left, James Mill dismissed both reviews as representers of the same aristocracy, the *Quarterly* more candid about that fact than the evasive *Edinburgh*. From the right, De Quincey put a similar point in his organicist terms: the quarterlies are nothing less than the "the antagonist forces of the English constitution."[37]

But the *Edinburgh* was a much more powerful instrument for shaping a middle-class reading audience. Expensive and well-circulated (Francis Jeffrey estimated its 14,000 paid circulation reached three times as many readers in Britain's coffeehouses and parlors) the *Edinburgh* wove every outlook into its corporate voice.[38] Its skilled, well-paid writers composed a veritable ideological repertory company, deploying the "work" under review as the merest pretext for their own discourse. In the hierarchy of early-nineteenth-century publishing, the quarterly review at every point situates its reader atop a simulacrum of social order, turning nearly any subject into an intellectual surveyor's social map. This sense of total vision encourages a totalizing rhetoric, the elaboration of sweeping metaphors the writer can use to "read" everything else. At their most extreme, such metaphors diagnose catastrophe, driving the critique of signs toward that medical semiotic of social health and decay Carlyle would sketch out most dramatically in "Characteristics." In such texts, the usual complications of public signs and meanings disappear as the writer extracts a fundamental thread, which, when unravelled, unfolds the entire social fabric along with it. This insistent metaphor becomes a monolithic sign through which we can read all other signs. Naming all the registers of this sign is inherently critical, for such a reading always reveals the emptiness formerly populated by an abundant world of signs, but a world where the older distinctions of social and intellectual life now appear to have collapsed.

A particularly lucid form of this most extreme of critical discourses comes at the end of the 1820s, a decade in which social prophecies have filled the land: "the Millenarians have come forth on the right hand, and the Millites on the left." So the writer himself will come forth with his own discourse of catastrophe to counter the darkly clouded visions of the popular prophets: "Day after day, in all manner of periodical or perennial publications, the most lugubrious predictions are sent forth. The king has virtually abdicated; the church is a widow, without jointure; public principle is gone; private honesty is going; society, in short, is fast falling in pieces; and a time of unmixed evil is come on us."[39] Such prophecies merely make denser the "perplexity" of the times. To cut through this fog requires a special lens through which the "deeper tendencies" of these times "reveal themselves." In Thomas Carlyle's first *Edinburgh Review* essay, "Signs of the Times," this sign is "mechanism." The peculiar but vastly influential *kind* of discourse modelled in this essay must be quoted at length:

> Nothing is now done directly, or by hand; all is by rule and calculated contrivance. For the simplest operation, some helps and accompaniments, some cunning, abbreviating process is in readiness. Our old modes of exertion are all discredited, and thrown aside. On every hand, the living artisan is driven from his workshop, to make room for a speedier, inanimate one. The shuttle drops from the fingers of the weaver, and falls into iron fingers that ply it faster. . . . There is no end to machinery. Even the horse is stripped of his harness, and finds a fleet firehorse yoked in his stead. Nay, we have an artist that hatches chickens by steam; the very brood-hen is to be superseded! For all earthly, and for some unearthly purposes, we have machines and mechanic furtherances; for mincing our cabbages; for casting us into magnetic sleep.
> . . .
> But leaving these matters for the present, let us observe how the mechanical genius of our time has diffused itself into quite other provinces. Not the external and physical alone is now managed by machinery, but the internal and spiritual also. Here, too, nothing follows its

spontaneous course, nothing is left to be accomplished by old, natural methods. Everything has its cunningly devised implements, its pre-established apparatus; it is not done by hand, but by machinery. Thus we have machines for Education: Lancastrian machines, Hamiltonian machines—monitors, maps and emblems. . . . Then, we have Religious machines, of all imaginable varieties—the Bible Society, professing a far higher and heavenly structure, is found, on enquiry, to be altogether an earthly contrivance: supported by collection of monies, by foment-ing of vanities, by putting, intrigue, and chicane—and yet, in effect, a very excellent machine for converting the heathen. . . . Then every machine must have its moving power, in some of the great currents of society: every little sect among us, Unitarians, Utilitarians, Anabap-tists, Phrenologists, must each have its periodical, its monthly or quar-terly magazine—hanging out, like its windmill, into the *popularis aura*, to grind meal for the society. . . .

We may trace this tendency, we think, very distinctly, in all the great manifestations of our time; in its intellectual aspect; the studies it most favours, and its manner of conducting them; in its practical as-pects, its politics, arts, religion, morals; in the whole sources, and throughout the whole currents, of its spiritual, no less than its material activity. ("Signs of the Times," 442–44)

Tracing the sign of mechanism through scientific, religious, political, ethi-cal, and literary regions leaves no social or private realm undisturbed. The "times" are to be cataloged according to how mechanism patterns and per-vades them. As evidence of the modern, "the times" will be cited as so many voided signs lined up and penetrated by the master sign called "mechanism." Often in "Signs of the Times," these empty signs appear as labels of particular ideologies or methods associated with personal names: "To the eye of a Smith, a Hume, or a Constant, all is well that works qui-etly. An Order of Ignatius Loyola, a Presbyterianism of John Knox, a Wick-liffe, or a Henry the Eighth, are simply so many mechanical phenomena, caused or causing" (453).

"Mechanism" is here no ordinary sign, but a powerful master sign. A master sign deprives objects, ideas, or ideologies of their apparent distinc-tiveness: beneath the seemingly irreducible proper nouns lurks a leveling, homogenizing process that works the same way in each of its dissimilar hosts. "Mechanism" deprives relationships of their "mystery": "Instruc-tion, that mysterious communing of Wisdom with Ignorance, is no longer an indefinable tentative process...but a secure, universal, straightforward business, to be conducted in the gross, by proper mechanism" (443). Likewise, Mechanism corrodes and finally obliterates customary social relationships (ranks, degrees, gradations) so that inequality loses its tangible, face-to-face character. Not only ineffable mysteries, but also class conflict arises from Mechanism's power to permeate all social and private realms and reduce them to various ciphers of itself. "Wealth has more and more increased, and at the same time gathered itself more and more into masses, strangely altering the old relations, and increasing the distance between rich and the poor" (442). As the writer turns the object mechanism into the master sign "Mechanism," the deeper tendencies it creates in a now-diseased social body—a virus and its various hosts—become visible to consciousness.

Readers often recognize a master-sign discourse by its characteristic rhetoric: a repetitive noun-verb-object syntax, an exploitation of absolute determiners ("nothing, everything, every, all, none"), its repeated use of "not only, but also" constructions, its prophetic or oracular tone, and its frequent rhetorical catalogs. But its peculiar power lies in the way it produces a sign potent enough to represent all other signs. Rhetorically, this sign, like money, translates a whole series of discrete and unequal signs into some abstract, homogeneous quantity. "Mechanism," for example, is abstracted from the various fields it inhabits—philosophical doctrines, political relations, literary production, educational practices—so that it can be made the privileged sign that explains all these objects. Far from merely manipulating cultural sign systems, as earlier writers had done, the *Edinburgh Review*'s writer can actually seem to *create* a sign out of the obscure, opaque "times." Such an act freezes temporality, the times themselves, as it disengages from them the essence of modern practices and turns it into a medium of knowledge. It becomes the measure of all signs; bearing a special authenticity, it has "the ring of truth." This rhetorical operation has its epistemological equivalent—best known, perhaps, as "empiricism" in Louis Althusser's critique of Hegel.[40] But in the everyday sense of that term, Carlyle's discourse of the master sign obeys no common empirical limits. The more heuristic power is forced on a master sign, the more debased a reality it signifies. Thus the master sign generates a new form of social critique, a powerful new way to see through the foggy "perplexity" this writer set out to penetrate.

Readers of this essay in the *Edinburgh Review*'s June 1829 edition must have recognized in "Signs of the Times" a rather extreme version of so many writers' efforts in the 1820s to read modern times through the social and cultural signs they forged. Both readers and writers searched the empire of signs for a map, a stance, a code with which to grasp historical transformation and a middle-class audience's role in it. The master-sign discourse represents this search most recognizably for a later-twentieth-century reader because it remains today so popular a form of social criticism for a middle-class reading audience. Such mid-twentieth-century social critiques as Vance Packard's "hidden persuaders" or "wastemakers," Philip Wylie's "momism," or Christopher Lasch's "narcissism" all serve the mission of the diagnostic master sign. In *The Culture of Narcissism*, for instance, Lasch uses language only slightly more restrained than Carlyle's to uncover the "narcissistic personality" in the structure of modern sports, politics, psychology movements, education, sexuality, and business practices. For months a bestseller, the book derived its unexpectedly popular success not only from its skillful topicality, but equally from its vigorous update of a mode of discourse well-known to middle-class readers since at least the 1820s.[41] To this undialectical but potent rhetoric, English and American culture owes its most scathing self-criticism.

VI

The middle-class audience achieves its sense of cultural power by continually dismantling and reconstituting signs, but not without a recurring anxiety about its own act. The *Athenaeum* sounds the typical refrain: flooded by newspapers, periodicals, and novels, modern British readers are "saturated and overwhelmed with details, and opinions, and thoughts, not born of reason, and feelings which are fancies, the produce and stock-in-trade of the present hour. We live not in the duration of time but amid a succession of moments. There is no continuous movement, but a repetition of ephemeral impulses; and England has become a mighty stockbroker, to whom ages past and future are nothing, and whose sole purpose and taste is to watch the news."[42] The deluge of writing appears to dissolve cultural duration into mere random impulses, smudging past and future into an endlessly repetitive, disorganized present. The reader of such texts becomes, as Baudelaire called the modern negotiator of city streets, a "*kaleidoscope* equipped with consciousness."[43] From Coleridge to Matthew Arnold, this fear of saturation, repetition, and fragmentation haunts the middle-class audience and its critics even as its writers form the affirming and critical interpretive modes of its cultural power.

In 1816 Coleridge pleaded, "From a popular philosophy and a philosophic populace, Good Sense deliver us!" Not only good sense, but the new audience Coleridge sought in the *Statesman's Manual* would have to deliver England from the philosophic populace being shaped in middle-class as well as radical journals. Coleridge rigorously distinguished the prose styles through which he addressed these diverging audiences, insisting that *A Lay Sermon* could be read by "any man of common education and information," any reader of the *New Monthly Magazine*, the *Edinburgh Review*, or *Blackwood's*.[44] Certainly he needed a means to separate his readership from theirs, for to all appearances his own stance might be difficult to distinguish from that, say, of *Blackwood's Magazine* in its tortuous attempt to grasp intellectual desire. At least William Blackwood recognized in Coleridge a potential contributor and begged Coleridge to write for him. Balking, Coleridge quoted back to Blackwood "the words which Mr. Wordsworth once used to Longman: 'You pay others, sir, for what they write; but you must pay me for what I do not write, for it is in this (i.e. the omissions, erasures, &c.) that costs me both time and toil.' "[45] Coleridge's omissions and erasures would have been vast, since he could not address the audience of journals like *Blackwood's* without sermonizing to it, lecturing in a mode that could only violate the stance toward an audience formed by the discourse of *Blackwood's* and other middle-class journals.

What they constructed was a "reader" who learns to negotiate the positive and negative hermeneutics of reading the social text. In the positive moment, the psychological mind expands along the stylistic, often contorted corridors of the textual pursuit of Mind; negatively, the social mind forms and collapses distinctions, the power of its critical act becoming the measure of its own distinction from all the social signs it encounters. Sublimely enlarged at one extreme, severely reduced when it makes critical judgments of taste (the parodic echo of Kant's Third Critique seems unavoidable) the reader formed in such texts discovers himself both individuated and generalized, both a solitary interpreter and, by a silent extension, part of a greater collective interpreter mapping out the cultural landscape where it is both everywhere and nowhere. This reader tends to be absorbed into the discourse, neither addressed nor spoken for, but situated all along the curve of his reading, unlocalizable in a space that can be read about—in a word, *unrepresentable*. This elusiveness corresponds to a peculiar subjectivity, one also being formed elsewhere in the late eighteenth and nineteenth centuries by paintings and novels. An art historian contemplating a peculiar form of this subjectivity in French painting between 1750

1850 calls it a mode of "absorption," a means of recruiting the beholder into the painting without seeming to do so. Against the absorptive stance toward a reader—one which always posits his deep subjectivity—can be arrayed the alternative modes of the rhetorical, the spectacular, or the "theatrical."[46] But while the latter acknowledge the audience as a popular or collective formation, the mode of self-conscious middle-class reading elides such a formation by constructing a sovereign "reader" without visible ground, a reader who is constituted as everywhere and nowhere by means of the affirmative and critical hermeneutics worked out in his public texts.

That such a reader belongs historically to a specifically "middle-class" audience becomes evident only when that audience is understood to acquire its peculiar interpretive strategies against the pressure of other audiences' interpretive modes. The English mass audience formed in the 1820s, for example, never learns to constitute its own signs. Rather, it faces in its texts an allegorical world already overcrowded with signs. This audience learns to recuperate the meanings and confirm the desires of a well-nigh mythological world anterior to public signs. There it attempts to recover a sense of human community and natural benevolence seemingly lost in the rush of the nineteenth century. Yet it can "find" those desperately necessary values only within the outward signs of alienation, class domination, and imperial aggressiveness. Still another audience—the radical readership of William Cobbett, Richard Carlile and the later Chartist writers—resists the power of signs altogether. The radical text tries to locate itself outside the making and unmaking of signs, opposing to them the blunt, experienced facts of historical change itself. This is also an interpretive stance, one whose adequacy both middle-class thought and later Marxist theory will challenge.

The middle-class audience, however, always remains within an interpretive world, tirelessly remapping its textual terrain. Equally self-confirming and self-critical, it moves repeatedly from verbal to social texts and back again, always redefining what it means to be "middle class." Unlike an older aristocratic order or an inchoate, insurgent working-class movement, writers and readers of the middle class cannot finally proclaim their own social, political, or historical identity without already having discredited it. Their historical restlessness, their perpetual self-displacement, their hunger for permanent reinterpretation all find articulation in the mooring and unmooring of the sign.

Three

From Crowd to Mass Audience

> O Friend! one feeling was there which belonged
> To this great city, by exclusive right;
> How often, in the overflowing streets,
> Have I gone forwards with the crowd, and said
> Unto myself, "The face of every one
> That passes by me is a mystery!"
>
> —Wordsworth, *The Prelude* (1805)

> The spectacle is not identifiable with mere gazing, even combined
> with hearing. It is that which escapes the activity of men, that which
> escapes reconsideration and correction by their work. It is the
> opposite of dialogue. Wherever there is independent *representation*,
> the spectacle reconstitutes itself.
>
> —Guy Debord, *Society of the Spectacle*

ENGLISH readers in the early nineteenth century confronted the burgeoning powers of machines, spectacular industrial creation, a reenergized capitalist city. A new kind of audience had to be invented to negotiate these powers, a "mass" audience that would discover its own image in what it read:

> The crowd—no subject was more entitled to the attention of nineteenth-century writers. It was getting ready to take shape as a public in broad strata who had acquired facility in reading. It became a customer; it wished to find itself portrayed in the contemporary novel, as

the patrons did in the paintings of the Middle Ages. The most success-
ful author of the century met this demand out of inner necessity. To
him, the crowd meant—almost in the ancient sense—the crowd of cli-
ents, the public. Victor Hugo was the first to address the crowd in his
titles: *Les Misérables, Les Travailleurs de la mer*.[1]

Walter Benjamin's portrait of the French writer's created public also fits the
audience formed by England's "cheap" journals that both addressed and
imaged a mass readership: the *Mirror of Literature, Amusement, and Instruction*; the *Hive*; the *Penny Magazine*; *Chambers' Edinburgh Journal*; and
countless more. The crowd's other images in the eighteenth and nineteenth centuries—as the mob, the rabble, *la canaille*—would have to be
transformed into a representation of a new popular audience whose past
and future could momentarily be glimpsed.

As a strategy for shaping a mass audience, the image of the crowd is a
veritable anthology of all social classes and types. Workers jostle in the
same crowds aristocrats do; prostitutes mingle with captains of industry. It
is often a very strange crowd, which the writer portrays as though it were
self-consciously posing for its own portrait. Collectively the crowd is un-
fathomably mysterious, as Wordsworth had most jarringly painted it, but
the mass writer can turn it into a taxonomy in which each of its members
reveals a singular desire with a mere gesture. Accounts of this crowd share
the cheap journal's pages with descriptions of inexplicable natural phenomena; strange predatory animals; obscure but dramatic historical events;
exotic Eastern figures; and biographies of such staple commodities as sugar,
tobacco, paper, and beer. But in this unique discursive space, the mass
reader never becomes the interlocutor of political or philosophical argument. The new popular journals transubstantiate dialogue in a universe of
discourse that seems to seal off the immediate political world from its own
mythological realm. Yet as we shall see, this writing also confronts the most
overwhelming historical energies of the nineteenth century.

Mapped on a disparate group of possible readers, the mass public as an
idea must be continuously tested, questioned, or reimagined. If, as T. J.
Clark has written, the idea of a public is a "prescience or phantasy within a
work and within the process of its production,"[2] the new audience is doubly
invented as the mass writer works to create a *kind* of reader, yet imagines a
public of all classes and all psychological or social types. This reader is not
to be abstracted from his audience in a singular act of literary production.

Rather, he must be incessantly situated among actual and possible social formations, less as an individual than as a human or social type for whom the question of *belonging* requires continuous answer. For this reason the enigmatic crowd appears again and again in these writings, openly or in some displaced form. Around the crowd or its individual human types the writer articulates a stance toward the complex nineteenth-century city, toward mechanical powers of the steam press or the gas light works, toward all the forces of some profound historical transformation that the mass writer's language constantly attempts to mythologically recontain. The crowd itself is also being historically transformed: for the first time, it is being consciously addressed as a public. In this myriad figure the relation of the individual to the collectivity, the conflict of social classes, and the reader's own place in an emerging, bewildering social order that baffles human desire will be explored, rearranged, even fantasized.

I

As if to confirm what Coleridge called the "Overbalance of Commercial Spirit," Charles Knight's *Penny Magazine* (1832) was the first to address the English reader as a *buyer*. Knight and the Society for the Diffusion of Useful Knowledge calculated popular discourse by a new economics of mass publishing on thin profit margins and the plotting of complex financial curves.[3] But this was neither England's first mass public, nor the first attempt to shape one. Two earlier, short-lived cheap publications—James Losh's *The Oeconomist* (1798–99) and George Miller's *Cheap Magazine* (1813–14)—imagined their audiences as victims of war, poverty, crime; both failed to galvanize large audiences. No doubt the vision of a vast commercial audience was inspired instead by Cobbett and the English radical writers Wooler, Wade, Carlile, and Hone, whose lively political journals gathered huge readerships between 1816 and 1820, ranging from ten to a hundred thousand or more artisan radical readers. Charles Knight tracked the making of England's radical public, believing there was much to learn from a man like Cobbett: "There is a *new power* entrusted to the great mass of the working people. . . .[Cobbett's] 'two-penny trash,' as it is called, has seen farther, with the quick perception of avarice or ambition, into the intellectual wants of the working classes."[4]   Against the radicals Knight brought out his own *Plain Englishman* in 1820, "directing the affections to what is reverend and beautiful in national manners and institutions." Reverend but unrewarding, Knight's *Plain Englishman* and its "small voice of popular knowledge" whispered ineffectually to a London "gone mad" about William Hone's popular *Political House That Jack Built* and Queen Anne's sensational trial. But in September 1822 appeared the *Hive* (1822–24), a two-pence illustrated journal registering such "remarkable events" as "execution by the knout," or the "Black Hole at Calcutta," spectacles incommensurate with Knight's pieties of popular knowledge. By November 1822 John Limbird launched the *Mirror of Literature, Amusement, and Instruction* (1822–47), a sixteen-page, two-pence journal modeled on the *Hive*. The *Mirror* became the standard text among 1820s "cheap" journals, its initial issues reputed to sell eighty thousand to a hundred thousand copies and widely imitated during the next ten years.[5]

The new popular journals combined crude woodcuts with texts, but such images did not simply illustrate the text. They required interpretation by the text, which had to position its public to read them. The *Mirror* established the mass journal as collage, a strangely constructed sequence of verbal and graphic images. A world would be reflected here, but it would be mirrored in discontinuous shards with no visible principle of continuity. Unlike *Blackwood's* or the *Edinburgh Review*, the mass journals make no attempt to present a corporate discourse. Their reader is plunged into anthologies without a panoptic vantage on the textual whole. Beside "The History of Manufacture of Writing Paper," "The Adventures of Michael Doherty, Soldier of Misfortune," "Customs at Whitsuntide," and "The Snake Charmer," the *Mirror*'s reader also finds Byron's "On the Greeks Who Lately Fell at Thermopylae," a chapter of Scott's *Quentin Durward*, or a passage from the *London Magazine*. The *Mirror* helped popularize writers like Byron and Scott, but also imported texts from the journals meant for middle-class readers: *Blackwood's*, the *Monthly* and *New Monthly* magazines, the *Edinburgh* and *Quarterly* reviews. What often appears in the latter journals as textual decor becomes for the mass reader the very essence of middle-class reading. This refracted language seems to offer a fountain of verbal possibilities:

> A Poor Relation is—the most irrelevant thing in nature—a piece of impertinent correspondency—an odious approximation—a haunting conscience—a preposterous shadow, lengthening in the noontide of your prosperity—an unwelcome remembrancer—a drain on your purse—a more intolerable dun on your pride—a drawback upon success—a rebuke to your rising—a stain in your blood—a blot on scutcheon—a rent in your garment.[6]

Breathing forth fragments of cultural codes, such language appears to exhaust the possibilities of naming and lodges the social reference in a seam-
less web of conscious symbolic stereotypes.[7] Like condensations the later
mass reader finds in the *Reader's Digest*, these passages from the middle-
class journals reappear in the mass text to give its own audience the sense
of reading what the middle class reads. Hence the mass journal seems to
vastly expand the possibilities of reading itself. All those texts "original to
the *Mirror*" signal a cultural plenum in which this audience includes but
exceeds the worldliness of its exemplar, the cultivated middle-class public.

Still, it is not enough to quote the texts of the middle-class audience:
the mass journal reaches out to cite the dialects of the whole social sphere,
those "modern phrases" that distinguish modern speakers but at the same
time reveal what lies beneath their diverse social dialects:

> Killing an innocent man in a duel (according to the present phraseol-
> ogy) is called, an affair of honour; violating the rights of wedlock, an
> affair of gallantry; defrauding honest tradesmen, out-running the con-
> stable; reducing a family to beggary by gaming, shaking the elbows; a
> drunkard, the worst of all livers, is a *bon vivant*; disturbing a whole
> street and breaking a watchman's head, a midnight frolic; exposing
> some harmless personage to insults, annoyances, and losses, a good
> hoax; uttering deliberate falsehoods, shooting the long bow, &c, &c.[8]

Here the writer preserves the linguistic peculiarity of London's social languages, only to translate them back into a bland *lingua communis*. This collection of "modern phrases" has been detached from its corresponding
ensemble of speakers, who will reappear in the form of the mass writer's
crowd. When "crowd" becomes "audience," it must be quieted, the dialogic
murmer of its innumerable voices displaced by proxy of the mass writer
himself.

Thus multiplying the social dialects this audience can assimilate, the
mass journal also multiplies the very objects of discourse. The mass reader
becomes the focal point for countless "mirrored" discourses bound by a bi-
zarre principle of order. Pages of the *Mirror*, the *Hive*, or the *Penny Magazine* read like pages fallen out of an eighteenth-century encyclopedia and
reassembled in a new "world book." One passage catalogs the cityscape of
Paris ("1,100 Streets, 10 Lanes, 111 Passages, 32 Quays, 18 Boulevards...");

another tells of "James II and His Second Queen"; a third describes "The Table in the Middle Ages."[9] Past and present, the remote and the nearby, are set side by side; biographies of historical figures and staple commodities inhabit the same narrative space.

This bricolage of popular writing is a conscious configuration of colliding objects, events, and styles. Drawing on the flotsam of eighteenth-century descriptive forms, the mass journal affords an early example of what Richard Hoggart calls the "working-class baroque": "the richness showing well and undisguisedly in an abundance of odds-and-ends . . . a melange whose unifying principle is the sense of an elaborate and colorful sufficiency."[10] The *Mirror* and other mass journals compose this cultural melange from all centuries, nations, classes, and types. But its "unifying principle" is less random than the accumulation of objects Hoggart discovers in modern working-class homes. The mass journal's strange encyclopedia displaces all discourses of political argument, philosophical speculation, and cultural discrimination one finds in *Blackwood's Magazine* or *Edinburgh Review*. Excluded from the dialogues of cultural power, the mass reader discovers an allegorical world overcrowded with signs. As Hoggart remarks of what often appears to be merely working-class materialism, the style of the working-class baroque is "less an expression of a desire for a heavily material and possession-laden life than an elementary, allegorical, and brief statement of a better, fuller life." The *Mirror*'s crowding of cultural fragments betrays beneath its clutter a longing, a utopian desire.

II

Nowhere is this imaginary plenitude more important to the mass writer's intended audience than in his typology of the London crowd:

A sameness in London! Preposterous! Every street, every square, every public walk, and every theatre, presents novelty and variety. The very shops with their shopmen and shopwomen, their proprietors and customers, offer a world of information and a wide field for remarks.

Neither the elegante, who canters through the streets to be admired, the debauché who half sleeps over his curricle horses, or by the side of his tilbury-groom, nor the rich subject for the gout, who lolls stupidly in his carriage, see much of this; but the man who studies his fellow-creatures, and whose active mind finds employment in all classes of life, can draw experience and knowledge from every character and from every scene in the eventful drama of existence. Such a man must be able to pass from the senate to the coffee-house, from the gay lounge of morning amusement to the busy scene of a Stock Exchange, and from taking the living portraits of titled idlers at auctions and in ice-shops, to the toil and bustle of trade and commerce.

. . . Shops, countenances—but above all, manners will all pass by him like the magic lanthorn. Without light it would produce no effect; —without a ray of genius he would see nothing but uninteresting men and women, crowded streets, busy and imposing tradespeople, by whom he is pressed and jostled, without deriving any benefit from his intercourse with the world, or his collision with mankind. But, blest with observation, life itself seems compressed for him into the abridgment of a morning walk.[11]

The "abridgment of a morning walk," like the mass journal's anthology of cultural pieces, condenses the fathomless crowd into a rich array of socially individuated types. Eighteenth-century writers had represented this crowd as a mass shape moving through London streets. Defoe's Crusoe, returning from isolation, feels more lonely in London's crowds than in natural exile; Addison's crowd calls "off his Attention" and wears out "his Mind"; Johnson's crowd at Charing Cross is a collective emblem ("the full tide of human existence"). More threateningly, Wordsworth's crowd streams by mysteriously, breaking out riotously in grotesque carnival shapes.[12] But whether the crowd elicits Johnson's joy or Wordsworth's fear, it always appears to them en masse, clearly outlined or formlessly congealed, displacing communal relationships or dissolving individual boundaries. The mass writer's crowd, however, is anthologized according to its individual energies:

The ruffian at Tattersall's, the half-pay officer hanging out for an invitation, the mercenary beauty fishing for a gudgeon, the adventure hunter casting about by chance, the park saunterer, the dinner hunter, the beau, or belle, on their road to an assignation, the minor or the young female on the road to ruin, the yawning time-killer, the reader on a bench under a tree, rooks and sharpers on the look out, the author feasting on his own brain, and the alderman in such a state of repletion that a doctor must inevitably be called in, the gaping countryman and the pert studier of fashion—surely these are subjects enough for contemplation.

Then suppose a man...strikes into Bond Street, and pursues his course down the Strand. How many various characters will he see in one linen-draper's shop! The superb dame who is there from idleness, and buys every thing, the fickle, troublesome fashionable, who shops from vacancy of mind and habit, and who turns over every thing without the least intention of purchasing, the boarding-school miss who looks wistfully at a rich aunt, but cannot soften her aunt into the purchase of a lace veil or a French shawl, the arch cyprian who eyes an embroidered gown and the linen-draper, or some chance male customer in the shop, with equal fondness—and, lastly, the adroit shop-lifter, with Argus eyes on every side. ("Life in London," 173)

The "ruffian," the "rooks and sharpers," the "cyprian"—these quaint common nouns carry a charge like those of Dickens's proper names, which already spell out his characters' predictable tendencies toward action. These types are not only stereotypical, predictable by their very names, but above all *purposive*. Like first rough drafts of a Balzacian population, the men and women in these passages act out designs and desires upon each other—with sexual or pecuniary motives—or upon objects. In their various stances toward the linen-draper's commodities, the customers in the shop betray their revealing, individualizing gestures, including the "arch cyprian" whose desires for a man and a commodity are the same. The figure of the prostitute, appearing in many euphemistic guises in the crowd, is the human type who herself doubles as a commodity among the *Mirror*'s idols of the marketplace.

These pickpockets, captains of industry, prostitutes, shopkeepers, and shoppers are not crowded atoms bouncing aimlessly against each other in an unfathomable gray sameness: they are the avatars of urban desire, embodiments of a pervasive human supply and demand. Their variously charged desires make them immediately visible. The crowd no longer threatens in its otherness; now it comforts and becomes friendly by spontaneously giving up the identities and secret desires of its members.[13] Reshaping traditional images of the crowd, the early-nineteenth-century popular writer reaches out to it as a public, renders the crowd personal and friendly, turns the anonymous massing of people in cities into social types whose characteristic acts express inward selves.

Thus the crowd "speaks" itself—yet it is silent. The mass writer always imputes to the crowd what he cannot hear; he fabricates meanings for expressions that remain just out of earshot. The commodity with its unexpectedly rich history, the Hindu snake charmer, the man about to be executed who makes a revealing move at the moment before death—these objects of the mass writer's attention share with the crowd an otherness that yet seems about to speak, to reveal itself. Never speaking in his own "voice," the writer inhabits the dramatized voices of others that displace his own presence to the reader. The mass writer appears to report the inner speech of the crowd, a potential and revealing speech only his own text can articulate. Gestural intimacies abound in this text of revelation: the writer opens up the insides of all those things or human figures that customarily display only their outsides.

Unnervingly noisy, the traditional crowd's tumult of voices drowned out the barely audible murmur of one's own inner speech. At such spectacles as public executions, the crowd's collective shouts could be interpreted as a lust for executive violence.[14] Writers of the 1820s still reported "noisy mobs beneath the gallows at the Old Bailey," but in the mass journals they described executions in Russia or India that evoked from their beholders a profound silence. Wherever the writer represents an execution or an atrocity, there is an speechless audience, a "silent group (and awful indeed was their silence)." Intensely visual, the punitive spectacle—"Execution by the Knout"—calls forth from its viewers a fascinated quiet:

> Women in Russia have undergone the punishment of the knout. The Abbé Chappe D'Auteroche, relates an execution of a female in the reign of Elizabeth the cruel.... The beautiful culprit mounted the scaffold in an elegant undress. She was surrounded by the executioners, on whom she gazed with astonishment, and seemed to doubt that she was the object of such cruel preparations. One of the executioners pulled off a cloak which covered her bosom, at which her modesty took alarm; she started back, turned pale, and burst into tears. Her clothes were soon stripped off, and she was naked to the waist, before the eager eyes of an immense concourse of people, profoundly silent.[15]

The profoundly silenced audience must be spoken for. To coordinate the reader's inner speech with the crowd's noisy tumult, the mass writer sublates the language of the crowd into his indirect, imputed language of individual desires. What makes this possible is the writer's erasure of all dialogue. He bridges with his own discourse the private, unheard speech of his represented figures and the silence of his reading audience.

III

But the task of making the crowd legible is never easy, for the writer must grapple with two kinds of conflict. He must ease the brutal otherness of the crowd for the lone individual. Yet he must also negotiate the distance between classes that one experiences within the crowd. Standing outside the crowd as isolated onlooker or wading into its jostling mix of people from all classes, the reader-subject needs to be reconciled to otherness in both its forms. Hence in journals like *Chambers' Edinburgh Journal*, writers often look in the city crowd for some analogue of the self: "What can be more interesting than 'the passing crowd'? Does not this tide of human beings, which we daily see passing along the ways of this world, consist of persons animated by the same spark of the divine essence, and partaking of the same high destinies with ourselves?"[16] In 1844 Friedrich Engels, stunned by his bruising contact with the London crowd, also asked, "Are they not all human beings with the same innate characteristics and potentialities?"[17] Yet notions of the crowd's latent humanity did not explain his perceptions of the crowd's "war of all against all" in the London streets, and so he went on to describe there a displaced form of class warfare.

The mass writer, however, evokes psychological paradigms to penetrate the outward mysteries of what he calls "The Passing Crowd":

How many tales of human weal and woe, of glory and of humiliation, could be told by those beings, whom, in passing, we regard not! Unvalued as they are by us, how many as good as ourselves repose upon them the affections of bounteous hearts, and would not want them for any earthly compensation! Every one of these persons, in all probability, retains in his bosom the cherished recollections of early happy days, spent in some scene which "they ne'er forget, though there they are forgot," with friends and fellows who, though now far removed in distance and in fortune, are never to be given up by the heart. Every one of these individuals, in all probability, nurses still deeper in the recesses of feeling, the remembrance of that chapter of romance in the life of every man, an early earnest attachment, conceived in the fervour of youth, unstained by the slightest thought of self, and for a time purifying and elevating the character far above its ordinary standard. Beneath all this gloss of the world—this cold conventional aspect, which all more or less present, and which the business of life renders necessary—there resides for certain a fountain of goodness, pure in its inner depths as the lymph rock-distilled, and ready on every proper occasion to well out in the exercise of the noblest duties. Though all may seem but a hunt after worldly objects, the great majority of these individuals can, at the proper time, cast aside all earthly thoughts, and communicate directly with the Being whom their fathers have taught them to worship, and whose will and attributes have been taught to man immediately by Himself. ("The Passing Crowd," 33)

Associatively the writer moves his reader from the alien, atomistic crowd to a different collectivity of personal intimacy and comfort. Against the crowd's sameness he balances the sameness of personal histories, their roots lying in earlier communal experience "with friends and fellows." Here the isolated self becomes a fulcrum between inner and outer figures of community—one anchored in his own breast, some "early earnest attachment. . .unstained by the slightest thought of self"; the other out in the world, now positioned to reveal the "fountain of goodness" within it. Going out of the self in romantic attachment and "losing" oneself in the crowd become parallel events, the personal experience taking the fear out of the public melting into the London crowd.

   Yet burrowing into the recesses of self to discover communion with the crowd does not resolve the other conflict always at the center of the mass writer's awareness. Sliding from metaphor to metaphor, the writer looks for those terms—circle of friends, romantic bond, fountain of goodness—which will fix his analogy between individual and crowd. Finally, however, he cannot avoid colliding with the perceptible barriers between classes one always finds in the crowd:

Perhaps many of these persons are of loftier aspect than ourselves, and belong to a sphere removed above our own. But, nevertheless, if the barrier of mere wordly form were taken out of the way, it is probable that we could interchange sympathies with these persons as freely and cordially as with any of our own class. Perhaps they are of an inferior order; but they are only inferior in certain circumstances, which should never interpose to prevent the flow of feeling for our kind. The great common features of human nature remain; and let us never forget how much respect is due to the very impress of humanity—the type of the divine nature itself! Even where our fellow creatures are degraded by

vice and poverty, let us still be gentle in our judging. The various fortunes which we every day see befalling the members of a single family,
after they part off in their several paths through life, teach us, that it is
not to every one that success in the career of existence is destined. Be-
sides, do not the arrangements of society at once necessitate the sub-
jection of an immense multitude to humble toil, and give rise to
temptations, before which the weak and uninstructed can scarcely escape falling? But even beneath the soiled face of the poor artizan there
may be aspirations after some vague excellence, which hard fate has denied him the means of attaining, though the very wish to obtain it is
itself ennobling. (33)

The mass writer does not ignore class separation but accentuates it. For this
is the needed passage from the crowd's alienating facelessness to the hidden
community's comforting sameness—the class structure that differentiates
one from those above and those below. "Above" and "below" momentarily
situate the mass reader in the topographical site of a social class. This is not
to distinguish the reader from all possible social classifications, as the
middle-class writer attempts to abstract his reader from any particular social
or economic rank. One must here be put momentarily *within* the class order
in order to recognize what lies beyond it. The very class difference that
seems to separate one from the "worldly" form of the upper-middle-class or
aristocratic figure, or from the "soiled face" of the artisan or laborer, must
be made the essential framework of some deeper "impress of humanity" beneath it. Class differences only mask the common human core within, yet
they are absolutely needed in order to find that core. Paradoxically, trivial-
izing class order is another way to reveal its necessity, for only by its agency
can a "true" classlessness emerge from the phenomenal flux.

Thus a singular enigma of the "popular": between an alien "mass"
(the faceless crowd) and an equally collective but internalized and now
comforting "humanity" mediates the sense of class difference that can neither be lived with, nor lived without.[18] Just as the crowd's alien temporality
(the "passing" crowd) turns into its opposite—the timeless communal spirit
hidden in each individual's breast—so the spatial arrangement of contrasting classes ("lofty" and low) frames the radiant sign, or "impress," of humanity for which all individual men and women are so many
reproductions. This special type of types—the great original of all those individualized social and psychological "types" the crowd constantly throws
forward for inspection—must always be "found," reconstructed, and reas-

serted within what the mass journal paints as a universe of astonishing variety, foreign and domestic, age-old and brand new, class-divided and classless. For a public inescapably facing bewildering historical transformations in the rush of the nineteenth century, what the mass journal must do is register and recuperate what was *always* there.

IV

"What the stage-coach has become to the middle classes, we hope our Penny Magazine will be to all classes."[19] Thus begins Charles Knight's *Penny Magazine*, which makes the seventeenth-century invention of stagecoaches, for a small but mobile middle class, analogous to early-nineteenth-century steam presses. In the early 1830s, the mass journal turns to the steam press already employed by daily newspapers, harnessing its expansive power that will shoot out cheap publications to all provinces and classes.[20] But the mass journal from the early 1820s had already professed fascination with mechanical power and industrial creation. Awed at the productive energy of the commercial city, industrial workplace, and busy machine, the mass writer brings these structures within the purview of the crowd. Still a central figure, the crowd with its individual human types now expands to gigantic proportions that include public and economic as well as private and intimate gestures. Revelation of the inwardly human within its outward and often alien social forms here shifts its gears to the role of the human and social within mechanical and economic spheres. Meanwhile, all the desires we have seen revealingly expressed in figures of the crowd will now, switched to a higher form of public dynamism, discover their transformation into the characteristic energies of the nineteenth century itself.

At night the London crowd swarmed under the gas lights. This new way to illuminate city streets, only gradually replacing older forms of lighting from 1800 to the 1820s, offered an immediate sign of what industrial power meant for the urban audience.[21] The *Hive* takes its mass reader to "The Gas Light Works," where text and illustration portray industrial spectacle as dramatically as the world's creation imagined in myth. The woodcut shows laborers stoking the retorts that separate gas from coal and propel it through labyrinthine conduits toward the streets. In the foreground looms a darkened figure with arms outstreched imperiously toward workers in the background, who themselves stretch melodramatically toward gap-

ing furnaces. Above these figures rises dense smoke in a chiaroscuro spectacle of shadow and firelight reflection. The reader's eye moves from the dim
foreground to the brilliantly lit background, where smoke, fire, and hercu-
lean labors form a presentiment of creation itself. Above all this, through
an opening in the roof, a crescent moon punctuates the dark night.

The text that interprets this picture elaborates three perceptual types:
casual observer, man of science, and an "educated man" standing in for the
reader. At issue is what stance, what power of description, what social or
class position will be able to take in this spectacle without being swept up
in it:

> The man of science contemplates it with a feeling of exultation: he
> sees in the retort-house, the heart, the living principle which gives ef-
> fect to a magnificent system, alike honourable in its place among the
> discoveries of the age, and excellent for its usefulness to the commu-
> nity.
>
> The casual spectator, ignorant perhaps, or heedless of the use of
> what he sees, finds himself surprised into an admiration of its effects;
> he is alternately engulphed in smoke, dust and darkness, and dazzled by
> the effulgence of flame, of brilliancy too great for his organs of sight: he
> sees men labouring under an uniform temperature, very far exceeding
> that of any known climate of the earth, he is encompassed by fiery en-
> gines which continually startle him by their explosions. . . .
>
> An educated man, of a poetic imagination, will at a glance over
> the scene, raise a perfect Tartarus before him; here he will find yawning
> mouths, belching flames, and pouring ignited matter into caverns of
> fire below; here he will see in terrific indistinctness the wheel of Ixion
> with its serpents; and monstrous chimerae without end. All gradations
> of light are exhibited from impenetrable darkness to the finest possible
> coruscations of flame; "forms dimly seen" flit in the gloomy recesses of
> the place, while the human figure in its finest athletic character is dis-
> played before him in an infinite variety of action, and under circum-
> stances of light and shadow, and of grandeur in the general effect,
> probably unnoticed and unintelligible to all but persons of his own
> class; and his imagination is assisted by the Babel-like confusion of
> tongues which occasionally arises, loud explosions from every quarter,
> remote as well as present, and the various discordant noises which pre-
> vail. He sees the blackened form of the toiling and uneducated laborer,

and he perhaps contrasts this figure with that of a directing engineer who stands beside him; the first seems hardly conscious of his nature, and is certainly ignorant of the extent of its capabilities; the other is a man of science, and practical skill, who by the mere effect of cultivation is enabled to take the whole of this wonderful arrangement, as it were in his grasp at once, from the development of its first principles, through all the ramified calculations of effect, and the minutiae of organization to a given practical result. The striking difference of this colouring would induce him to lament the violent inequality of their conditions, but the jocund laugh of the former in the intervals of his labour, awakes him from his philosophical dream, and reminds him that these objects of his attention are alike the creatures of circumstance, and that they are respectively content.[22]

There are three ways to perceive such a spectacle: having the senses engulfed by it (casual observer); seeing into its inner principle (man of science); or associatively replacing it with mythic figures of the imagination (educated man). Between the poles of sensual and intellectual response, the imaginative reading ranges among mythological associations to find "all gradations" and "infinite variety" between the extremes of blindness and insight. Language itself is hardly adequate to signify this spectacle. Indeed, the very "Babel-like confusion of tongues" helps the imaginative mind work, for it can take its own confused perceptions as signs of "grandeur" and power. The educated man needs oppositions (light/day, ignorance/knowledge) between which he can interpretively move. At the same time, the writer's own language oscillates between two extremes of representation. Often hesitant and speculative when describing the reader's imputed interpretations ("probably...perhaps...seems"), it also insists on hyperbolic superlatives ("finest athletic character") to validate its sense of meaning. Both unsteady and vehement, his language forms oppositions even when it thematically insists on variety and gradation.

When the writer moves inside the gas light works, the casual observer and man of science become the laborers working the furnace and the directing engineer. Like the observer whose senses are engulfed, the laborer is utterly determined, "unconscious of his nature." The foreman/engineer now represents intellectual comprehension, that knowledge of the whole industrial process required by the new industrial order's division of labor. But this figure of knowledge is likewise determined. Director and laborer once again form the poles of industrial activity. Consciousness and unconsciousness, insight and blindness, knowledge and ignorance, dominator and dominated—these are the opposites whose tension produces creative industrial energy, and the reader who is to comprehend the powers of industrial production must move between these poles. Here "violent inequality" becomes the lamentable but essential precondition of knowledge; once recognized, it diminishes before the greater order it makes possible. Hence the educated man's eye moves transcendently above the panorama of technical creation to the crescent moon above, the sign of a Nature that encloses violent oppositions below it in an unexpected concord.

A persistent pattern runs through all these writings on the crowd, its perceptual and social types, and the urban industrial order framing them. Direct confrontation of social classes, whether jostling in the crowd or set in opposition on the factory floor, has to be met with another figure: unquenchable human desire, or a well of deep inner goodness, or the symbolism of a benign nature. None of these signs of a latent authenticity in the world can be perceived by the pure intellectual power. While the middle-class reader of *Blackwood's* or the *Edinburgh Review* asserts intellectual and cultural power in the act of reading itself, the mass reader recovers another sense of power: the recurrent discovery of a genuine human naturalness beneath all the appearances of the nineteenth century, which presents itself in turn as a series of mechanisms that first thwart such a discovery, then reveal the very means of realizing it. Always confronted with dehumanizing forces, the mass reader can yet be led through them toward something essentially, eternally human which these forces help organize. It is not a question of denouncing the crowd, the industrial workplace, or the order of classes; rather it is to dis-cover them, reveal what they hide, at last find a "human" rationale for the palpably inhuman surfaces they present.

Indeed, what natural history, strange animals, Hindu snake charmers, commodities with their own biographies, historical portraits, or discourses on city, crowd, and factory have in common is that their mysterious outward shells can all be penetrated to expose something common to a now reconstructed "human experience." The mass reader thus enters something wholly inclusive, a "society" that draws into its orbit the most private human expressions as well as the most forbidding impersonal public structures. Addressed in terms of the crowd, the mass audience negotiates discontinuities between the private and natural, and the public and seemingly unnatural. This is why the mass magazine can become in the 1830s the instrument for opposing all those attempts to *change* social order by a resurgent radical movement in its most coherent form, Chartism. Against the radical writings of Cobbett, Henry Hetherington, and Ernest Jones, both widely circulated journals like the *Penny Magazine* and *Chambers' Edinburgh Journal* and more provincial ones like the *Bristol Job Nott* wield a potent metaphor of society within which human desire and economic demand, human nature and historical change can be imaginatively fused.

V

When it tries to define society itself, the mass journal looks not only to the crowd but to the great commercial city that houses it. Here the writer must adapt an older discourse of the city, for which the crowd itself appeared as James Thomson's "seditious herd," Hogarth's crowd of Gin Lane, or, more threateningly, the "mob" whose spontaneous riots challenge the city's civilized order.[23] At the same time, the city had been traditionally opposed to the country, the peaceful rural seat or country house to which an Addison gladly escaped from a city that pressed too hard on his senses. As Raymond Williams has shown, the positive city against the disheveled crowd and the negative city against the organic country can both appear in the same text, as in Thomson's *The Seasons*.[24] To represent the city as the "mechanism of society," as we read in the provincial *Bristol Job Nott* (1831), the writer must wrestle with traditional contradictions between the city and crowd on the one hand, the city and country on the other. Yet he must also capture that intrinsic energy only the city possesses:

> Then commerce brought into the public walk
> The busy merchant; the big warehouse built;
> Raised the strong crane; choked up the loaded street
> With foreign plenty; and thy stream, O Thames,
> Large, gentle, deep, majestic, king of floods!
>
> (*The Seasons*, "Autumn," 118–22)

Explaining to his public how society is ordered like a machine, the writer of "The Mechanism of Society" thus turns his readers toward the exemplary city:

Now, observe the general activity and the vast variety of employments in a large mercantile community; for example, in London, the chief of cities, with its 1,200,000 inhabitants. What a constant influx there is of droves of cattle, and waggon loads of provisions, from all parts of the kingdom. Richly laden vessels are borne along the Thames with every tide, containing cargoes of native produce from all parts of the coast, and the productions of every country in the world. Long before the great mass of the population are awake, the markets for meat, fish, vegetables, etc. present a stirring scene, being crowded with country people and salesmen. The neighboring streets are nearly impassable, from the numerous carts and vans that are ranged along to carry off to shops and stalls throughout the city, the supplies for the tables of the wealthy, and the poor man's homelier meal.... Presently foot-passengers, carts, cabs, waggons, and coaches traverse the city, and thread their way through the crowded streets. The shops are opened, and all the commodities which the combined industry of thousands has been able to collect, their ingenuity to invent, their skill to execute, pass in rapid succession from the ship to the warehouse, the manufactory, the shopkeeper and the consumer. Here we find the most skillful workmen employed at the highest wages; merchants in the different branches of trade arranging their exports and imports, and trafficking with the retail dealers; statesmen deliberating, and deciding the most momentous questions of foreign and domestic policy. Here are the acquirers of wealth; there the possessors of property which industry has already accumulated; the learned and the literary; the busy and the idle; the sober and the dissipated; the prosperous and the wretched. However opposite their characters and circumstances, however unknown to each other are the individuals composing this vast multitude, they mutually depend on one another for the necessaries and enjoyments of life.[25]

Eighteenth-century writers who apostrophized the city as Thomson did also called up the image of a prelapsarian country against which the modern city is only a sign of "these Iron Times."[26] But as the passage above suggests, the nineteenth-century writer's city swallows up the country. "Meat, fish, vegetables" and the "country people" themselves become arms of the city, gears in its social machine. No longer outside the city, the country's produce and producers take their place as a "stirring scene" within the metropolis. Incorporating signs of the country within the city's inclusive scope, the mass writer also implicitly confronts the radical writer like William Cobbett, whose prose of the 1820s and 1830s politicizes the opposition of city and country, defending rural community against the atomism of parasitic, misshapen urban "wens." Meanwhile the mass writer celebrates the victorious city, its surging mechanical energy, its power to turn all other topographic sites into satellites of itself.

To valorize the city as a vast, pulsating social machine, the writer employs a remarkable rhetorical enumeratio cataloging its multitude of activities. The city's commodities, laborers, traders, governors, and even figures of the crowd all have their machinelike functions. The writer nominalizes verbs and adjectives so they make streams of balanced nouns and noun phrases—"foot passengers, carts, cabs...skillful workmen employed... merchants arranging...statesmen deliberating...the busy and the idle, the sober and the dissipated." Thus figures of the crowd balance each other, merchants balance workers, and the august statesman earns no more descriptive privilege than soiled country people. The noun-based style equates process and product, labor and commodity, idler and governor. No longer a congealed shape that threatens urban order, the crowd can here be cataloged, balanced, and finally fitted into categories that make up the social machine; democratically, all parts have irreplaceable roles. The mass writer's mechanical metaphor levels older hierarchies within the city, his language making all urban activities a metonymic chain of interrelated acts.

But while it makes London itself a balanced order equating social opposites in a smoothly working mechanism, the mass journal also tilts this energized city toward the outside foreign world. All this human and mechanical power is moving toward some greater purpose. Eighteenth-century writers often pictured London as a world center, where goods from all countries mixed on its cosmopolitan table. Addison, for example, plunges into the Royal Exchange, what he calls "the private Business of Mankind, making this Metropolis a kind of Emporium for the whole Earth." Here, as vicarious world citizen, the writer is "jostled among a Body of Armenians... lost in a Crowd of Jews...I am a Dane, Swede, or Frenchman at different times." Addison's city is London as center of the mercantile, benevolent empire in which the city receives and bestows gifts. "The Fruits of Portugal are corrected by the Products of Barbadoes.... Our Rooms are filled with Pyramids of china, and adorned with the Workmanship of Japan." The eighteenth-century writer paints the city as the world's passive commercial center, its imports balancing each other just as the merchant himself balances classes to "find Work for the Poor, add Wealth to the Rich, and Magnificence to the Great."[27]

But the *Bristol Job Nott*'s writer shifts his emphasis from those "merchants. . . arranging their exports" to the third and perhaps most emphatic of his essential urban actors: "statesmen deliberating, and deciding the most momentous questions of foreign. . . policy." Addison's was an empire made by "Men thriving in their own private Fortunes and at the same time promoting the Public Stock." But the new city of the nineteenth century does not depend on the private pursuit of gain to regulate domestic and foreign affairs. Turning from empire's passive center to its active directorate, the mass writer's city is armed with "foreign policy," a subtle but decisive movement. The city drives a social *machine*, whose intricately balanced internal workings produce an energy directed out into the greater world, transforming it, shaping it in the English city's own image. The eighteenth-century writer's urban benevolence yields to the mass writer's implicit aggressiveness, where even his habitual superlatives take on a suggestively nationalistic ring ("the most skillful workmen. . . at the highest wages; . . . the most momentous questions of foreign and domestic policy"). Thus the figure of the crowd, elaborated in terms of its most private desires, its hidden stores of goodness, or its productive role within the city, finds here an intimation of its greater function in historical development, to be at the structural center of the very transformation of the world itself.

VI

Among architects of the mass public, William Chambers most searchingly asked what it meant to create a broad popular audience in the nineteenth century. For him it meant reaching working-class readers as well as those of the middle class, and such intentions made more honest and more pained what, after careful investigation, he finally had to report: *Chambers' Journal*, he said, is read by "the elite of the laboring community; those who think, conduct themselves respectably, and are anxious to improve their circumstances by judicious means. But below this worthy order of men, our work, except in a few particular cases, does not go far. A fatal mistake is committed in the notion that the lower classes read." In larger towns, Chambers reported, "a vast proportion of the mercantile and professional persons of every rank and order are its regular purchasers"; but he was also forced to admit that among his more affluent subscribers, "a few express themselves dissatisfied with the homeliness of those articles which fall under the description of sketches of society. This kind of society, they say, is not theirs; it is that of our tradesmen."[28]

Despite its great expectations, the mass journal was finding its public largely among tradesmen and shopkeepers. This lower-middle-class audience dreamed less of cultural domination or political revolt than of a simpler social rapprochement between classes. Indeed, the mass journal's "crowd" is always the crowd visible from a shopkeeper's store window. While the mass writer impersonates a *flâneur* moving in and out of the crowd, the shopkeeper observes the crowd from within the firm, gazing out a window at the crowd of possible buyers. That figural window organizes the optical structure of the crowd but screens out the audible; a framing device, it produces what it appears transparently to reveal. Mass discourse transforms an abstractly impersonal mass into individualized types, who must in later developments of mass culture be surveyed, profiled, half-invented as consuming types by the pollster and the advertising researcher. In the 1820s and '30s those types appear immediately human in their deeply preoccupied, distinguishing excess. Each type displays a controlling function that situates him in the audience, the crowd, the "mass." No member of the crowd has an identity outside his perceived relation to the structured group, which oscillates between a faceless "mass" and the all-too-human. Thus the odd conditional-potential mood of so many verbs in these texts, particularly in the discourse of the crowd. Constructing the imputed inner speech of all its members, the mass writer fabricates in his verbs—"may," "can," "will," "would in all probability"—a discourse of what *remains* to be revealed amidst all the circumstances of the nineteenth century.

The fact that Chambers's careful sifting of readers' responses found so narrow an actual audience hardly vitiates the notion of a "mass public" itself. The crowd is an extraordinarily supple image. Writers for more cultivated middle-class audiences persistently isolate the crowd as an indecipherable rabble, while the radical writers refuse the thematics of the crowd altogether and speak a different language of the "productive and parasitic classes." But by making the crowd a metonymy for personal and national togetherness, the mass writer can sidestep both class conflict and cultural alienation. In its fecund capacity to incorporate signs and desires of all classes, the crowd becomes a way to see through class structure into a suggestive classlessness. Similarly the mass writer can elaborate discourses that unfold inner secrets concealed by remote phenomenal appearances. His texts continually renew the promise that every reader can find the image of his own desire here, whether for communal connection, participation in imperial national motion, or innumerable other desires the mass writer can articulate. Thus the mass writer's representation of society itself:

a structure that initially hides but, the reader learns, is so organized as finally to disclose the conditions of realizing human desire. All this, like members of the crowd themselves, remains mute, unable to speak itself. The mass writer must divulge it. "They cannot represent themselves," as Marx wrote of the French lower middle class that brought Napoleon to power; "they must be represented."[29] Hence the mass writer represents them in inexhaustible images and a ceaseless stream of discourse.

Four

Radical Representations

> *Miranda:*   Abhorred slave,
> Which any print of goodness will not take
> Being capable of all ill: I pitied thee,
> Took pains to make thee speak, taught thee each hour
> One thing or other: when thou didst not—savage!—
> Know thine own meaning, but wouldst gabble like
> A thing most brutish, I endowed thy purposes
> With words that made them known. But thy vile race,
> Though thou didst learn, had that in't which good natures
> Could not abide to be with; therefore wast thou
> Deservedly confined to this rock,
> Who hadst deserved more than a prison.
> *Caliban:* You taught me language, and my profit on't
> Is, I know how to curse: the red-plague rid you,
> For learning me your language. (1.2.353–66)
>
> —Shakespeare, *The Tempest*

THE modern sense of the "public" as audience obscures its original sense, as the ancients regarded it: the body politic, the state.[1] As England's radical public formed by the principle of political opposition to the state, first in the mid-1790s, and then in the years between Waterloo and Peterloo, artisans, weavers, and factory laborers began reading the texts of political writers who worked out a withering critique of England's ancien régime. By 1819 English writers faced not a single but two national reading publics, implacably opposed in their politics and language. Drawn from disparate intellectual and rhetorical traditions, radical discourse shaped an audience it finally could not sustain after the collapse of Chartism. Like Caliban—that familiar figure of cultural abhorrence who cannot learn to use verbal signs without at the same time being turned into a social sign—radical writers and their audience would become both subjects and objects of English cultural power.

This radical public did not develop separately from middle-class reading and writing; it was not sealed off in its own social sphere. The idea of a radical audience presupposed a dominant public, and by declaring themselves dominated, English radical writers and readers also helped *produce* a self-consciously dominant culture. Against a real or imagined radical antagonist, middle-class writers had to redefine the ethos that distinguished them from "those below." Often the cultivated public and its writers made the gesture of pushing away the radical public into some sphere it could call the vulgar, the "infidel," or the propagandistic. Yet the radical public was not only a demonstrable audience in the late eighteenth and early nineteenth century: it was also something irritatingly lodged inside middle-class consciousness itself.

Like the mass writer's imagined public, the radical writer's audience bore resemblance to the eighteenth-century crowd, the riotous mob that could spontaneously revolt to defend traditional values and rights by what E. P. Thompson has called a "moral economy of the English crowd."[2] But unlike the mass writer's public, the radical audience was a *focused* gathering. Between the eighteenth-century "crowd" and the radical writer's "audience" intervened another collective form, that of the radical "meeting," whether the formal meetings of the London Corresponding Society in 1792, the Hampden Clubs of 1817, or the open-air meetings attended by thousands of artisans at St. George's Field in 1795, the Spa Fields in 1816, or St. Peter's Field near Manchester in August 1819. Small or large, such meetings echoed conventions of classical rhetoric, and the making of a radical audience in the early nineteenth century must be understood partly in terms of rhetorical tradition and its transformations. For "rhetoric" itself, as a mode of public discourse increasingly felt to be culturally outmoded and theoretically indefensible, would become attached to a new cultural site in the late eighteenth and early nineteenth centuries, as the language of radicalism in all its political and linguistic "excess."

This was the audience Coleridge, despite his plans for three Lay Sermons, could not bring himself address. The sermon he postponed found its way into the silence of his notebooks, where it becomes evident that his strategy was to disengage radical discourse from its laboring audience:

> The Demagogues address the lower orders as if each Individual were an *inseparable* part of the order—always to remain, *nolens volens*, poor & ignorant... That the Cobbetts & Hunts address you (= the lower Ranks) as beasts who have no future Selves—as if by a natural necessity you must all for ever remain poor & slaving. But what is the fact? How many scores might each of you point out in your own neighborhood of men raised to wealth or comfort from your own ranks?[3]

The pedagogic radical writer surely had no stake in keeping his audience ignorant. But what Coleridge found most tellingly absent from radical discourse was the individuated reader, a "future self" who could be formed in a dialectic of text, reader, and audience, and to whose careful making Coleridge devoted the inimitable labor of his own prose. No such "implied reader" haunts the radicals' texts. They confront their readers as collectives and representatives of collectives—"an *inseparable* part" of the social order, undetachable members of an audience contesting its position in social and cultural space. The radical text was not meant to form a singular bond between reader and writer, but to bind one reader to another *as* audience, a readership the radical writer both confronted and spoke for in a complex rhetorical act of "representation."

In stark contrast to the mass journals, where no one speaks but everyone is spoken for, the radical text is all talk, a stormy representation of one social discourse by another. Here, no voice is unsituated; each has a position, an argument, something to maintain. These texts work out strategies of quoting, parodying, rewriting, or inflicting semantic wounds upon the language of middle-class and aristocratic readers. Radical writers turn restive artisans from machine wreckers into Luddites of language, savage parodists of the dominant culture's ideological texts. In such writings, as Bakhtin remarked of social heteroglossia in the novel, "the dialogue of voices *arises directly out of* a social dialogue of 'languages.'"[4] But unlike the novelist, the radical writer always claims the last word, laying bare the rhetorical stance which his middle-class interlocutors find intolerably fixed. Necessarily so, for amid the proliferation of signs in the nineteenth century that makes urgent the struggle for their control, the real or imagined reference point must be that discourse and its audience whose position is never in doubt, the agons of the social text.

I

The English working class was "making itself," in E. P. Thompson's ambiguous phrase, throughout the late eighteenth and early nineteenth centuries, but it could not spontaneously generate its own discourse. A public for radical writing developed fitfully between 1791 and 1795, from the exhilarating first days of the French Revolution to the final prison doors that swung shut on radical leaders prosecuted for treason. Thomas Paine, Daniel Eaton, John Thelwall, Joseph Spence, William Taylor, and others formed greater or smaller artisan audiences, although no periodical or political tract could approach the reputed 200,000 circulation of Paine's *Rights of Man*.[5] From 1796, the year of Coleridge's *Watchman* and the *Monthly Magazine*, to 1816, when Cobbett published a two-pence version of his *Political Register*, it is difficult to speak in any sense of a popular radical audience. Cobbett himself had shifted from Tory to radical political allegiances by 1805, but his *Register* remained comparatively expensive (1s. 1/2d.) and narrowly circulated. Among middle-class intellectuals who had read Godwin in the 1790s, Leigh and John Hunt's *Examiner* (1809) formed a small audience of liberal reformers whom Hazlitt and Shelley addressed, a readership parallel to the radical artisan public.[6] Then, beginning with Cobbett's two-pence "Penny Trash" version of the *Political Register* in November 1816, artisans and laborers in tens of thousands read Cobbett, T. J. Wooler's *Black Dwarf* (1817), Richard Carlile's *Republican* (1819), John Wade's *Gorgon* (1818), Thomas Sherwin's *Sherwin's Political Register* (1817), William Hone's *Reformist's Register* (1817), Robert Wedderburn's "*Forlorn Hope*" (1817), and Thomas Davison's *Medusa* (1819). Readership of these journals ranged from 10,000 to 12,000 for the *Black Dwarf* to some 150,000 to 200,000 for the earliest two-pence editions of Cobbett's register. For each copy circulated, anxious aristocrats imagined assemblies of seditious readers gathered round the radicals' texts.[7] After 1820 the radical audience dwindled into handfuls; the *Black Dwarf* ended its harangues in 1824, the *Republican* in 1826. Only Cobbett's *Register* survived in the 1820s, Cobbett himself turning from the political arena to trace marks of class division in the English countryside in articles that were bound in 1830 to become his best-known work, *Rural Rides*.

Composing the radical public were, according to the *Crisis*, the "producers of all wealth"—agricultural and mining workers; umbrella makers, chair coverers, lace workers, and other artisans; mechanics and manufacturing workers—and then the occasional shopkeeper, artist, or sculptor, and more distant aristocratic sympathizers like Byron and Shelley. Such producers numbered just over ten million English men and women in 1812; the "radical public" itself numbered some four million by 1830.[8] Within this audience, the radical writers distinguished particular readerships: Cobbett's rural weavers, the *Black Dwarf*'s northern miners and urban artisans, the *Republican*'s and the *Gorgon*'s factory workers. The *Gorgon* and the *Republican* were read largely in the urban centers of London and Manchester. But Cobbett's *Register* and Wooler's *Dwarf* spanned the breadth of English labor, claiming a radical public of national scale.

Such journals did not yet speak to the internationalist, socialist, and propertyless working-class movement whose greatest theorist would wish his carbuncles on the bourgeoisie. Early English radicalism plagued the house of the "swaggering aristocrat" rather than the shop of the mercantile capitalist, and it only slowly and searchingly formed a labor theory of value that would make capital rather than hereditary privilege the antagonist of the "useful and productive" classes. But it is no longer clear that this earlier radical discourse was a mere prelude to the socialist thrust of Chartism. Gareth Stedman Jones, in his provoking essay "Rethinking Chartism," persuasively argues that for both this earlier Regency radicalism and Chartism itself, "the dividing line between classes was not that between employer and employed, but that between the represented and the unrepresented."[9] Hence, as Jones rightly points out, it is the language and the *kind* of discourse they engender that give Regency radical journals their ambition to shape what will become a militant English working-class public. Unrepresented, unsignified in the political realm, England's artisans and laborers had to be represented in and by their political texts. To enter the empire of signs as critic and interlocutor means to demystify all those signs that misrepresent them within a larger dissymmetry of signs and meanings, representers and represented. It is also a figure like Cobbett who, read with as much curiosity among aristocrats and middle-class readers as with conviction among weavers, makes the radicals' text a sign for the very separation of publics and the deeper division of classes it designates.

The history of other audiences rarely shows how they responded to their writers' works, but we know in voluminous detail how publicly, how exhaustingly the artisan audience agreed with or dissented from their strongest texts. This is already the best-documented of nineteenth-century publics, the subject of a powerful British historiography extending from the Fabian socialist historians to Marxist writers and more recently, to Albert J.

Goodwin, J. Ann Hone, and Olivia Smith.[10] E. P. Thompson's conception of this public leads carefully from its class bearings to its political consciousness, and then to its constitution as audience: as expression of a nascent class, radical discourse was its way of "handling" the experience of class. Thus "a reading public which was increasingly working class in character was forced to *organize itself.*"[11] But no audience in the early nineteenth century could be formed without the intense mutual pressure of opposing publics, particularly an audience so conscious of itself as an excluded "other." The English radical public assumed a critically bordering stance, inhabiting a zone where, to borrow Bahktin's language, "discourse lives. . . on the boundary between its own context and another, alien, context." At such a border, one class-based culture can define itself only by becoming imbricated in another.[12] Radical discourse was not as much "expressed" by a nascent working class as it formed the latter's ideological and interpretive map. Yet, like an atlas in which one map overlaps another, fitting its figural territory within another frame, the boundaries between middle-class and working-class discourses were not immobile lines but strategic, shifting latitudes of force.

II

The French Revolution could be imagined theatrically, Edmund Burke shrewdly reminded his readers in *Reflections on the Revolution in France*, as an erratically authored spectacle for the benefit of a bewildered English audience. Burke turns French revolutionaries into failed world-historical authors, playwrights of a tragedy that spills off the stage, thus negating the laws of Aristotelian dramatism by failing to resolve their violent struggles in any satisfyingly symbolic way.[13] Burke recoups that symbolic power in the *Reflections*, bringing to bear in his now sublime, now sexually charged representations of the revolution the very resources of authorship he cannot afford to concede, politically or textually, to the militant *philosophes* themselves. The *Reflections* makes a counter-claim for authorship, one for Burke's own text and one for England's unwritten text, the Constitution. It is not hard to perceive an intention to make his own writing, offered up as an "open letter" to a French aristocrat, the visible supplement of what must remain invisible and unwritten, the English Constitution that would violently unravel should it be committed to a real reading.

Hence the hyperbole of these "reflections," the grandest display of classical rhetoric, for which there is no better example than Burke's defense of the "original" social contract:

> Society is indeed a contract. Subordinate contracts for objects of mere occasional interest may be dissolved at pleasure—but the state ought not to be considered as nothing better than a partnership agreement in a trade of pepper and coffee, callico or tobacco, or some other such low concern, to be taken up for a little temporary interest, and to be dissolved by the fancy of the parties. It is to be looked on with other reverence; because it is not a partnership in things subservient only to the gross animal existence of a temporary and perishable nature. It is a partnership in all science; a partnership in all art; a partnership in every virtue, and in all perfection. As the ends of such a partnership cannot be obtained in many generations, it becomes a partnership not only between those who are living, but between those who are living, those who are dead, and those who are to be born. Each contract of each particular state is but a clause in the great primaeval contract of eternal society, linking the lower with the higher natures, connecting the visible and invisible world, according to a fixed compact sanctioned by the inviolable oath which holds all physical and all moral natures, each in their appointed place. This law is not subject to the will of those, who by an obligation above them, and infinitely superior, are bound to submit their will to that law. The municipal corporations of that universal kingdom are not morally at liberty at their pleasure, and on their speculations of a contingent improvement, wholly to separate and tear asunder the bands of their subordinate community, and to dissolve it into an unsocial, uncivil, unconnected chaos of elementary principles. It is the first and supreme necessity only, a necessity that is not chosen but chooses, a necessity paramount to deliberation, that admits no discussion, and demands no evidence, which alone can justify a resort to anarchy. This necessity is no exception to the rule; because this necessity itself is a part too of that moral and physical disposition of things to which man must be obedient by consent or force; but if that which is only submission to necessity should be made the object of choice, the law is broken, nature is disobeyed, and the rebellious are outlawed, cast forth, and exiled, from this world of reason, and order, and peace, and virtue, and fruitful penitence, into the antagonistic world of madness, discord, vice, confusion, and unavailing sorrow. (*Reflections*, 194–95)

Burke's rolling periods gather force toward an apocalyptic contrast between a polysyndetic "world of reason, and order, and peace, and virtue, and fruit-ful penitence," and its demonic asyndetic opposite, "the antagonistic world of madness, discord, vice, confusion, and unavailing sorrow." But this is pre-cisely the kind of opposition Burke's thinking is intended to avoid. Throughout the passage, adjectives, adjectival phrases, and finally whole clauses accumulate in triads: "To separate...tear...and to dissolve," "linking the lower with the higher...connecting the visible and invisible ...according to a fixed compact," "unsocial, uncivil, unconnected chaos," or "outlawed, cast forth, and exiled." Often such oppositions as "lower/ higher" and "visible/invisible" are restructured by triadic participles ("link-ing...connecting...according"). The passage builds architecturally upon these inclusive triangles, which first structure phrases and then, in the last sentence, expand paratactically to include a triadic series of main clauses ("the law is broken, nature is disobeyed, and the rebellious are outlawed"). Such triads often subsume antithetic terms into larger wholes: "between those who are living, those who are dead, and those who are to be born." Burke's syntactic logic depends on collapsing conflict into terms of order, so that he arrives at a sense of closure by positing purely rhetorical resolu-tions of opposites. For the same purpose Burke's language also transforms verbs into adjectival or nominal qualities, while absolute determiners code his nouns as eternal verities already inscribed in an immobile universe of value.

Triumphantly authorial, this language appears to incarnate all its prior authors, a historicist rhetoric thick with precedents, customs, institutions, and habits. Human history can only be represented "reflectively," through what Paine will call a "pathless wilderness" of mixed narrative and argu-mentative modes, of intermediated metaphors packed in Burke's periodic sentences. The blinding rays of light so characteristic of Revolutionary iconography—evident in Blake's etchings as well as Paine's prose—must be refracted back through all the mediators until the light of the Enlighten-ment has been reflexively dimmed away. Authorized by history, Burke's book turns the Revolution into a text so that he may outstrip it as a text, overwriting the revolutionaries' work in a superior act of authorship. Thomas Paine's reply, which Thompson calls the "founding text" of En-glish radical discourse, will not merely simplify Burke's terms by inventing an "intellectual vernacular," but will found radical discourse upon a radical critique of such authorship itself.[14]

Paine seems to have approached the English public in 1791 uncertain who his readers would be. He waited eleven months before publishing the second part of *The Rights of Man*, explaining that "I wished to know the manner in which a work, written in a style of thinking and expression different to what had been customary in England, would be received before I proceeded farther." Once it was clear that Part I of his pamphlet was being read most attentively by artisans, tradesmen, and laborers, Paine more consciously conceived the second part of his work for the plebeian public with which he is now identified.[15] When Paine quotes a particularly convoluted Burkean passage and claims "I will undertake to be its interpreter," Paine thinks of a great popular public, not yet a specific audience of artisans. His ambitions, more profound than merely to "translate" Burke into simple, common language, are to transform the terms of rhetorical tradition without abandoning them, to radicalize the Enlightenment in terms which might offend taste (as Paine's prose unfailingly did) but would remain strictly recognizable within the rhetorical tradition. To use rhetoric against itself will be to establish an alternative rhetorical and political style that contests all claims of authority and domination based on authorship. The passage of such authority from generation to generation has its foundations in primogeniture:

> That, then, which is called Aristocracy in some countries and nobility in others, arose out of the governments founded on conquest. It was originally a military order for the purpose of supporting military government (for such were all governments founded in conquest); and to keep up a succession of this order for the purpose for which it was established, all the younger branches of those families were disinherited and the law of *primogenitureship* set up.
>
> The nature and character of Aristocracy shows itself to us in this law. It is a law against every law of nature, and Nature herself calls for its destruction. Establish family justice and Aristocracy falls. By the aristocratical law of primogenitureship, in a family of six children five are exposed. Aristocracy has never more than one child. The rest are begotten to be devoured. They are thrown to the cannibal for prey, and the natural parent prepares the unnatural repast.
>
> As everything which is out of nature in man affects, more or less, the interest of society, so does this. All the children which the aristocracy disowns (which are all except the eldest) are, in general, cast like orphans on a parish, to be provided for by the public, but at a greater

charge. Unnecessary offices and places in Governments and Courts are created at the expense of the public to maintain them.

With what kind of parental reflections can the father or mother contemplate their younger offspring? By Nature they are children, and by Marriage they are heirs; but by Aristocracy they are bastards and orphans. They are the flesh and blood of their parents in one line, and nothing akin to them in the other. To restore, therefore, parents to their children, and children to their parents—relations to each other, and man to society—and to exterminate the monster Aristocracy, root and branch—the French Constitution has destroyed the law of primogenitureship. Here then lies the monster; and Mr. Burke, if he pleases, may write its epitaph. (*Rights of Man*, 104)

Paine's contemporaries did not greet his experimental language as "common" or ordinary; they recorded a sense of shock.[16] Startingly understated by contrast to Burke's baroque hyperbole, Paine's style could only accentuate what it left unsaid. This epigrammatical style, suppressing logical and syntactic connectives, foregrounds its antithetical syntax. "It is a law against every law of nature.... The rest are begotten to be devoured...the natural parent prepares the unnatural repast." In such sentences, instance ("it is a law") is prepositionally opposed to category ("every law"), verbs are opposed by transformation into verbals ("are begotten...to be devoured"), and nouns by their contrasting adjectives ("natural parent...unnatural repast"). By always framing sentence elements antithetically, Paine parodies facile Burkean resolutions: "By Nature they are children, and by Marriage they are heirs; but by Aristocracy they are bastards and orphans." Antitheses, as Paine uses them, bare contradictions which cannot be resolved in the text or in the imagination. Thus politicized, they force choices rather than resolve conflicts. The text offers no symbolic surplus beyond what it claims to represent. This paratactic style attempts to disentangle the complex webbing of Burke's prose, a prose in which the adjectival phrase loads on the sentence an overbearing weight, a calculated sense of historical determinacy. The difference in their stances toward language is suggested in Hazlitt's report of how Burke incessantly revised the galleys of his *Reflections*, adding so many metaphorical resonances to his sentences that the printer had to reset page proofs from scratch. Meanwhile, Paine "used to walk out, compose a sentence or paragraph in his head, come home and write it down, and never altered it afterward. He then added another, and

so on, till the whole was completed."[17] Enclosed and self-sufficient, the antithetical epigram punctuates the discourse, halting the proliferation of verbal signs at the point of conflicting principles and implied political
choices. Hence the opening of a "path" through Burke's "pathless wilderness of rhapsodies"—but a path *away* from the text. Against a discourse
that appropriated temporality as its immutable historic precedent and authority, Paine's antithetical violence wrenches political language from its
authoritative, historicist moorings.

But to displace Burke's historically authorized stance, Paine must institute a series of "beginnings," in Edward Said's sense of the word: invented
origins whose authority cannot depend on historic precedent. One way to
conceive such beginnings is to use a style—the epigrammatic—as an instance of self-division. Paine's "Man" has been divided from himself by
power, by "false Government," by a "succession of barriers, or sort of turn-
pike gates." Mediated to himself by kings, parliaments, magistrates, priests,
and nobles, man becomes enemy to himself (89). If history is this long
chain of mediations, the aristocratic thinker cannot find the historical "origin" upon which all his precedents must be based. At the origin, there was
always a theft:

> A monarchical reasoner never traces Government to its source, or from
> its source. It is one of the *shibboleths* by which he may be known. A
> thousand years hence, those who shall live in America or in France
> will look back with contemplative pride on the origin of their Govern-
> ments and say, This was the work of our glorious ancestors! But what
> can a monarchical talker say? What has he to exult in? Alas! he has
> nothing. A certain something forbids him to look back to a beginning,
> lest some robber, or some Robin Hood, should rise from the long ob-
> scurity of time and say, *I am the origin*. Hard as Mr. Burke laboured the
> Regency Bill and hereditary succession two years ago, and much as he
> dived for precedents, he still had not boldness enough to bring up Wil-
> liam of Normandy, and say, *There is the head of the list, there is the foun-
> tain of honour*; the son of a prostitute and the plunderer of the English
> nation. (103–104)

Unlike later radicals who appealed to the theory of the Norman yoke, Paine
uses it against all historical accounting. All precedents lead back to an original theft, but a stolen origin has, strictly speaking, no identity; man cannot
find his own constitutive properties in an origin based on robbery.

In place of the precedent, Paine installs the *model*. Government is to be constructed: "This was the *work* of our ancestors." An autodidactic model-bridge builder and amateur engineer, Paine opposes "construction"—model-making, political labor—to the dense historical weight inscribed in Burke's adjectival, parallel-laden rhetorical style. The "source" must be a construction, not a reconstruction. Nor, in a polemical war where all invocation of history appears to serve the ancien régime, can Paine's construction be a form of *production*. The "production" of Marx will be determined by the level of previous historical production; it will be unthinkable outside a severe measurement of history and the limits it imposes. But the model represents the heretofore unrepresented; it represents what *will* be made of it. The model has no author, engages no line of prior succession. "Such a beginning," Said writes, itself "authorizes; it constitutes an authorization for what follows it."[18]

The language of this beginning is the language of principle, asserted nakedly in the pointed, Anglo-Gallican style. Principle, as Jean Starobinski writes of French revolutionary discourse, constitutes "the word of beginning, the founding utterance that tries to contain and fix in itself beginning's bright authority."[19] As intellectual model, the principle contains its field of possibilities against the unprincipled, the excessive. In *The Rights of Man* that excess is constitutional monarchy, the compromise with the Constitution that negates the possibility of principle and its power to constitute. Hence, when Paine seizes one of Burke's more tenacious metaphors—the nation as organic body—he superimposes upon it a characteristic geometric figure: "A Nation is not a body, the figure of which is to be represented by the human body, but is like a body contained within a circle, having a common centre in which every radius meets; and that centre is formed by representation. To connect representation with what is called Monarchy is eccentric Government" (178). The "eccentric" Monarch claims to govern the national sphere from a point outside that sphere, "representing" it by substituting himself for it. This excessive, supplemental point of power forms the political surplus of the national sphere, a symbolic surplus exercising real effects.[20] Thus "constitutional monarchy" forms a self-divided representation, partly within the circle, partly without. Resisting this usurping supplement, Paine attempts to close the circle of representation against all its substitutes, invoking the geometry of the radical Enlightenment to distribute power among the newly represented and their representers.

Even Paine's most sympathetic readers in the London Corresponding Society could not assent to beheading the king.[21] But they disagreed with

Paine *within* the new Girondinist model of a representation that would recontain excess, if not quite lop it off, whether that excess appeared as the
head of a monarch, the grotesque physique of the aristocrat, or the baroque
language of a Burke. Absorbing Burke's language of "veils," "mystery," or
"pantomimical contrivance" into the symbolic surplus of monarchy, the
radical writer claims for his own language a firm representative order that
"exists not by fraud and mystery; it deals not in cant and sophistry; but in-
spires a language that, passing from heart to heart, is felt and understood"
(179). Both England's constitutional monarchy and Paine's Girondinist republicanism "represent," but a totalized representation eliminates all surplus, all excess; partial representation accumulates it. No English writer of
the 1790s advocates a truly Jacobin direct democracy in which all representation would be finally effaced. But Paine's extreme representational parity
frightened England's liberal as well as conservative writers. Arthur Young
would understand Paine's discourse as a language that "disseminates"
among its audience, a propaganda that propagates principles without circulating meanings. It is not recuperated in a continuous circuit of signs and
their readings; it does not accumulate cultural capital.[22] If Burke's symbolic
triads resolve oppositions in transcendent third terms, sublating contradictions in the imagination, Paine's antithetical epigrams close the play of
signs in another way, forcing political language to clarify its oppositions
without resolving them in the text. Such contradictions must be settled beyond political language, in a realm beyond signs yet constituted and clari-
fied by signs.

Thus the first of those radical critiques that identify the surplus of
power with the surplus of signs, of their meanings and their exploitable
tendency to generate the mysteries of "interpretation." Against this "metaphysics" of the sign the radical writers will cast other metaphysical
weapons—principles, common sense, lived experience, empirical facts—or
what Coleridge will paradoxically denounce as merely the "verbal truth."
The radicals' verbal truth insists upon its reference, the squaring of signs
with things and writers with the readers they represent. To it, the cultural
conservative must impose Coleridge's "moral truth," which, like Burke's
metaphysical historicism, will accumulate within signs the innumerable intentions, earlier texts, and contexts through which they have "lived."[23]

As a model of reading and writing, Paine's ideology of representation
makes political discourse accessible to the unrepresented, as Paine's admirers argue. Yet it is a thoroughly rhetorical model and implies a rhetorical relationship between readers and writers. One of Paine's ablest commentators

believes that Paine's syntactic "signposts convey a sense of progress and intimacy by disrupting the distinction between writers and readers. By using
the present tense and the pronoun 'we,' Paine presents the illusion that he
and the readers share the activity of constructing an argument." Yet such
intimacy between reader and writer is hardly characteristic of the radical
text, which on the contrary accentuates the distinction between reading
and writing.[24] The pedagogic radical text cannot be "representative" if it
conflates reader and writer in the act of reading, and both Shelley and
Coleridge, from opposing political and cultural stances, would recognize
more clearly what is at stake in distinguishing or merging reader and writer.
From Paine to Brecht, the radical text radically distinguishes reader and
writer, actor and role, performer and audience, speaker and listener, the
representer and the represented. This essentially rhetorical stance conflicts
with all those complex mechanisms of "identification" and "absorption"
which a quite different political and aesthetic tradition locates in the act of
"reading."[25]

III

Burke's classical and Paine's experimental rhetoric do not exhaust the
late eighteenth century's politics of style: between them lies another language that abandons rhetorical tradition altogether to embark on a suggestive yet still inchoate way for the writer to address a middle-class audience
fearful of what Paine's public represents. Arthur Young's ideology of "circulation," a map of reading and writing poised against its "disseminating"
radical antagonist, requires a style that neither accumulates the echoing
cultural authority and symbolic capital of Burke's eloquence nor poses the
disruptive choices of Paine's "principles." Young's own language gives us a
sense of how the liberal but antiradical writer tactically handles the struggle for political discourse. Like the classical and radical rhetoricians, Young
also claims principles, but they do not emerge the same way in his texts,
which call for an entirely different relation between writer and reader. In
frequent passages like the following from *Travels in France*, the cultural
strategist tracks closely behind the inquisitive traveller:

The importance of a country producing twenty-five bushels per acre instead of eighteen, is prodigious; but it is an idle deception to speak of
twenty-five, for the superiority of English spring corn (barley and oats)

is doubly greater than that of wheat and rye, and would justify me in proportioning the corn products of England, in general, compared with those of France, as twenty-eight to eighteen; and I am well persuaded, that such a ratio would be no exaggeration. Ten millions of acres produce more corn than fifteen millions; consequently a territory of one hundred millions of acres more than equals another of one hundred and fifty millions. It is from such facts that we must seek for an explanation of the power of England, which has ventured to measure itself with that of a country so much more populous, extensive, and more favored by nature as France really is; and it is a lesson to all governments whatever, that if they would be powerful, they must encourage the only real and permanent basis of power, *agriculture*. By enlarging the quantity of the products of land in a nation, all those advantages flow which have been attributed to a great population, but which ought, with much more truth, to have been assigned to a great consumption; since it is not the mere number of people, but their ease and welfare, which constitute national prosperity. The difference between the corn products of France and England is so great, that it would justify some degree of surprise, how any political writer could ever express any degree of amazement, that a territory, naturally so inconsiderable as the British Isles, on comparison with France, should ever become equally powerful; yet this sentiment, founded in mere ignorance, has been very common.[26]

What is most striking in this polemical statement of Young's central principle—the primacy of cultivated land as English wealth—is its cautious antirhetorical stance. The principle of agricultural power seems to emerge out of a careful journey through calculations as, hesitantly, Young draws conclusions from the distinction between producing twenty-five and eighteen bushels of corn products. The modal and passive verb constructions ("would justify me," "I am persuaded") suggest a mind drawing out principles only "from such facts." By a deliberate hesitancy, Young recruits the reader as a partner in reasoning, a persuasive stance which labors to avoid any appearance of rhetorical manipulating. Typically Young nominalizes sentences so that the abstract subject noun ("difference," "importance") and the verb of being throw semantic weight forward to a tangled succession of subordinate clauses and phrasal modifiers; these bear the more concrete terms and statements of value. Underplaying the writer's sense of self, Young uses modal verbs as a means of inviting the reader to shore up his apparent skepticism. Such a style attempts to reverse the rhetorical roles of writer and reader; now the writer himself seems disbelieving, hard to convince, while the reader, formally drawn into the discourse, supplements the needed conviction. Validating the very process of thinking, reader couples with writer in a common movement toward hard-won judgment. Between the writer's confident empiricism and his rhetoric of insecurity, the implied reader silently intervenes to complete the arrival at certainty.

As Young conflates writer and reader in a common process, his prose sprawls. Here there are no Paineite antithetical structures, no Burkean parallelisms, no sense of a larger order that eighteenth-century prose often tries to reproduce. Young's syntax, suggestively drawing out an unending, continuous flow of reflections from some initial point of fact, moves outward and away from any sense of a firm structure underlying thought. Like other late-eighteenth- and early-nineteenth-century writers, Young is trying to define his relation to middle-class readers, exploring ways to edge closer to these readers which prefigure the far more developed and self-conscious methods of the Victorian prose sages.[27] But as he moves toward his readers by inviting them to share the motions of thought, Young also moves away from those orderly structures which eighteenth-century writers used to categorize their own relations with readers—the essentially rhetorical structures we have seen operate in both Burke's and Paine's texts. Such shifts in stylistic patterns work together with shifts in relations between writer and audience, and nowhere more so than in this writer so conscious of what it means to write and to read.

IV

"We stand on the brink of ruin," the *Black Dwarf* wrote in 1817, "and contemplate the abyss beneath us with a fearless eye."[28] The English laborer's "season of dismay" after the Napoleonic wars saw rising inflation, depressed wages, unemployment, bread riots, and accelerated movement of rural artisans and laborers to crowded factory towns. But even these dislocations of capitalist growth and recession paled before aristocratic corruption and its web of pensioners, sinecurists, and "boroughmongers" Cobbett called Old Corruption. Power used commercial hands but wore an aristocratic face which radical writers of 1816 to 1820 painted in the most grotesque terms. Lively and dramatic, the radical journals project the conflict between "parasitic classes" extracting surplus wealth from "useful and productive classes." Unlike the mass journal's social and psychological types, the radical periodicals portray both classes according to productive func-

tions and power relationships. Yet theirs is less a class analysis than an anatomical discourse of producers and parasites, the corrupt and the accursed,
the represented and the unrepresented. The radical anatomy will become
more subtle and detailed in such texts as John Wade's utilitarian sociologies
of English labor, but in the most widely read journals—Cobbett's *Political
Register* and Wooler's *Black Dwarf*—radical writers reach across the diverging occupations and economic interests of English shipwrights, cotton
spinners, miners, factory mechanics, and day laborers to shape this public
by "haranguing" their readers—this is Cobbett's self-described stance—in a
newly heightened vocabulary of resistance. As early as 1807 Cobbett was
writing: "England has long groaned under a *commercial system*, which is the
most oppressive of all possible systems; and it is, too, a quiet, silent, smoth-
ering oppression that it produces, which is more hateful than all others."[29]
The *Black Dwarf*, the *Gorgon*, the *Republican*, and other journals of 1817 to
1820 arose from such sentences. They accentuate the radical writer's role as
what Gramsci would call the "organic intellectual," not the detached figure of eloquence but the intellectual directly involved in strategic practice,
the pedagogue of social position, a "specialist and director."[30]

Likewise, the radical writer keeps his reader "an inseparable part" of an
artisan audience by driving against one another the discourses of socially
contentious readers and their writers—a riotous panoply of voices,
speeches, quotations, answers, questions, mockeries, parodies, and harangues. Wooler, Cobbett, Hone, and others claimed as literary anteced-
ents the dominant culture's most indigestible texts. William Cobbett
reported his own intellectual awakening as a boyhood reading of a cheap
edition of Swift's *Tale of a Tub*; Wooler borrowed Pope's vow to deploy satire
as strategic move "in a land of Hectors, Thieves, Supercargoes, Sharpers &
Directors." Of all radical satires of the time, Wooler's was perhaps the most
energetic and often the bitterest. The invented correspondents of the *Black
Dwarf* form a gallery of radical grotesques—the Dwarf, the Yellow Bonze,
the Black Neb—whose personae permit a complex range of satiric viewpoints. Thus, Wooler can range through a number of discursive registers,
from an editorial abstractly formulating criticism to the more concrete iro-
nies of the Dwarf or the "Blue Devil" at St. James.[31] Alternating between
the collective editorial judgments and individual predicaments of these
grotesque characters, the *Black Dwarf*'s satiric dialectic brings the Paineite
argument jarringly down to earth; the argument of Wooler's editorial finds
its immediate consequences in the shock of the naive Black Dwarf, who
runs blindly and often amusingly into the ancient régime's punitive power.

The journal deploys an extraordinary symbolic violence, its pages erupting in a panoply of exclamation points, italics, and large capitals. "You are designed to earn money, for those who have time to spend it," the *Black Dwarf* storms in an early editorial:

It would derange *your* habits; and injure your morals, to become *rich*. But their habits are to spend; and as to their morals, everybody knows that *they cannot be injured*. Learn then your duty ye hewers of wood, and drawers of water! Buckle to the wheel of necessity, and draw your lordly superiors through the dirt. They have kindly consented to provide for all your wants. They have given you laws to keep you good members of society. They have removed far from you all the benefits of the world, lest you should be puffed up with pride, and be vain glorious, and deny the LORDS. They have taken from you all temptation to sin; and to remedy the inherent and deeprooted depravity of your nature, they have provided for you seventy-thousand priests to pray for you, and to shew you the way to heaven. They have appointed lawyers to secure your property, lest ye should waste it, without thought, and tax-gatherers to collect quarterly your savings, in that root of all evil—*money*. This they deposit in the treasury for your good, for when you become so numerous, that it might be feared heaven would not send enough provisions for you; or what would be the same thing, that you have no means to purchase them with, they contrive to declare some righteous and holy war, in which you are killed as fast as the glory of God and the welfare of the state requires. And does not all this claim your gratitude? Does not this melt you into extacies, at the boundless benevolence of such generous superiors? And will you still grumble at a few lords of the bed-chamber, who thus toil for your good, and exert themselves for your welfare? No, no you will not. You will be thankful to them for their attention to you. You will commiserate their toil, and applaud their diligence. When you meet them in the public way, you will fall down before them, and worship them, saying—"The LORD giveth, and the LORDS take away. Blessed be the way of the *Lords*." This sentence, which is now rendered as it ought to be, from the original, contains the whole of your business and your duty. It speaks all the law, and the prophets which concerns you. It is plain and easy. It involves no sophistry. Read it attentively, learn it, and engrave it on the tablets of your heart. It is of the *last* consequence to you, for to its acknowledgment you must come at last.[32]

Drawing contemporary political experience into a recognizable textual pattern, Wooler parodies the accents of the King James Version so that the scriptural text appears to unmask its own corruption: "The Lord giveth, and the Lords take away. Blessed be the way of the *Lords*." The mock-biblical harangue bristles with explicit rhetorical gestures. Anaphora, rhetorical questions, and collective pronouns ("you"/"they") create a rhetorical relationship between reader and writer, whose own voice assumes the tone of a scriptural prophet denouncing the priesthood. Parodically inhabiting the same text he shows has been corrupted by an aristocracy, the writer fuses apparently distinct forms of power and privilege—laws against political dissent, taxation, boroughmongering, public deference, military service—into a single dialectic of lordship and bondage, for which the Bible unexpectedly provides the exemplary text.

Thus the radical writer wages a struggle over what Voloshinov called the "multi-accentuality" of signs, their protean capacity to be rewritten according to the strategy of social position.[33] The *Black Dwarf* represents not the biblical text but its strategic reading by the ministry for its own, less skeptical audience. Radical writers deployed such alien readings and motivated misreadings in a simultaneous social space, reopening in their language that distance between English discourses and their readerships which the signs of official power constantly aimed to close.

This language attempts no subtlety. The *Black Dwarf* adopts the most extreme verbal forms, using typography to press words themselves toward an almost extralinguistic force straining at the very limit of written language. Partly an attempt to reproduce in print the emphatic gesture and timbre of voice, this energy is also a means to render the opaque sources of power and powerlessness legible. The radical writer's well-nigh melodramatic language works to clarify his terms of power. As John Wade explained to his readers in 1818, the "labouring classes" who felt the "iron hand that was crushing them to the earth" had no way to judge causes or comprehend the relationships of this "misery, poverty, and embarrassment."[34] Wade himself would use Bentham's utilitarian thought and Ricardo's political economy to help readers determine causes; Wooler, deeply influenced by the popular theater, turned toward more symbolic and perhaps desperate means.

His version of the Peterloo massacre is a telling example. Both English reformers and middle-class observers were appalled at the violence a yeoman cavalry visited upon men, women and children during a peaceful protest meeting held near Manchester in August 1819. Peterloo signalled to Richard Carlile the long awaited crisis of English class conflict: "Already

we can see the howling storm, emanating from those black misdeeds, encir-
cling the very seat of government."[35] Wooler's "Black Dwarf" records an
apocalyptic fear and loathing:

> I am, my friend, petrified with horror and disgust. I am awakened, as
> from a frightful dream, and I find myself surrounded with a sea of
> blood, in which are floating mangled carcases, and mutilated limbs.
> Did not indignation overpower horror, my blood would freeze at the
> carnage as my eyes drank in the horrible detail. Blood, innocent blood
> has been wantonly shed. The drought of the season has been allayed at
> Manchester by a shower of gore. The dogs have been fed with human
> blood; and the desolation of war has been exhibited in what was called
> a period of peace. Talk not to me of the horrors of Japan, of Morroco, or
> Algiers! What is it to me, whether the human victim be sacrificed to
> the great idol, Juggernaut, or to the cruelty of an eastern despot, or an
> English Boroughmonger? I see the blood flowing down the streets, and
> I detest the abominable agent who has poured it living from the veins.
>   An immense assembly of men, women and children were congre-
> gated together, on the subject of their sufferings, and their wrongs.
> Shall I be believed, when I tell thee, that a ferocious company of armed
> men, rushed with sabres upon this assembly, and commenced the work
> of indiscriminate slaughter! Yet this is recorded in the annals of this
> country in letters of blood, which will never be erased from the page of
> its history. Ah, my friend, civilization is worse than barbarity: for it de-
> ceives our hopes, and blasts the expectations it has raised.... Fiends
> have been dressed in the uniform of soldiers, to do what devils would
> have scorned to do. They *have trampled* on and SABRED WOMEN—
> Children have been bathed in their mother's blood—and the peace-
> able citizen has been butchered at noon day, when he deemed himself
> walking under the protection of the day, as in the beams of the smiling
> sun. But what is law, when power would trample it under foot? What is
> justice, when a boroughmonger can kill it with his frowns? I will some-
> day particularize to thee, this monster, called here a boroughmonger. It
> far surpasses in voracity and rapacious guilt, anything thou has heard,
> or read of, in ancient and modern history. But the thing has hitherto
> been deemed a coward. It has often drank blood in *secret*, and fed upon
> the *tears* and *sighs* of its victims, when it could only incarcerate them in
> its horrible dens. But the thing has become braver. It has been driven
> to the courage of despair; and being on the eve of capture, trial, and

conviction, it has rushed out of its cell at noon-day, and torn to pieces all that came within its grasp![36]

Cobbett often called the boroughmonger a "monster," but here the epithet becomes an extended metaphor fitting the language of bloody violation and drawing powerfully on the imagery of London's melodramatic theater and the darker moments of the Elizabethan tragedies that played Drury Lane. Wooler was fascinated by the popular theater and its possibilities for staging sweeping public conflicts in concrete symbolic forms.[37] And the Dwarf's character allows the massacre to be imaged in more extravagant forms than Wooler himself could plausibly have used: "I find myself surrounded with a sea of blood...My eyes drank in the horrible detail": "floating mangled carcases," "mutilated limbs," "a shower of gore," "dogs ...fed with human blood." The *Black Dwarf* writes of political struggle as authority's violent destruction of the body. But this body is not only the human form: it is also the radical writer's own audience. Peterloo calls forth dire representations of the destruction of one's own readership, for those gathered at St. Peter's field formed the core of Wooler's public, who would now read about themselves shattered by the physical force of a potent ancien régime. Such dramaturgy registers an event involving mass forces within individual consciousness, a heightened, melodramatic consciousness waking into nightmare.

The mangled artisan body figures as the opposite of the radical writer's grotesque aristocratic body, but no description corresponding to Blake's robust, Orcian revolutionary body enters popular radical discourse. Yet what distinguishes all the radicals' representations of the body—in Blake, Wooler, Carlile, Cobbett, or George Cruikshank—from the mass writer's gestural body or the middle-class writer's decorated body is the telling mark on the flesh, its Blakean muscularity when liberated from shackles or its splayed, bloody fragments when breached by cavalry sabers. The radical's body signifies not by what it points toward or what it dons, but by the effects of class and power that indelibly stamp their imprint on its physical membranes.

The *Black Dwarf*'s incantatory language of blood, sacrifice, and demonology, personifying the boroughmongering system in terms that approach vampirism, evokes archaic roots of satire as a struggle against power itself. What Robert Elliott called the "power of satire" invests its symbolic violence with the language of the "curse," a trope the slave deploys helplessly against the master: "You taught me language," Caliban cries against his oppressors, "and my profit on't / Is, I know how to curse."[38] The curse becomes the self-imprisoning trope of Prometheus in Shelley's allegory of the master-slave dialectic, *Prometheus Unbound*, where the language of symbolic resistance becomes circular, mirrorlike, as the "slave" reproduces the "master" within the structure of his own discourse. The curse constitutes both the power and the risk of Wooler's radical language, a trope that at once clarifies the anatomical terms of power and, at the same time, locks radical discourse into its immutable dramatistic terms.

In the *Black Dwarf*'s frequent moments of heightened discursive anguish, the language of satire merges with the excessive language of melodrama itself. The most theatrical of radical writers, Wooler represents the British ancien régime as the ludicrous "State Theatricals," the farce of constitutional monarchy. But this is a stage in which the audience is also the victim-participant. Here the language of the curse makes its audience both the spectator of the state's political theater and its antagonist, reminding Wooler's readers that to be an "audience" is also to be a "public" in the ancient sense, a "body politic." Radical writing posits the moment of "expressionistic clarification," as Peter Brooks defines the effect of the French *melo-dramé*, when the polar terms of oppressor and oppressed can be symbolized in a perceptible rhetorical shape.[39] Thus, for instance, the melodramatic structure of feudal lords and oppressed slaves can become the expressionist form within which to criticize the religious drapery of power by inhabiting the biblical language such power corrupts. Inevitably binary in its anatomical structure, such radical writing clarifies the dynamic of mastery while also investing it with an almost supernatural power no longer attached to its material investments. The *Black Dwarf* searches for a language that will be capable of representing—and thus containing—the old regime's apparently limitless power. Thus it also risks imprisoning its own discourse within the perilous logic of the social sign.

Quite the opposite of Wooler's extravagant language, the style of John Wade's *Gorgon* is deliberately muted. Satire and melodrama recede in what Thompson calls this "most austere and intellectually reputable" of radical journals.[40] To its readers in London and the factory cities, Wade shifts radical argument from the political question of power toward the economic question of labor. His patient analysis of economic crisis examines particular urban vocations (tailor, typesetter, optician), studies particular areas of reform (legal, educational, penal), and calls for selective rather than general political struggles (suffrage for artisans rather than all producers). The *Gorgon* collects research, constructs tables and examines statistics. To such material Wade applies the economics of Adam Smith and David Ricardo, while Benthamism affords a theoretical framework for his careful research. Indeed, the *Gorgon* often uses the fruits of the middle-class philosopher and the capitalist political economist against Thomas Paine's theory of "natural rights," which from Wade's radical utilitarian viewpoint is a political metaphysics. Now radical demands will be formulated according to what "works," from practical arguments rather than from first principles.

Writing two years after Cobbett and Wooler began shaping a wide radical audience, Wade assumes a certain tradition of radical style, to which he now adds a new conceptual ground:

> Labour is the superabundant produce of this country; and it is the chief commodity we export. Whatever, therefore, affects the price of labour, inasmuch as it may operate upon a principal article of our trade, is of the very first importance. Of the four staple manufactures, namely, cotton, linen, cloth, and iron, perhaps, on an average, the raw material does not constitute one-tenth of their value, the remaining nine-tenths being created by the labours of the weaver, spinner, dyer, smith, cutler, and fifty others, employed in different departments. The labours of these men form the chief article of traffic in this country. It is by trading in the blood and bones of the journeymen and labourers of England, that our merchants have derived their riches, and the country its glory and importance. They laid the foundation of our naval triumphs, in our commercial superiority;—they created the wealth of the aristocracy, and made agriculture to flourish, by purchasing its produce;—they enabled the country to support a weight of taxes never before supported—yet, though they have been the foundation of our national glory and riches, and although the arms of English labourers have been a more prolific source of wealth than the soil of Britain, are they daily abused, by an *ignorant* and *hireling* crew; and all classes combine to abridge the miserable pittance necessary to their support.[41]

Throughout 1818 Wade filled in this sketch of labor's value with detailed studies of journeymen tailors, opticians, and other trades. The passage above, from an article on exports, begins with an exposition of economic principle. Characteristically Wade names specific commodities, finds a ratio, and lists the trades needed in his calculation. His phrase "of the very first importance" is an understatement one would expect of an Arthur Young carefully calculating relative values. But this exposition becomes the premise for conclusions in which the radical rhetorician emerges with "the blood and bones" of English workers, the gestural anaphora ("They laid . . . they created . . . they enabled") and the signal epithets ("an *ignorant* and *hireling* crew"). Here, rather than casting aside radical style, the *Gorgon* tries to ground it in a discourse of fact and measurable certainty. Wade is searching for a way out of a political and rhetorical impasse. His language works against both Paine's ahistorical sense of human rights and the rhetorical stance that poses melodramatic terms of power. The development of English class consciousness will require the terms of labor, the methods of empirical research, the patient analysis that lies behind Wade's *Gorgon* and later Marx's *Capital*. But these are not the essential terms of the early-nineteenth-century radical audience, for whom the representational theater of the political sign essays its role in the greater social text.

V

When northern English miners tucked the *Black Dwarf* prominently in their hats for all to see, they constituted radical discourse as a sign of their resistance, a sign the middle class and aristocracy found threatening, if textually opaque.[42] But one radical writer spanned as well as accentuated the gulf between middle-class and radical audiences, a writer with an uncommon belief in the powers of writing who set out to show the middle-class reader what the militant laborer and the disaffected weaver were reading and how they conceived the social order in which they were inscribed. William Cobbett formed an intentionally ambiguous, "populist" stance whose characteristic style would appear both idiomatically personal and the very sign of an emerging social class.

Between 1802 and 1816, he directed his *Political Register* to ministers, the rural gentry, and middle-class merchants and manufacturers, a maverick reformer preaching against paper money, boroughmongering, and the "commercial system." As it became increasingly clear to him that country gentlemen would do nothing to restore power to the "natural magistracy" of landowners, Cobbett began looking toward a new kind of reader, one who was by 1816 subscribing to the still expensive *Political Register* in northern factory towns. A prolific writer without an effective audience, Cobbett turned to the laborers with a two-penny version of the *Register*. In November 1816 the "Address to the Journeymen and Labourers" appeared in the first of the cheap radical papers; it addressed English workers as though they could now, by direct peaceful action, expel the stockjobbers and boroughmongers by pressing for parliamentary reform. "At this time the writings of William Cobbett suddenly became of great authority," a radical weaver later wrote; "they were read on nearly every cottage hearth in the manufacturing districts...Riots soon became scarce...The Labourers... soon became deliberate and systematic in their proceedings."[43] Rejecting the sporadic violence of Luddism, Cobbett also argued against the formation of radical clubs and associations, a perverse stance that became notorious among other radicals and their readers because it seemed to undercut the very foundation of the radical audience. He wrote his *Register* as though it were itself an institution which would shape workers' disorganized energies for parliamentary reform, as though there were an unmediated link between writing and action which did not require laborers to organize themselves. If other radicals saw in Paine a metaphysics of natural right, they saw in Cobbett an equally tenuous metaphysics of the political word. To middle-class writers and readers, William Cobbett became the very emblem of an English radical public. He forced them to become its interlocutors. *Blackwood's Magazine* parodied his style; the right-wing *Anti-Cobbett* (1817) and the *Bristol Job Nott* imitated it against him.[44] For such readers, the question of Cobbett was always the question of his language. Cobbett seemed to write more like a "writer" than a rhetorician; he could always be singled out from the "mob writers," as the *Athenaeum* called Carlile, Wooler, Wade, and other radicals. At the center of Cobbett's language is an "I," not a panoply of satiric voices but an ego, in Hazlitt's phrase, "always full of matter." But it is an individuality without individualism; "There is no blindman's bluff, no conscious hints, no awkward ventriloquism....He writes himself plain William Cobbett."[45] Admirers and opponents alike felt themselves drawn to this supremely egoistic voice which yet spoke "plain, broad downright English," which seemed to be "the natural outgrowth of our soil," which was finally an impersonal voice enunciating the "plain" English mind itself. This is not the only contradiction in Cobbett—he writes with convictions yet without principles; his very nature is "contradiction"—but it is the one to which his readers again and again allude. Other radical writers, more principled and systematic, can be separated from their public in a maneuver that opposes the radical's ideological intention to the honest, apolitical impulses of the working-class reader. But "Mr. Cobbett's personal consciousness of all which is concealed from our eyes by grey jackets and clouted shoes has kept alive his sympathy with the majority of mankind."[46] Somehow, his most virulent critics confess, Cobbett's language "speaks" the English working class.

This "original" style resists assimilation to prior models of public discourse. Alternately descriptive, narrative, argumentative, or satirical, Cobbett's language moves through these discursive modes in a restless production of sentences. No biblical phraseology, no epigrammatic structures, no rhetorical encoding, no cultivation of figures lead Cobbett's writing toward stylistic closure. "Paine tries to enclose his ideas in a fold for security and repose," Hazlitt remarked; "Cobbett lets *his* pour out upon a plain."[47] Cobbett does not practice "style" as such; rather, certain phrases and verbal formulas become raw materials for his own peculiar linguistic practice. From the mouths or texts of Canning, Castlereagh, or other ministers, these formulas are always abstract nominal units that Cobbett unravels by setting them in sentences:

> I have never been able clearly to comprehend what the beastly Scotch *feelosofers* mean by their 'national wealth'; but, as far as I can understand them, this is their meaning: that national wealth means, that which is *left* of the products of the country over and above what is *consumed*, or *used*, by those whose labour causes the products to be. This being the notion, it follows, of course, that the *fewer* poor devils you can screw the products out of, the *richer* the nation is.[48]

Phrases like "vast improvements," "increased capital," or Canning's "sum of prosperity" undergo the same crude translation. These are always symptomatic rather than systematic readings; the phrase is taken to be the congealed sign of a way of thinking rather than part of an actual critique of Smith's economics or Canning's politics. Against the condensed phrase or the typical abstraction, Cobbett unleashes a series of sentences that pin it down to a determinate sequence of actions. Typically, a word like *tendency* will be taken apart not because it is simply false, misleading, or ideological, but because it is too interpretable:

> If the magistrates find that any publications, which *they may deem* to be of an irreligious, immoral, or seditious TENDENCY, is kept in any such place, they may take away the *License* and put an end to the business of the man who keeps the Room or Place for reading.... And, only think of the extent of this word *tendency*! Only think of the boundless extent

of such a word, and of such a word being left to the interpretations of thousands of men! Suppose the editor of a newspaper to insert an article, which article recommended *the reduction of the salt tax.* What does this *tend* to? Why, to be sure, a Magistrate might *think*, to make the people *discontented* with the salt tax; to make them discontented with the salt tax would be, he might think, to make them discontented *with those who compel the people to pay it*; those who compel the people to pay it are *King, Lords* and *Commons*; and, therefore, here is an article which *tends* to make the people *discontented with kings, lords, and commons*, and which, of course, *tends* to produce hatred of them, and to bring about insurrection, treason, revolution, and blood and carnage. There is no bounds to this word *tendency*.[49]

Cobbett seizes the symptomatic word or phrase and then imagines a syllogism in which the term unfolds its concrete consequences. Here the word *tendency* develops into a typical "interpretation" as it will be used to censor political writing. Cobbett is measuring the distance between a particular act—an article on reducing the salt tax—and the train of reasoning through which this act will be linked with "treason, revolution, and blood and carnage." The nominal abstraction ("national wealth" or "seditious tendency") will be forced to collide with a determinate activity (extracting surplus from laborers, censoring political texts), so that Cobbett's critique of official formulas always resolves them into a certain relationship, a concrete act whose blunt description ("the *fewer* poor devils you can screw the products out of") rhetorically measures the quality of exploitation. Such "demystifying" is perhaps no different than Orwell's critique of political phraseology in "Politics and the English Language." For Cobbett, however, symptomatic reading of the phrase of power opens up a space for his own political language, a certain ideological space which Cobbett's language fills in with a tireless production of sentences. There is something inevitable about the way Cobbett's language "pours out on the plain." Unlike Paine, Wooler, or Wade, whose systematic exposition contests one body of principles with another, Cobbett opposes a code of political and economic *language* to what at first seems to be an incommensurate level of concrete social effects. Between the official phrase and the "real," Cobbett's language, in his own words, "will contain a spring, in its inside, to set it and keep it in motion."[50] Thus Cobbett defines his radical writing: the elaboration of a countercode of political description which both measures the distance between the language of power and its social consequences and, on the other hand, makes this language the subject of a long discursive sentence whose verbs and adjectives will discredit it.

The late Victorians read Cobbett for his rural descriptions, not his politics; Fabian socialists like G.D.H Cole and conservatives like Chesterton valued Cobbett's nostalgic political attack on the "commercial system." More recently Raymond Williams and Edward Thompson have emphasized Cobbett's unequivocal adoption of a working-class stance.[51] These divergent readings do not speak as much to different Cobbetts as to different discourses within Cobbett, a writer whose "inconsistency" allowed him to traverse particular political and rhetorical modes within a peculiar personal style. Rewriting "England" against all its contemporary representations, Cobbett's splenetic language contests them by making every act of naming an act of judgment. His Juvenalian portrait of Cheltenham, for instance, seems aimed at the alternate representations that could be made of the city and its urban types:

> [This] is what they call a 'watering place'; that is to say, a place to which East India plunderers, West India floggers, English tax-gorgers, together with gluttons, drunkards and debauchees of all descriptions, *female* as well as male, resort, at the suggestion of silently laughing quacks, in the hope of getting rid of the bodily consequences of their manifold sins and iniquities.... To places like this come all that is knavish and all that is foolish and all that is base; gamesters, pickpockets, and harlots; young wife-hunters in search of rich and ugly and old women, and young husband-hunters in search of rich and wrinkled or half-rotten men, the former resolutely bent, be the means what they may, to give the latter heirs to their lands and tenements.[52]

These are the same characters who inhabit the *Mirror of Literature* and other cheap urban journals, where they are fascinating types cataloged without moral judgment. But for Cobbett these types signify the city as moral excrescence, the human equivalent of the corrupt "Thing," as Cobbett called the aristocratic financial system. Here the traditional excoriation of the city and its amoral crowd has not been superseded but politicized. The mass writer's city crowd stands at the center of the busy commercial city and the greater foreign empire, while for a radical public Cobbett's internally corrupt crowd comically tries to wash itself clean. The mass writer's "rooks and sharpers" are Cobbett's "East India plunderers" and "West India floggers," agents of English imperialism; and his "wife-hunters" and "husband-hunters" pursue each other not out of desire—Cobbett's aristocrats, like Wooler's and Wade's, suffer advanced physical decay—but to give "heirs to their lands and tenements," to reproduce the ancien régime itself. As he extends the eighteenth century's demonology of the urban crowd, Cobbett reverses what the crowd signifies. No longer the emblem of an amoral, anarchic, potentially violent lower class, the crowd is now an amoral, congealed form of the aristocracy.

What all readers of Cobbett find indelible is the extraordinary concreteness of a language that weaves its way through narrative, descriptive, and argumentative modes. The concrete detail becomes a representative point that his own language will then give a history, a greater social pattern, a means of grasping historical movement. The simplest quotidian act—bleaching linen, for example—can be made the sign of a vast historical transformation from rural artisanal labor into the emerging industrial order:

> Today, near a place called Wesborough Green, I saw a woman bleaching her *home-spun* and *home-woven linen*. I have not seen such a thing before, since I left Long Island. There, and, indeed, all over the American States, North of Maryland, and especially in the New England States, almost the whole of both linen and woollen, used in the country, and a large part of that used in towns, is made in the farm-houses. There are thousands and thousands of families who never use either, except of their own making. All but the *weaving* is done by the family. There is a loom in the house, and the weaver goes from house to house. I once saw about three thousand farmers, or rather country people, at a horse-race in Long Island, and my opinion was, that there were not five hundred who were not dressed in *home-spun coats*. As to *linen*, no farmer's family thinks of *buying linen*. The *Lords of the Loom* have taken *from the land*, in England, *this part of its due*; and hence one cause of the poverty, misery and pauperism, that are becoming so frightful throughout the country. A national debt, and all the taxation and gambling belonging to it have a natural tendency *to draw wealth into great masses*. These masses produce a power of *congregating* manufacturers, and of making the many work at them, *for the gain of a few*. The taxing Government finds great convenience in these congregations. It can lay its hand easily upon a part of the produce; as ours does with much effect.

But, the land suffers greatly from this, and the country must finally feel the fatal effects of it. The country people lose part of their natural employment. The women and children, who ought to provide a great part of the raiment, have nothing to do. The fields *must have men and boys*; but, where there are men and boys there will be *women* and *girls*; and, as the Lords of the Loom have now a set of *real slaves*, by the means of whom they take away a great part of the employment of the country-*women* and *girls*, these must be kept by poor-rates in whatever degree they lose employment through the Lords of the Loom. (*Rural Rides*, 117–18)

Alternately synecdochic or metonymic, the detail or the part always unfolds its connections: "Take any considerable circle *where you know everybody*, and the condition of that circle will teach you how to judge pretty correctly of the condition of every other part of the country" (106). This representationalism, turning the typical action into a sign, also works historically. When Cobbett selects a woman washing "homespun linen" or a turnip-hoer eating a good breakfast of "household bread and not a very small piece of bacon" (126), these figures represent something about to vanish, or a survival of a social arrangement already sundered by the requirements of capital. Cobbett's nostalgic longing for the return of an older England is less consciously medieval in *Rural Rides* than in his other works.[53] Here it acts more as a pressure to yield up the symptoms of historical change. Wherever Cobbett senses something valuable about to be dispersed and then replaced—whether by the massing of laborers in factories or by the oatmeal and water which replace bread and bacon among the northern industrial workers—he turns it into another symptom of the "devouring Wens," the insatiable "Thing."

The method of significant detail, forced into meaningfulness by its increasingly tenuous survival, gives Cobbett's political discourse the sense of the novelistic, as Raymond Williams points out, and connects Cobbett to the Victorian novelists who will extend this "new method in literature."[54] As a political writer, however, Cobbett forms another kind of discourse. In one moment, the political word or phrase will be critically brought to bear against a sequence of concrete historical actions. At another, simple quotidian acts clash against massive, sweeping social and political shifts between whole forms of social organization and, indeed, modes of production. Cobbett's language finds its "spring" between these specific and general points. It discovers a series of hidden links between apparently incommensurate realities, realities it can then bring forcefully and unexpectedly together.[55] To be sure, it is an undisciplined and theoretically unguided way of explaining historical transformations and political struggles. Cobbett must always fall back on what Alice Chandler calls a "feudal dream of order" to make historical sense of what he ineluctably perceives and writes about.[56] But despite its reactionary theory of history, Cobbett's stance allows the radical reader to make connections between hitherto separate orders of experience, affording him a strategic position between cultural utterance and concrete act, quotidian experience and structural change. This vantage point shapes a discourse that brings rural and urban, northern and southern, handcraft and artisan laborers within a broader, national sense of being a public, since the kind of historical change Cobbett's language implies leaves no geographic or occupational realm untouched. Everything is connected, brought into a pattern, given a sense of historical movement—a movement Cobbett registers against his own desires—within which members of an audience find common ground.

Hence Cobbett attempts to locate his audience both within and without a world of signs. When he disperses the language of the ministry against its concrete social effects, he seeks a stance outside the social text, a ground where all representations become inadequate to their pragmatic effects. Yet it is from the field of practices that he selects those telling acts that become signs for sweeping historical transformations. What is absent from Cobbett's political sign-making is what readers of both middle-class and mass audiences in the early nineteenth century were shaped to seek in *their* texts, something which arises out of the tangible and discovers a world elsewhere. This protean radical writer, complain his critics, mercilessly disappoints one's desire for "imagination,"

> a faculty that can only exist as the organ and interpreter of deep feelings and much-embracing thoughts: it is denied to ribald levity and systematic dogmatism: it is like the allegories of ancient mythology, or the temple of the Lord at Jerusalem, a rich treasure-house of symbols for things infinite and invisible. . . . But in the author whom we are now considering, as there are none of these expansive and pregnant convictions, none of these consciousnesses of the master laws of the universe; so is there none of that power whereby they might be embodied and made palpable. . . . He scarcely ever takes us away from those wretched and trivial tumults of the hour, in which our feelings come in contact with nothing but the follies and selfishness, the outward accidents and unhappy frivolities of our kind.[57]

The imagination has no home in the political *melo-dramé*, the radicals' carnivalesque levity, or Cobbett's social pragmatics that bind the sign within what the *Athenaeum* sourly calls "the weary and bleeding world...the same thorny round of faction." But it is just this difference from all other makers and readers of the social text that turns Cobbett into must reading for England's men of power. Peers, bishops, parliamentary orators, and university professors are all urged to read Cobbett for his "portrait, thrilling with all the pulses of animation, of the thoughts and desires of a class, the largest and therefore the most important in society, among whom that which is universal and eternal in our nature displays itself under a totally different aspect from that which it wears among us. Mr. Cobbett's personal consciousness of all which is concealed from our eyes by grey jackets and clouted shoes, has kept alive his sympathy with the majority of mankind" (*Athenaeum*, 98). After Cobbett's emergence as England's most widely read radical writer, middle-class writers opposed him, denounced him, parodied him. Still unable to ignore Cobbett, they would finally turn him into a sign, absorbing into the social text that audience whose presence he had shaped and made palpable to other publics. Attempting to neutralize that audience, the *Athenaeum* only underscores the way early-nineteenth-century publics separated from one another by means of their paradoxically intense consciousness of one another.

VI

Reading Cobbett, Shelley was of two minds: "What a pity that so powerful a genius should be combined with the most odious moral qualities."[58] Shelley's morning post in Italy was incomplete without the *Political Register*; but he would no more have sat down to lunch with the Botley radical than supped with Cobbett's gray-jacketed readers. Shelley leaned heavily on his economics; "A Philosophical View Reform" combines Hume and Condorcet with strong doses of Cobbett's critique of paper money and the national debt. But Shelley's distance from the radical movement compelled him to think out his own relation to radical writing and its audience, as a literary intellectual whose practice of writing did not long conceal an extraordinary claim: "Poets are the unacknowledged *legislators* of the world." While radical writers pitched their "unrepresented" audience against the legislating of English life by boroughmongers and the represented class of property owners, Shelley made his own intervention in the shifting politics of the sign.

Paper money, for instance, was not only what Cobbett believed it was, an efflux of the national debt. It was also, Shelley thought, a semiotic mode, treacherously arbitrary:

The modern scheme of public credit is a far subtler and more compli-cated contrivance of misrule. All great transactions of personal prop-erty in England are managed by signs and that is by the authority of the possessor expressed upon paper, thus representing in a compendi-ous form his right to so much gold, which represents his right to so much labor. A man may write on a piece of paper what he pleases; he may say he is worth a thousand when he is not worth a hundred pounds. . . . One of the vaunted effects of this system is to increase the national industry: that is, to increase the labors of the poor and those luxuries of the rich which they supply; to make a manufacturer work 16 hours where he only worked 8; to turn children into lifeless and blood-less machines at an age when otherwise they would be at play before the cottage doors of their parents; to augment indefinitely the propor-tion of those who enjoy the profit of the labor of others as compared with those who exercise this labor.[59]

Thus the making of a "new aristocracy, which has its basis in fraud as the old one has its basis in force." The new financial aristocracy inflates the public signs of money. But this wealthy middle class also inflates the private signs of literature. It expects to find, as part of the new middle-class audi-ence, "the antitype of their own mediocrity in books, or such stupid and distorted and inharmonious idealisms as alone have the power to stir their torpid imaginations" ("Philosophical View," 245). Shelley's sociology of reading borrows Wordsworth's literary sociology of 1800 and the radical writers' economics, his analytic stance traversing economic and textual realms by means of the singularity of the sign. Earlier the misuse of signs appeared to Shelley as the task of philosophy to extirpate: philosophy "re-duces the mind to that freedom in which it would have acted but for the misuse of words and signs, the instruments of its own creation."[60] But in the writings of 1818 to 1820, the sign assumes a greater burden than merely "an education of error": the burden of its surplus in the struggle for cultural and economic power.

If the sign is subject to the vagaries of power, language itself may either elude or capitulate to the logic of signs. A "vitally metaphorical" language apprehends "the before unapprehended relations of things," yet historically the "words which represent them become, through time, signs for portions or classes of thoughts instead of pictures of integral thoughts." Shelley's "Defence of Poetry" navigates with difficulty between language as reduced to reified signs and language that becomes, as it were, tran-sign-dental, apprehending the relations between things without becoming merely a collection of "things" itself. In its ideal plasticity, language becomes "a more direct representation of the actions and passions of our internal being and is susceptible of more various and delicate combinations than color, form, or motion. . . all other materials, instruments, and conditions of art have relations among each other which limit and interpose between conception and expression."[61] Because it admits less resistant materiality between conception and expression, language can represent not only things as they are but also as they should be: the "future in the present." Hence at this moment language is a more powerful and profound *political* medium than others, for the "unapprehended relations of things" means most crucially the unapprehended relation of the present to the future, the quotidian to the utopian. But when it falls into the condition of "signs," language collapses either into representations of things as their possessors, like the possessors of paper money, want them to appear—or, at best, into the dour determinism of Godwin's Caleb Williams as he suffers "things as they are."

The distinction between language and signs reappears in "The Mask of Anarchy" and *Prometheus Unbound*, two poems that recognize England's division between middle-class and radical audiences and their discourses. Written to readers of the *Political Register*, the *Black Dwarf*, and Carlile's *Republican*, "The Mask of Anarchy" adopts the accents of the radical journals, but not their stance toward the power of signs. "Slavery" will here be defined both as the subjugation the radical writers criticize and the mode in which radical writing conceives its resistance:

> "'Tis to let the Ghost of Gold
> Take from Toil a thousandfold
> More than e'er its substance could
> In the tyrannies of old.

> "Paper coin—that forgery
> Of the title-deeds, which ye
> Hold to something of the worth
> Of the inheritance of Earth.

> "'Tis to be a slave in soul
> And to hold no strong control
> Over your own wills, but be
> All that others make of ye.
>
> "And at length when ye complain
> With a murmur weak and vain
> 'Tis to see the Tyrant's crew
> Ride over your wives and you—
> Blood is on the grass like dew.
>
> "Then it is to feel revenge
> Fiercely thirsting to exchange
> Blood for blood—and wrong for wrong—
> Do not thus when ye are strong.
>
>   ("Mask of Anarchy," lines 176–96)

Rule by signs reaps greater exploitation than rule by force, as the indefinite slippage of value in paper money makes clear. But this power of a representation over what it represents becomes most insidious when it makes "a slave in soul," when the "free-born Englishman" cannot resist the power of signs to make him "all that others make of ye." Slave of all representations of themselves, England's artisans and workers may—Shelley feared in late 1819—turn to that form of vengeance already prepared for in the logic of the sign, namely a fierce "thirsting to exchange / Blood for blood—and wrong for wrong."

The image calls forth its counterimage. If Murder wears the "mask" of Castlereagh, that reified sign seems to invite its abolition in a countersign, whether that sign be an act of physical violence or merely the heightened cries against Castlereagh echoed in the radical press. "The Mask of Anarchy" opposes to such "revenge" the puzzling counsel of passive resistance:

> "Rise like Lions after slumber
> In unvanquishable number—
> Shake your chains to earth like dew
> which in sleep had fallen on you—
> Ye are many—they are few."
>
>   (368–71)

More than a century of Shelley's critics have mused over whether he pays allegiance to violent revolution, nonviolent symbolic resistance, or at

different times both.[62] But the choice between such modes had to be as un-
decidable for Shelley as for Cobbett, Carlile, and other radical writers; only
in the Marxist inflection of radical discourse would a *narrative* of the revolution be worked out, one which entails a lengthy transition between spontaneous resistance and an educated, disciplinary revolutionary act—a
transition which would also entail the intractable problem of the revolutionary "party." In "The Mask of Anarchy," no such transitional narrative is
visible, but its possibility in *some* form seems prefigured in Shelley's insis-
tence that the great mass of English artisans and laborers become aware
that their strength against power's signs and sabers lies in a patiently collective stance rather than in some one-to-one struggle against the signifying "mask."

For a more cultivated audience whose intertextual frame was Aeschy-
lean mythography rather than plebeian radical journalism, the politics of
the sign assumes the problematic form of Promethean symbolic resistance:
"the curse." The "five or six" readers of this drama cannot be expected, like
artisan readers, to make one-to-one connections between poetic figures and
contemporary political tyrants. These liberal middle-class readers cannot
grapple with their contemporary political crisis without first apprehending
the implications of their own *cultural* position, their experience as educated readers. This is why Shelley makes the problem of domination depend on the question of language, whose cultural mastery distinguishes the
readers of *Prometheus Unbound* from other social audiences, but also proves
far more complex than the middle-class reader would assume. Wordsworth
turned his middle-class readers away from the "poetic diction" that had
blinded them to Milton and Shakespeare, but Shelley forces his audience
to confront the cultural inheritance that both confers power upon them,
yet also binds them to a fiercer power they haplessly reproduce. Such readers cannot perceive the possibility of their "freedom" until they have recognized how their own culturally accredited acts—the power to name,
declare, classify, and curse—have created the mind-forg'd manacle that had
appeared to them as the very source of their own cultural distinction.

Sometimes opaquely, the poem navigates between clearly articulate
words or images and hazy, half-formed sounds and shapes. All language
arises from and returns to a material substratum of pure sound. As countless
commentaries have noted, Prometheus recants his "curse" against the en-
slaving Jupiter as a form of self-enslavement, reproducing within the discourse of the "slave" the empowering sign of the master himself. The
difficulty of *Prometheus Unbound* seems to lie in its imagined alternative to
the semiotic dualism of a linguistic master-slave relation, the variously im-

palpable shapes and sounds which represent an airy something, yet nothing distinct enough to call an image or a name. Shapeless forms, wordless converse: "a voice / Is wanting, the deep truth is imageless."[63] It is as though power plays on its definite signs, its visual and verbal representations whose renunciation rather than denunciation—by a steely indifference rather than a sharp retort—calls forth finally the visible alternative to the political language of the curse, which in Act 4 emerges as the collective, untrammeled language of *song*. Such singing hardly brings down the empire: that act takes place off the stage of language, by an implied act of force that, in terms of the poem's problematic of language and ideological enslavement, seems literally neither here nor there. But Jupiter does not sink into Demogorgon's darkness without recognizing he is no longer being answered, neither faithfully by his minions nor angrily by his victims (3.1). The spell of signs broken, his power becomes, as it were, only physical, a sceptre without magic.

What no radical writer of the Regency period produces, but Shelley at least prefigures in these poems, is an unanswerable demand, a response to power that is not a "response" because it cannot be answered in the semiotic terms power uses to define itself. Cobbett's sneering term "feelosophers" parodies the pretensions of those who use abstractions to mask relations of exploitation. But it turns over the philosopher's stone rather than burying it. Shelley veers to the right and the left of the radical journals, now cautious, now utopian, at once careful and extravagant. This is less a contradiction than a constant maneuvering to deflect the entrapment of the social sign, which middle-class writers and ministerial rulers used to absorb English radicalism, turn it inside out as unbearable "excess," or, at last resort, make it the very index of their own force.

CHAPTER

Five

Romantic Theory and English Reading Audiences

W ORDSWORTH and Coleridge came to believe—as Shelley did not—that reading redeems us. Wordsworth struggled to save this faith against institutions, the journals and reviewers who identified his 1800 poems with political Jacobinism and his theory of poetic language with a "metaphysical system." Out of his prefaces, supplements, and letters emerged a whole vocabulary with which literary history and the sociology of culture came to distinguish the transmission of cultural works: their "reception" by some readers, their "consumption" by many others, and the abyss between serious and mass culture that has only recently begun to be critically explored. For what Wordsworth called the task of "*creating*" taste was not a matter of poetic practice alone. It required theory, a reflective space in which Wordsworth, never comfortable with abstruse speculations, groped toward a systematic conception of his cultural aims, while Coleridge, addicted to metaphysics, constructed the most complex notion of an "audience" in the nineteenth century. Perhaps only in theory—resisted stubbornly by the reviewing institutions that safeguarded English cultural power at the end of the eighteenth century—could the complex relations between textuality, social structure, and cultural institutions themselves come strikingly into view.

The great social audiences of the early nineteenth century thrived within institutional bounds. The middle-class audience "dieted," in Coleridge's terms, at the "two public *ordinaries* of Literature, the circulating libraries and the periodical press."[1] The new mass audience combined these institutions with the Society for the Diffusion of Useful Knowledge, while the radical artisan audience formed within alternative institutions of the radical clubs and corresponding societies. Coleridge turned to greater institutions: the class-ordered state and the purely individual, morally ordered church. The clerisy, Carlyle's "Writing and Teaching Heroes," were to compose a great body of readers, virtuosos of symbolic texts. At the same time they were, as Coleridge urged his readers of the *Friend*, "to *influence* the multitude," make them its audience, train their capacities to read for themselves. Coleridge's theoretical clerisy never fully found a home among the practical clerics of modern academies. Yet the model has underwritten a politics of interpretation that maintains great power, particularly among those who tax themselves with deciding the clerical function at the present time. Even where his organicism is discredited, his notions of art consigned to metaphysical dustbins, or his social commitments discarded as threadbare ideologies, Coleridge's ethos of reading reappears in unusual and apparently innovative forms of contemporary clerical work. The aim of that ethos remains largely unchanged: to rule in and rule out the possible readings of social and cultural discourses contested throughout the social realm.

Writers between 1790 and 1830 could not organize their readers as audiences without mediating them through other collective forms: the crowd, the radical meeting, the chain of ranks, or the social text itself. Wordsworth's alien culture of English peasants, Coleridge's clergymen who move fluidly among the rich and poor, or Shelley's bands of patient rebels form similar social mediators who gave Romantic theorists tangible collective forms to help imagine and write to another, more difficult form, the audience they wished to construct. The most often-represented collective form in the early nineteenth century was doubtless that of social class itself. Yet only the radical writer attempted to make an audience that would coincide with a class; middle-class and mass writers ceaselessly represented figures of class order, only to define their readers as an audience apart from it. Coleridge's clerisy corresponds to no social class, yet it would be inconceivable without a firmly structured class order against which the clerisy finds its spiritually classless form. Nor does Wordsworth's project to transcend all languages of class make sense without the conviction that cultural and social languages of the 1790s were severely, almost grotesquely constrained by the material effects of class society. Thus the intensity of the great illusion about reading that informs the discourse of the Romantic Imagination: it frees us from a materially intolerable social world.

I. "Fit Audience Find": Reception and Consumption in Wordsworth

Wordsworth's 1800 Preface attempts to explain how the cultural condition of the 1790s came to pass. The terms of his famous diagnosis deserve close attention:

> For a multitude of causes, unknown to former times, are now acting with a combined force to blunt the discriminating powers of the mind, and, unfitting it for all voluntary exertion, to reduce it to a state of almost savage torpor. The most effective of these causes are the great national events which are daily taking place, and the increasing accumulation of men in cities, where the uniformity of their occupations produces a craving for extraordinary incident, which the rapid communication of intelligence hourly gratifies. To this tendency of life and manners the literature and theatrical exhibitions of the country have conformed themselves.[2]

Wordsworth imagines a popular public that "craves" but cannot truly "prefer" what it reads; its unconscious desires parade as its conscious cultural choices. This is perhaps the first functionalist view of cultural acts, and it is no wonder that middle-class readers and reviewers of 1800 resented having what seemed to them freely chosen preferences painted as a narcotic reflex. Reviewers objected bitterly to Wordsworth's "system," his "metaphysic" that ensnared modern readers in a remorseless cultural and social determinism.[3] Even worse, from their point of view, Wordsworth squares this audience's cultural cravings with the design of its languages: either a careless, "rapid communication of intelligence" or a calculated literary language, "poetic diction." Hence he describes the crude, almost behaviorist circle of a historically-conditioned need, a demand for "gratification," and a language that basely satisfies by creating ever greater need. What Wordsworth supplies the sociologist of mass culture, he also gives the literary theorist. Displacing the reading of Milton, the brutal sphere of textual consumption overwhelms the gentler world of textual "reception." The cultural commodity shoulders aside the cultural gift, overpowering the symbolic acts of giving and receiving. In a few broad strokes, the Romantic theorist establishes those antithetic modes of reading that will come in the next two centuries, under rubrics of "consumption" and "reception," to signify the realms of mass and high culture themselves.

The 1802 Appendix crucially qualifies this perspective. The *language* of the middle-class audience is not, like the audience itself, utterly situated by historical circumstance, but rather floats free of any material attachment. Repeated from poet to poet, the original language of men loses its primordial referentiality: "A language was thus insensibly produced, differing materially from the real language of men *in any situation.*" This language belongs nowhere, to no one. Yet "poetic diction" appears to all the senses a "real language" because it arrests just those faculties which might distinguish its falseness:

> The Reader or Hearer of this distorted language found himself in a perturbed and unusual state of mind: when affected by the genuine language of passion he had been in a perturbed and unusual state of mind also: in both cases he was willing that his common judgment and understanding should be laid asleep, and he had no instinctive and infallible perception of the true to make him reject the false; the one served as a passport for the other. (*Prose Works*, 1:160)

The loss of referentials suspends the poetic sign between "true" and "false"; in the realm of the passions, the counterfeit silently displaces the real thing. Wordsworth adheres unswervingly to the distinction between genuine and counterfeit that gives his ideological analysis its force. He attempts here to explain how the status of signs has changed, how the confusion between "true" and "false" signs marks the class distinction of the middle-class writer. "The true and the false were inseparably interwoven until, the taste of men becoming gradually perverted, this language was received as a natural language: and at length, by the influence of books upon men, did to a certain degree really become so" (1:161). To the 1800 Preface and its historical determinism, the 1802 Appendix adds Wordsworth's account of cultural production and its formative power. The historical transformation of the audience connects to a disturbing shift in the power of signs to merge the genuine into the counterfeit and the existential into the merely "literary." This position is hardly an empiricist one, as it is often described. Longing for recovery of all the referentials, Wordsworth comes to a position unmistakably "modern": a belief in the power of signs to transform the real itself.

The 1800 Preface claims no naive mimesis. What will be represented in the *Lyrical Ballads* is not the "real" but a "real language" all but inaccessible to the middle-class mind. The language of Wordsworth's own poems therefore becomes a metalanguage, a framework of highly qualified "poetic" language that carefully "selects," "adapts," "adopts," or "imitates" a "real language of men" as its object. Deprived of the real by the corruption of his own language, the self-conscious poet must now hypothesize another language—the language of the peasant poor—that preserves all the crucial referentials the poet can no longer summon himself. But Wordsworth's hope to recover a "real" language by representing it involves him in an infinite theoretical regress. In order to be *perceived* as representing the real language of men, Wordsworth's poems require the further, extraordinary step of a theoretical Preface—a second metalanguage to theorize the conditions of the first. The 1802 Appendix shows that no modern audience could distinguish "real" language from its counterfeit without such a preface. A theory of poetic signs has become absolutely necessary to arrest the historical, semiotic spiral in which it has become impossible for readers to distinguish true signs of value from the false. Still, even a theoretical preface cannot suffice. It, in turn, demands a larger theory of language, social order, and historical development that Wordsworth, in the opening of the Preface, apologizes for *not* writing:

> For, to treat the subject with the clearness and coherence of which it is susceptible, it would be necessary to give a full account of the present state of the public taste in this country, and to determine how far this taste is healthy or depraved; which, again, could not be determined, without pointing out in what manner language and the human mind act and react on each other, and without tracing the revolutions not of literature alone, but likewise of society itself. (1:121)

This is a breathtaking prospectus. It has now become impossible to write the smallest, humblest poem of worth without framing it with an ambitious theory of social transformation, individual and collective psychology, literature and the interpretation of signs. A whole sociology of literature is outlined here, greater and more eventful than much of what has since passed under that name. It was to be abortive: Wordsworth's struggle against the reviewing institutions over the next fifteen years reduced this grand surview to the lofty but hollow prospect of the 1815 "Essay, Supplementary to the

Preface." Once the agent of a momentous social and moral transformation, poetry will come to appear possible only in a realm apart from any society and its reading audiences.

Still, the resistance of the reviewing institutions alone cannot explain Wordsworth's retreat from cultural activism to a lonely, reactionary isolation. No matter how self-conscious his struggle to transform middle-class culture was, it argued something inherently contradictory, perhaps impossible. At its root lay the transcendent faith that reading itself may raise us above the social struggles that define us. At first, Wordsworth's argument is thoroughly materialist. To the displeasure of readers who wish to preserve the apparent freedom of their cultural preferences from social limit and cultural habit, Wordsworth claims that a distinctive "language" forms around each particular, class-shaped set of experiences and habitual predispositions. How can we deny, he wrote to John Wilson in 1802, that the audience poets address with "poetic diction" mistakes itself for humanity when it is only a part, a class: "Gentlemen, persons of fortune, professional men, ladies, persons who can afford to buy, or can easily procure, books of half a guinea price, hot-pressed, and printed upon superfine paper"? This class falsely proclaims its universality, "supposing that human nature and the persons they associate with are one and the same thing."[4] Rustics also compose a class and also generate a distinctive language. But this language, whose users have no power to proclaim themselves universal, admixes elements of a "real language of men" with gross provincialisms, profanities, and sentimentalities. Wordsworth now argues that one class-shaped language can be changed so that it represents another, socially alien language; the middle-class poet's language can "adopt" or "imitate" the peasant's. This is also the moment, however, when what is class-specific to *both* languages suddenly disappears. By reading one "language" through the frame of another, the materially imposed limits of both socially conditioned languages may be overcome in the revelatory palimpsest of a common "human" discourse. To "select" from, "adopt," or "adapt," above all to "imitate" a "real language" of the peasant poor, is to assert that such a language exists ontologically apart from the language of the urban middle class, and that the very framework of representation—where one language "imitates" another—will at last reveal yet a third language. Neither peasant nor middle-class, this language is the very "music of humanity." Here the ambitious, profoundly moral act of writing produces an audience that may escape its unacknowledged prisonhouse of language, its own class-limited cultural position, and gaze into the far freer realm of a humanity that "suffers" rather than "craves."

This humanist, apparently democratic project faces two great difficulties. The most familiar is the idealist's complaint. Far from discovering an alternative language of the poor, Coleridge argues in the *Biographia Literaria*, Wordsworth has in fact unconsciously *produced* one from within the grid of his own language. No language of the poor could be imagined that is not already a truncated projection of one's own: "I conclude, therefore, that the attempt is impracticable; and that, were it not impracticable, it would still be useless. For the very power of making the selection implies the previous possession of the language selected."[5] Likewise, the representationalist vocabulary Wordsworth wields—"select, imitate, adopt" and elsewhere "represent"—must give way to Coleridge's phenomenological vocabulary of connection and separation. At issue is not whether language can represent "reality" but whether one social language can represent another. Coleridge's strategy is to maintain that rustic language cannot be "sufficient"; it cannot be conceded the wholeness which would make it *a* language and thus representable by another. Such a language—if it exists— is radically incomplete:

> The rustic. . . aims almost solely to convey *insulated facts*, either those of his scanty experience or his traditional belief; while the educated man chiefly seeks to discover and express those *connections* of things, or those relative *bearings* of fact to fact, from which some more or less general law is deducible. . . . There is a want of that prospectiveness of mind, that *surview*, which enables a man to foresee the whole of what he is to convey, appertaining to any one point; and by this means so to subordinate and arrange the different parts according to their relative importance, as to convey it at once, and as an organized whole. (BL, 2:52–53, 58)

All attempts to make contact with a language truly *other* by "imitating" it constantly give way to the uncontrollable powers of Wordsworth's own linguistic productivity. The peasant's "culture" is not truly alien to the educated man's. Thus, while sharing Wordsworth's sense of a debased, class-limited middlebrow culture, Coleridge cannot imagine transcending it except by widening yet further its inadequately ideal powers. These powers cannot be discovered in any class, they must be constructed in that ultimate institution of the mind, the National Church.

The surprising similarity of Coleridge's arguments to those made by contemporary reviewers, however, partly suggests why he needed to frame them in the imposing apparatus of German metaphysics. This passage from W. R. Lyall's 1815 essay in the *Quarterly Review*, for instance, begins with the argument familiar to any reader of Coleridge's "literary life," before it takes a wayward speculative turn:

> The truth is, if the language of low life be purified from what *we* should call its *real defects*, it will differ only in copiousness from the language of high life; as to the *rational and lasting causes of dislike and disgust*, it is plain that on the subject of language no such causes can, in any instance, be assigned.... Language, as everybody knows, consists merely of arbitrary signs which stand for whatever it may have pleased custom to enact, and whatever changes may happen among them are occasioned not by 'rational causes' but by accidental associations of one sort and and another, of which, in general, we defy the most profound metaphysician to give any philosophical account.[6]

In the *Biographia* Coleridge answers not only Wordsworth's purposive materialism of language, but also this random materialism that locates meaning in the happenstance collision of signs. It goes hand-in-hand with the reviewing institution's assault on *all* rational metaphysics and cultural theory. This willy-nilly notion of language and cultural history buttresses an entirely arbitrary institutional authority. The subtext of Coleridge's famous claim that language is both ideal and rational takes aim at a greater target than Wordsworth himself:

> The best part of human language, properly so called, is derived from reflection on the acts of the mind itself. It is formed by a voluntary association of fixed symbols to internal acts, to processes and results of imagination, the greater part of which have no place in the consciousness of uneducated man; though in civilized society, by imitation and passive remembrance of what they hear from their religious instructors and other superiors, the most uneducated share in the harvest which they neither sowed nor reaped. (BL 2:54)

Wordsworth's theory is not only self-contradictory, Coleridge claims. It unwittingly gives comfort to an ideology more powerful than any of Wordsworth's texts.

But the other difficulty of Wordsworth's effort to recover a genuine cultural language has greater consequences. Having described the middle-class audience as consumers of a brutalized popular culture fashioned for urban readers, Wordsworth seeks in the rustic's alternative culture a means to reverse that consumption into a form of "reception." He attempts to transform commodified textual relations into an older relation of symbolic exchange, opposing to popular German verse tragedies and the sentimental trash of the magazines new poems that call for an active, engaged response from the same readers. When he calls for a Reader who will answer the Writer's "power" with a matching power of response, in the 1815 Essay, he envisions a purely symbolic exchange that must stand in place of degraded commodity exchanges the middle-class public has become all too accustomed to accept. Despite its yearning for the cultural past, however, Wordsworth's proposed poetic language is irreversibly, in Jean Baudrillard's sense of the term, a "modern" sign: "[It] dreams of the sign anterior to it and fervently desires, in its reference to the real, to rediscover some binding obligation. But it finds only a *reason:* a referential reason, the real—the 'natural' on which it will feed. This lifeline of designation, however, is no more than a simulacrum of symbolic obligation."[7] Baudrillard's "modern sign" does not belong to those for whom representation still unproblematically binds words with things—the eighteenth century from which Wordsworth borrowed his associationist theory of language. It belongs to a new age in which the writer's language can at most only "represent" a truly representational language. This is the difficulty of attempting to return to the purely symbolic exchanges imagined in peasant culture with a language already saturated in the commodity logic that grips the middle-class audience of 1800. This Romantic writer yearns to return to the space of "reception" (symbolic exchange) from the historical ground of "consumption" (commodity exchange). Yet to restore the reading of Milton and thus to save literature itself, Wordsworth must ultimately produce the most paradoxical sense of "literature"—a discourse which can be "received" only in the absence of a real social audience. Wordsworth's effort to remake the existing audience of 1800 ends, in 1815, by inventing an audience in imagination he was unable to form in the world. Hoping to return his readers to the real activity of symbolic exchange, he unavoidably invents a now familiar notion of an audience, one utterly detached from social space. Under such conditions, the audience of literature can realize, to borrow Baudrillard's phrase, only a "simulacrum of symbolic obligation."

This crucial shift may best be glimpsed in Wordsworth's sense of the historical relations between the two worlds the 1800 Preface attempts to bridge. Wordsworth was well aware that these urban and rural cultures were not simply notional opposites yoked together by the ingenuity of his own Preface; one had been, for the past generation, *becoming* the other. The men and women whose "real language" he theorizes had already begun migrating toward the cities to become what he describes in an 1812 letter to Catherine Clarkson, written from London: "The lower orders [who] have been for upwards of 30 years accumulating in pestilential masses of ignorant population."[8] The late-eighteenth-century "agricultural revolution" celebrated by Arthur Young had already turned rural populations into city aggregates and peasant communities into ignorant London crowds. Some ten to twenty years after this letter, those "pestilential masses" would be formed as an audience—the first English mass audience shaped in such journals as the *Hive*, the *Penny Magazine*, and *Chambers' Edinburgh Journal*. Wordsworth often idealized the ground tilled by "Men who are the Owners of it," the very "ground" of a "real language of men." But what happens when that ground is enclosed and monopolized, when those speakers of a "real language" are expelled from its nourishing substance and forced to mass pestilentially in the overwhelming crowds first glimpsed in Book VII of *The Prelude*? As if to answer that question, Wordsworth reminds Catherine Clarkson that this is by no means a new historical development. Despite "unthinking people [who] cry out that the national character has been changed all at once," the poet insists, "the change has been silently going on ever since we were born; the disease has been growing, and now breaks out in all its danger and deformity." The birth of the writer coincides with the death of the only culture that gives value to writing itself. Such a death gives Wordsworth common cause with the ethnologist and the archaeologist, who, as Michel de Certeau puts it, "arrive at the moment a culture has lost its means of self-defense."[9]

Hence a new link between cultural past and future—and yet another appendix to the 1800 Preface—appears in his letters of 1812. The poems of 1800 are not merely textual relays between two autonomous cultures. They compose the textual countermove against that vast social transformation that since Wordsworth's birth has been turning one (full) culture into another (empty) culture, as the peasants who speak "the very language of men" become historically the future urban readers who, at further and further textual removes, can at best read only *about* such a language in the poems the poet offers them. Thus the increasingly bleak strategy of a writer who casts the act of *reading* against ineluctable historical development itself.

Perhaps this is why, though Wordsworth had set out to address an urban middle-class readership sorely in need of regeneration, he sometimes imagined writing *to* that very class whose language he only felt he could "imitate." Consulted as an authority on the culture of peasants, the author of *Lyrical Ballads* would advise ministers like Francis Wrangham that rustics themselves do little reading: "The labouring man in agriculture generally carries on his work either in solitude, or with his own Family, persons whose minds he is thoroughly acquainted with, and with whom he is under no temptation to enter into discussions, or to compare opinions."[10] No sphere of public discourse develops where the "narrow circle of their intercourse" connects mind to familiar mind. No "audience" displaces the face-to-face intercourse of a real community. Yet, Wordsworth acknowledges, there *is* a peasant's written culture:

I find, among the people I am speaking of, half-penny Ballads, and penny and two-penny histories, in great abundance; these are often bought as charitable tributes to the poor Persons who hawk them about (and it is the best way of procuring them); they are frequently stitched together in tolerably thick volumes, and such I have read; some of the contents, though not often religious, very good; others objectionable, either for the superstition in them (such as prophecies, fortune-telling, etc.) or more frequently for indelicacy. I have so much felt the influence of these straggling papers, that I have many a time wished I had talents to produce songs, poems, and little histories, that might circulate among other good things in this way, supplanting partly the bad; flowers and useful herbs to take place of weeds. Indeed some of the Poems which I have published were composed not without a hope that at some time or other they might answer this purpose. (*Letters*, 2:248)

Wordsworth imagines himself delicately intervening in this homegrown garden of "little histories." But he knows these chapbooks were the indigenous product of the peasant culture itself, not written for the peasants by outsiders attempting—like Francis Wrangham—to impose their own culture on the rustic. Thus he warns Wrangham that any effort to impose culture wholesale from above—in this case, through "religious books for the Poor"—will be largely, but not entirely, useless:

The kind of Library [of religious books for the poor] you recommend would not, I think, from the reasons given above, be of much direct use in any of the agricultural or pastoral districts of Cumberland or Westmoreland with which I am acquainted, though almost every person can read: I mean of *general* use as to morals or behavior; it might however with individuals do much in awakening enterprize, calling forth ingenuity, and fostering genius. . . . The knowledge thus acquired would also have spread, by being dealt about in conversation among their Neighbours, at the door, or by the fireside—so that it is not easy to foresee how far the good might extend; and harm I can see none which would not be greatly overbalanced by the advantage. (248)

This model of cultural transmission amplifies the 1800 Preface. Firmly inserted in his social audience, the "Reader," who is both mocked and assuaged in poems like "Simon Lee," filters the impact of a text through his community, and at length, the poems transform the peasant audience itself. But it is clearly not a matter, as Francis Wrangham seems to believe, of imposing doctrine or any particular textual *content* on these readers. What matters is the form of reading itself ("awakening enterprize, calling forth ingenuity, and fostering genius"), an encounter that slowly transforms the heart of a culture.

Thus Wordsworth imagines the possible reception of his own poems as he contributes to this marginal literature of the poor. A secret ambition of the *Ballads*—unconfessable in public prefaces—is to represent the rural poor to themselves, to work in reverse the difficult act he proposes in the 1800 Preface. His own "songs, poems, and little histories" would edge out the bad texts (superstitious, indelicate), thereby transforming the peasant's indigenous culture in the same way that he would, for the middle-class audience, subtly transform its "real language" by eliding all its "rational and lasting causes of dislike and disgust." By shifting the frame of his audience, Wordsworth in this letter momentarily rewrites the *Ballads* themselves. Their subjects and language are no longer leveled upward to make the middle class confront what is most human in themselves, but now refract the rural poor back to themselves. The middle-class writer can reveal to them, in his "little histories," that greater narrative in which they are all singly inscribed. No moment so distinguishes the middle-class writer from his sympathetically drawn subjects than this desire to make a peasant reader glimpse, in a sudden recognition of his type, what was always hidden from himself. The poems would uncover what was "inoperative and unvalued" in the peasant's own mind, suddenly made legible insofar as he is now the reader of a very special, very hypothetical audience. Even when it actually crosses the deep divides of culture and class, Wordsworth's cultural production cannot embrace its audience without transforming it, and always in the same way. Leveling the peasant culture "upward" or the haughty middle-class urban culture "down," Wordsworth's writing aims at last to make an audience somewhere beyond the determination of class and the material habitus it effects. The *Lyrical Ballads* thus becomes a text woven between two incommensurate audiences, the one in whose surprised face they are flung, insolently prefaced, and the one—perhaps the only one— who could ideally confirm what no middle-class audience would bring it- self to acknowledge, that "we have *all* one human heart." Wordsworth imagines what, in another way, the later mass writers will construct in the cities—an audience meant to recognize itself among its types and, in this way, fully absorb the text that Wordsworth's recalcitrant middle-class public can read only at arm's length, at every moment prepared to fling the text back.

Profoundly anthropological, Wordsworth's project seeks out an alien culture, the language of a remote social class, only to recover from it what was *always* there. To "represent" this language can mean only to rescue it from its otherness, like the modern anthropologist who tries to penetrate what is most opaque in an alien culture to make it familiar and unthreaten- ing to Western eyes. There is, indeed, a fine line between the gesture which brings together two social languages in what Mikhail Bakhtin called a "he- teroglot" encounter and the gesture that effaces their differences, rendering them "human" rather than social. Wordsworth rides this line throughout the Preface of 1800 and the letters of the next twelve years. The conflict within Wordsworth's conception is also, inescapably, the conflict among Bakhtin's own readers, for whom dialogic and heteroglot encounters appear either as "class struggle" in the "arena" of signs or, on the contrary, the ulti- mate human connection of "self" and "other." Wordsworth's critique of middle-class culture begins with his materialist calculation of taste and so- cial circumstance. It becomes idealist the moment his argument no longer tries to clarify the differences between social classes, but now attempts to bridge and erase them.[11]

These dialectics of cultural transmission mark the *Lyrical Ballads* them- selves as a veritable anthology of styles and cross-purposes, ranging from the *humilitas* of "Simon Lee" to the personal sublime of "Tintern Abbey." In those poems where the language of the self-conscious intellectual min- gles with the language of the female vagrant or the mad mother, readers en- ter into something like Bakhtin's dialogism, where the diverse dialects of persons and cultures play against each other. Yet the irresolvable "dialogue" theorized by Bakhtin finally shades into the Romantic poet's pluralist blending of differences, fused in a great high humanist style that shifts these dissonant, dialogical gears into the smoother workings of what Erich Auerbach called an Augustinian mode of *sermo humilis*, the humble sublime. It is this "real" Wordsworth—not the Wordsworth of heteroglot encounter between socially alien languages—that M. H. Abrams canonizes in *Natural Supernaturalism*. Wordsworth, he writes, "must therefore as poet establish that dominion over the spirits of Readers by which they are to be humbled and humanized, in order that they may be purified and exalted".[12] As the humble suffuses the sublime and the sublime exalts the humble, the encounter between alien languages translates into the mixture of styles, a representational language that "signifies" the human apart from all its social and historical configurations. Social conflicts reappear, in the mingling of social languages, as a liberal, comforting pluralism. Strikingly, it is the 1815 Essay through which Abrams reads Wordsworth, the text that projects both a humble-sublime mingling of styles and also sanctions a "Reader" apart from any historical audience in which he must be otherwise inscribed.

By 1815 Wordsworth had yielded up any relation between his "reader" and a historically situated audience for that "Reader" who will be realized in a distant prospect of time. Wherever he may alight in some unimaginable future, such a reader can be realized only as a prospective "power" commensurate with the agonized power the writer himself invested in his work. This difficult conception of a final symbolic exchange within the text concedes to the middle-class culture of commodity exchange its priority and enabling necessity. In 1815 it is no longer possible to conceive transforming that culture into its symbolic opposite. The 1815 Essay supplements the Preface only to replace it. Here the history of textual editions is oddly illuminating. The 1800 Preface dropped to the end of the 1815 two-volume *Poems*, with the Essay meant to be "supplementary" to the new 1815 Preface explaining how Wordsworth had ordered the latest sequence of poems. But in the 1836 edition of the *Poems*, the Essay shifts to follow the 1800 Preface, still at the end, in whose counterspirit it had always really been read. For the Essay announces that the fate of reading is no longer a question of reception *or* consumption, but of reception as the desperate dialectic *of* consumption. His project to remake the middle-class audience for poems now abandoned, Wordsworth imagines a readership that may arise only by renouncing its place among the Public that never ceases to "crave." This is, as Wordsworth writes, "the People, philosophically characterized" —philosophically, because it is now impossible to conceive it socially.

Hence it is both strange and revealing to see an 1815 reviewer of the Essay construe Wordsworth's "People" as the future, fully commodified mass audience yet to be born:

> Let our readers digest that which we are about to quote, and with which we shall be contented as an example of the author's prose performances, criticisms, or good auspices relating to his own future support from the *people*;—the *people*, whom he emphatically separates from the *public*; meaning, we presume, those who are hereafter to be taught to read, to *mox erudiendum vulgus*, the unborn children of Joseph Lancaster, as contradistinguished from the progeny of the universities or the literary swarm of the metropolis now in existence.[13]

Wrongheaded as this seems, the reviewer's mocking misreading bears its own ironic kernel of truth. The future development of mass culture will depend partly on precisely the formulation of "literature" Wordsworth proffers in the 1815 Essay. Literature is to be the dialectical negation of a fated world of textual commodity exchanges, a literature which never addresses itself to the social present but realizes its audience only at the end of time:

> 'Past and future, are the wings
> On whose support, harmoniously conjoined,
> Moves the great Spirit of human knowledge—'

. . . Towards the Public the writer hopes that he feels as much deference as it is entitled to: but to the People, philosophically characterized, and to the embodied spirit of their knowledge, so far as it exists and moves, at the present, faithfully supported by its two wings, the past and the future, his devout respect, his reverence is due. He offers it willingly and readily; and, this done, takes leave of his Readers, by assuring them—that if he were not persuaded that the contents of these Volumes, and the Work to which they are subsidiary, evince something of the 'Vision and Faculty divine'; and that, both in words and things, they will operate in their degree, to extend the domain of sensibility for the delight, the honour, and the benefit of human nature, notwithstanding the many happy hours which he has enjoyed in their composition, and the manifold comforts and enjoyments they have procured to him, he would not, if a wish could do it, save them from immediate destruction; —from becoming at this moment, to the world, as a thing that had never been. (*Prose Works*, 3:84)

Wordsworth's high hyperbole confronts the real structural impasse of the early-nineteenth-century British cultural sphere. The high humanist effort to bridge social and cultural difference in a powerful act of cultural transmission—explicit in the 1800 Preface, far less confidently confessed in the letters—founders against the deepening division of social audiences themselves. Even in 1815 the *Monthly Review* projects a degraded mass audience that has not yet fully come into being, yet is proleptically visible in the very dynamic of the powerful middle-class public Wordsworth has struggled to reform. Rewriting Wordsworth's national-spirit "People" as the middle-class reviewer's contemptuous mass-cultural "people," the journalist accentuates the cultural determinism Wordsworth now desperately seeks to escape.

In the event, Wordsworth found his audience. His growing "public," true to the 1815 Essay, came in the later nineteenth and twentieth centuries to read in him the quintessential "Romantic" unsituated in social space and time. What Jerome McGann calls the "Romantic ideology" displaces the real cultural and historical conflicts of the early nineteenth century with an essentialized "Romanticism," and Wordsworth, among others, successfully established the terms for that subliming of the historical in the ideal.[14] He did not do so without great pain. The choice he refers to at the end of the Essay—either *believe* in this suprahistorical audience he must hope for, or destroy all his own works—seemed forced on him. Forced it was, partly by a recalcitrant middle-class public and its defensive institutions of reading, and partly by Wordsworth's own commitment to an impossible faith. That the abyss between social classes and their cultures could be bridged in a heroic, high humanist act of writing, and that socially divided readers might transcend their differences in a morally renewing, redemptive act of reading—this belief failed him. Yet it survives in his works, and in the faiths of many who still read him.

II. COLERIDGE: THE INSTITUTIONS OF A MISREADING PUBLIC

Unlike Wordsworth, Coleridge could not conceive reading and writing except in the framework of institutions. He spoke late in life of "three silent revolutions in England: —first, when the professions fell off from the church; secondly, when literature fell off from the professions; and, thirdly, when the press fell off from literature."[15] What he meant was a historical fracturing of textual institutions, a "desynonymization" and weakening of their cultural authority. In response to this cultural confusion, whose product was "the luxuriant misgrowth of our activity, a Reading Public," Coleridge sought to construct an audience that was *also* an institution, a body of readers and writers capable of governing the relations between all the emerging audiences of the nineteenth century over whom, individually, no institution could claim control.

The clerisy was to be composed of protean readers capable of powerful symbolic interpretations, who were to instruct all other audiences, each according to its social space, how to read and how to distinguish between proper readings and those readings that must be ruled out. Coleridge recognized astutely the failure of earlier means of cultural control: censorship, the power of circulation, the exercise of taste. Crudest of all was the state's power to govern publication and propaganda by the force it levied against the radical public in 1794–95 and 1819–20. The censors' local success, as victims like Richard Carlile triumphantly pointed out, stood in inverse proportion to their moral legitimacy. By the early 1820s even the ministers' most apologetic acolytes recognized this corrosive delegitimation of the state, casting its hollow authority against the slippery resistance of a ubiquitous public text. More powerful appeared to be the grand arena of "circulation," in which tendentious viewpoints finally cancelled each other out in the greater consensus of a pluralistic public sphere. But Coleridge sharply perceived the internal contradictions of that circulation. Its attractive metaphoricity concealed a number of logical impasses and devastating moral and ideological evasions. Not least of these was the question of "taste," that overdetermined notion which for the previous hundred years had governed a complex discourse on the subject of cultural legitimacy and resistance to social change. This inward state—a state of grace—corresponded in its complexity and necessity to that outward political state whose cracked arches could no longer govern cultural production and reception in the postrhetorical, postrevolutionary world. Indeed the regeneration of taste—to which both Wordsworth and Coleridge were deeply committed—required for Coleridge the making of an interpretive institution that at once resituated the political state, reestablished a state of intellectual grace, and restructured the circulatory practices of reading and writing themselves. In the end, this institutional response, rather than Wordsworth's anthropological or Shelley's political strategies, would go furthest to recontain the explosiveness of nineteenth-century cultural conflict.

"I could not reconcile personality with infinity," Coleridge remarked of his own theological growth (*BL*, 1:201). "The *idea* of the Supreme Being appeared to me to be as necessarily implied in all particular modes of being as the idea of infinite space in all the geometrical figures by which space is limited" (*BL*, 1:200). Vacillating between the infinities of Spinozism and the palpable sense of personality he read in Paul and John, Coleridge sought in social theory as well as philosophy a figure for the embodied infinite, the whole within "each," and never more so than when he tried to imagine the reader who would embody a greater audience. As he surveyed the audience who attended the production of his first play, *Remorse*, he sought not their applause nor the beat of his language visibly on their pulses, but a sign, any sign, of personal recognition: "I can conscientiously declare, that the complete success of the *Remorse* on the first night of its representation did not give me as great or as heart-felt a pleasure, as the observation that the pit and boxes were crowded with faces familiar to me, though of individuals whose names I did not know, and of whom I knew nothing, but that they had attended one or other of my courses of lectures." (*BL*, 1:221). The contrary of this personal public is the public personified, oppressively totalized as "the multitudinous Public," who, "shaped into personal unity by the magic of abstraction, sits nominal despot on the throne of criticism" (*BL*, 1:59). The personal audience Coleridge seeks cannot become, like the great and pernicious reviews, the synecdoche of a reading public, substituting itself for the reading whole. In 1809 he would take up the *Friend* to shape an audience that is not only gathered personally from the greater middle class but prepared in its turn to actively direct the large public: "those who by Rank, or Fortune, or official Situation, or Talents and Habits of Reflection, are to *influence* the Multitude." The new readership has shifted its base from the *Watchman*'s inventors, amateur engineers, venture-capital entrepreneurs, and other vanguards of middle-class dissent to the *Friend*'s doctors, lawyers, lords, professors, clergymen, and landowners, all now prepared to become productive ideologists in their own right.[16]

This audience, still inchoately personal, must be forged through a prose style more convoluted than any periodical could reasonably withstand. It must be made a culturally *reproductive* body antithetical to the increasingly passive, consuming audiences who, as Wordsworth feared, acted as mere functions of the marketplace. Thus the complex "connected" style of the *Friend* becomes an audience-forming strategy to counter all other strategies being deployed in the early nineteenth century.[17] But this well-known distinction between the obscure "connected" prose style and its opposite, the "Anglo-Gallican unconnected" style, belongs to a larger method Coleridge dedicated to determining the cultural politics of discourse. This "rhematic" method, as we will see, corresponds to a choice of interpretive stances crucial to the ethos of the clerical institution Coleridge's personal audience ultimately must become.

Among his drafts of the *Logic* Coleridge included this brief, odd table:

A table of the formal sciences, or systematized arts, of which words are the subject and medium.

1. *Grammatice*—Fitting together of letters
2. *Rhematice*—Arrangement of words
3. *Rhetorice*—Putting together of persuasions
4. *Logice*—[Binding together] of reasonings.[18]

For those seeking entry to "the bar, the pulpit, or the senate," this preprofessional curriculum has a classical reading list for subjects 1, 3, and 4. But the required texts for subject 2 would evidently be the works of S. T. Coleridge himself, sole neologist of the term *rhematic*. The "rhe-matic" apparently bridges grammar and rhetoric. It is "the doctrine of arranging words and sentences perspicuously; an art which has hitherto had no appropriate title, having been confounded with all the others" (*Logic*, 22). No clearer definition of the "rhematic" appears in Coleridge's writings. Like the method of interpretation he can only define "by its negatives" in *The Statesman's Manual*, the rhematic mode always appears as an excluded and yet-to-be defined method or cultural "science." But a definition can be proposed on the basis of his sparse hints and recurring semiotic practice. If the rhematic lies somewhere between the purely linguistic sphere of grammar and the sociopolitical realm of rhetoric—between the law of language and the practice of discourse—it must be because this is a question of "legal practice." Its subject is neither language as a system, nor discrete social uses of speech, but rather the *certification* of political, social, and historical discourses.

Characteristically the rhematic mode involves what we should now call a form of stylistic analysis. But the category of "style," as Coleridge uses

it, cannot mean either the signature of an individual writer or the historical essence sometimes called a "period style."[19] Rhematic "styles" are for
Coleridge a matter both of significancy and persuasion, grammar and rhetoric. Above all they are collective categories, instanced in the case of this
or that particular writer, but ultimately rhetorical in the oldest classical
sense of a collective discursive framework. Thus rhematic analysis can be
properly practiced upon the often hidden solidarities Roland Barthes called
"modes of writing":

> A mode of writing is an act of historical solidarity . . . a function: it is
> the relationship between creation and society, the literary language
> transformed by its social finality, form considered as a human intention
> and thus linked to the great crises of History. . . . Since writing is the
> spectacular commitment of language, it contains at one and the same
> time, thanks to a valuable ambiguity, the reality and the appearance of
> power, what it is, and what it would like to be thought to be: a history
> of political modes of writing would therefore be the best of social phe-
> nomenologies.[20]

Coleridge attempts his own social phenomenology in a highly selective
history of writing governed by alternating rhematic polarities—the "connected" and "cementless" styles. Transforming the customarily grammatical "conjunction" into the now rhematic "copula" or "connection," the
theorist of writing solidarities confides one of the final aims of the rhematic mode: "I wish, in short, to connect by a moral *copula* natural history
with political history; or in other words, to make history scientific and science historical—to take from history its accidentality, and from science its
fatalism."[21]

Coleridge's political stylistics moves ceaselessly between fusion, or
connection, and separation, or cementlessness. For this reason, rhematic
analysis provides a powerful tactic against a certain kind of "representation," the kind best known as "allegory." At one extreme, allegorical representation embraces the uncategorical particulars of "accidentality," yoking
them to the other extreme, the systematic universals of "fatalism." Coleridge objects to allegory for the arbitrariness between its totalized system of
concepts and its "accidentalist" selection of images from objects themselves (*Statesman's Manual*, 30). For the allegorist, the caesura between sign
and meaning requires an *investment* that links them, an ideological invest-

ment that would reveal what David Hume uncovers in his histories: the *motives* of these investments. What an ideological analysis like Hume's always reveals is a calculus of interests and "selfish passions": "This inadequacy of the mere understanding to the apprehension of moral greatness we may trace in this historian's cool systematic attempt to steal away every feeling of reverence for every great name by a scheme of *motives,* in which as often as possible the efforts and enterprizes of heroic spirits are attributed to this or that paltry view of the most despicable selfishness" (*Statesman's Manual,* 22–23) Such motive analysis reduces the momentary saturation of the sign with meaning back to its allegorical elements, the sign-maker back to his frail, manipulative, existential, and *rhetorical* stance as an isolated self struggling on the contested terrain of interest and gain. But "rhematic" analysis situates itself on the nether side of rhetoric. It resists the reduction of style to ideological motive; it abstains from the battlefield of investments in which styles are transformed into weapons of criticism and defense. The allegorist and the radical or skeptical writer invest signs with strategically chosen meanings; likewise, they can unpack signs of meanings invested by others. But in Coleridge's politics of discourse, signs and styles come to us already loaded with meaning, before any possible investment.

The Anglo-Gallican "unconnected" style, for instance, could no more be used to serve a Coleridgean project than the "obscure" style could serve a radical rhetorician's. "The cementless periods of the modern Anglo-Gallican styles," Coleridge wrote to Robert Southey ". . . are not only understood *beforehand,* but, being free from all connections of logic, all the hooks and eyes of intellectual memory, never oppress the mind by any after recollections."[22] This style not only binds the French *philosophes* with their English radical interpreters: it is hardly distinguishable from the "cementless aggregates of the Oriental Sages" or from the "smooth and strong epigrammatic couplets" of Pope—"a conjunction disjunctive of epigrams" (*BL* 1:19). At once political, philosophical, and literary, the unit of rhematic analysis obeys no ordinary national, chronological, or disciplinary boundaries. Oriental, political, and poetical despots join along the arc of rhematic solidarity, so that Thomas Paine, whose Anglo-Gallican style becomes the necessary antithetical scaffolding of Coleridge the political essayist, can be no different than the Tartar despot whose geometrically cementless estate forms the crucially negative model for a raging Dionysiac poet.[23] Rhematic analysis reveals strange bedfellows and discloses surprising connections between hitherto remote cultural states. It is no ordinary mode of analysis that discovers the oriental sage bound to the English Jacobin writer. In

Hume's world, politics chooses a discourse; in Coleridge's, the discourse projects a politics.

Coleridge also imagines a rhematic historiography in which Western Europe distinguishes itself from Oriental culture at the Socratic point where the "connected" style veers off from the Asian "cementless" mode. Here is also the point at which the Platonic language of Reason must have individuated itself from the Sophistic language of Rhetoric.[24] As the "French style" forks again from the European in the seventeenth century, the English style suffers an internal split between the periodic language of the Anglican divines and the neo-Gallican style that dominates English discourse from the Restoration. Nowhere in this history can there appear a struggle between two or more factions over the meaning of the same style. Every style or discourse bears an internal ordering principle—like the inherent order that distinguishes the educated man's language from Wordsworth's rustic speech. This principle decisively seals it off from social contest. No social conflicts can be inflected *within* the style Coleridge calls "connected" or, for that matter, within the "Anglo-Gallican." Rhematic analysis is precisely what avoids such disruptive encounter. The unsettling clash of what Bakhtin calls "socio-ideological points of view" within the same discourse would fatally collapse the order that rhematic analysis is meant to discover. To open a discourse to conflicting readings is a socially explosive act; to close it off from such encounters is what rhematic analysis intends. For the great Romantic theorist of the Symbol and its multiple meanings, this resistance to multiple readings may appear paradoxical. So it is: it is precisely the closure of socio-ideological readings that will allow the opening of symbolic and interpretive readings.

In the first numbers of the 1809 *Friend*, Coleridge ponders the peril of "translating" the truth into discourse, a move which forces us into the dialogical realm, the place where one's own sense of truth is always in danger of being imbricated in another's. "Truth-in-language" may not only be misunderstood: worse, it can always be appropriated by another and rewritten according to the rhematic laws of *his* discourse. The "adequacy" of language to truth can be achieved only where that equation is not constantly interfered with by the language of the other. The only such adequate expression of truth, a style which embodies and embraces the "moral truth," will be the language which *already* includes and forestalls the possibilities of its expropriation by the other. At the opposite extreme is the style which addresses its reader as an "inseparable part" of the social order, the rhetoric of radical discourse:

> Bold, warm, and earnest assertions...arguments built on passing
> events...startling particular facts; the display of defects without ac-
> companying excellencies...chains of questions, especially of such
> questions as those best authorized to propose are the slowest in propos-
> ing; objections intelligible of themselves, the answers to which require
> the comprehension of a system; —all these a Demagogue might make
> use of, and in nothing deviate from the verbal truth.[25]

For it is not merely in the "verbal" truth that Truth is to be found: the radical writer, who is known by his "jerks of style" (the unconnected style), remains trapped in a purely representational language that lacks those
connectives, grammatical or logical, which open the way to a dialectical
rebounding upon the instruments of its own thought. The representational
style of the "verbal truth" cannot, whatever its rhetorical and logical resources, evade the possibility of misreading and misappropriation. This is
why the extraordinarily resourceful radical writer masters the scene of "verbal truth" by purposively "misreading" his ministerial and aristocratic antagonists with the unparalleled critical weapons of parody, satire, and
polemic. The verbal truth can be communicated indiscriminately to all audiences. But it marks one's truth as "moral" that it is shaped for a particular
audience, an audience internally prepared for a truth that extends beyond
words and encompasses the concrete discursive situation itself. "By *verbal*
truth we mean no more than the correspondence of a given fact to given
words. In *moral* truth, we moreover involve the intention of the speaker,
that his words should correspond to his thoughts in the sense in which he
expects them to be understood by others" (*Friend*, 2:42). Coleridge's truth is
absolute but the language that bears it is profoundly situational. This, however, is no contradiction: it is the very principle by which his own audience
must be formed. The connected style presupposes, and deflects, the various
interpretations that could be made of its truth. It allows no misreadings. It
will be *for* one audience and decidedly not for another.

In fact, the problem of communicating truth among contentious reading audiences is remarkably similar to the problem of getting a joke across.
When Freud considers the possibility of misreading the joke, he raises a
thoroughly Coleridgean question: "Is it the truth if we describe things as
they are without troubling to consider how our hearer will understand what
we say? Or is this only jesuitical truth, and does not genuine truth consist
in taking the hearer into account and giving him a faithful picture of our
own knowledge?" Everything is won or lost depending on one's strategic

position in the discursive act.[26] Freud's subject here is a special class of "skeptical" jokes which raise acutely the problem "of what determines the truth." These reflexive jokes point out in their content what all jokes assume in their form: that the joke is the most misreadable of texts, always in danger of being received by the wrong kind of listener. Doubly disastrous if they misfire are the "skeptical" jokes about the conditions of truth itself. But these jokes are also self-armed against the misreading that constantly threatens the joking act; they forestall misinterpretation by being about misinterpretation. Coleridge's truth is no joke; but it may, received by the wrong audience, become an unintended self-betrayal, a joke of the worst kind, misread for what it reveals about him rather than for what he is trying, in the precarious medium of language, to reveal himself.

The struggle against grave social and textual misinterpretations forms the social content of Coleridge's connected style: "representative and reward of our past conscious reasonings, insights and conclusions" which finally "acquires the name of Taste" (BL, 2:81). In the postrhetorical fluxion of audiences in the late eighteenth and early nineteenth centuries, "Taste" must be the conscious mode of cultural calculation, the infinitely wary act of communicating "Truth" to a particular audience so as to take into account all its possible interpretations, and to foreclose those that may destroy the very ground upon which one has chosen to speak. An important part of this calculation, rhematic analysis always establishes a pregiven ideological meaning for a particular stylistic or rhetorical mode. It assumes that forms and styles float above all their users, inscribed with the unchanging values, but never invested with them. The "meaning" of a style, and its social import, remains constant no matter who uses it, no matter what historical strategy it serves.

Whether it is aimed against Humean skepticism or Marxist suspicion, rhematic analysis always deflects ideological analysis. This cultural practice first detaches a reader from his socially defined and rhetorically shared audience, any audience in which he might otherwise remain an "inseparable" part of that order. But it also finds that reader's place in a new audience, a greater interpretive order. The complex connected style proves a tortuous path to membership in that new audience. It is an initiatory style, a rite of passage between all prior reading habits and some new cultural act of great consequence. It is easy now to smile at Coleridge's tortuous prose meanderings or at his unflappable faith that his readers might keep abreast of a style like the *Friend*'s. But in a larger sense, this style will prove to be the *standard*, in the legal terms of the "validity of interpretation," for all other conceivable relations between reading and writing. Hence, in one of many familiar formulations of its protocol, "the Coleridgean reader participates in the creation of what he reads.... Coleridge posits a close proximity, often approaching identity, between reader and writer." Some prose styles, and innumerable cultural theories after Coleridge, invite this "identity" of reader and writer, a kind of metaphysical postulate of post-Romantic critical discourse.[27]

Even a poststructuralism that has renounced Coleridge's ontological faiths can extend the authority of his rhematic mode and its central categories: audience versus reader, the social versus the detachment of Self from social being. The path from reader-response theory to Stanley Fish's "interpretive communities" and finally to an open-armed embrace of institutional authority follows the rhematic arc from style to the transformed reader to the interpretive institution itself. Coleridge's unacknowledged heir, in this regard, is the latter-day rhematic analyst whose distinction "self-satisfying" and "self-consuming" styles bears no accidental resemblance to Coleridge's Anglo-Gallican and connected styles or "verbal" and "moral" truths. For Stanley Fish, these seventeenth-century "rhetorical" and "dialectical" styles have, beyond any historical investment, the inherent values Fish echoes from both Coleridge and the other great theorist of the clerisy, Matthew Arnold. What Fish calls the "self-satisfying" style demonstrates, in all its users, the bad faith of "rhetoric." It "encourage[s] and speak[s] to that part of the mind which is in bondage to the sensible world," it "speak[s] to man's basest instincts," it treats "knowledge as the organization of items outside the mind of the respondent," and—perhaps worst of all—it "canonizes community values." Far better, from Fish's standpoint, the "self-consuming" style "strive[s] to free the mind from its enslavement to the material and visible." It regards "knowledge as the transformation of the mind *into* the object of knowledge." Most important, as Fish puts it in an Arnoldian phrase, it speaks to "man's best self." True, the latter-day theorist wages no Coleridgean campaign for Truth: it will suffice, in a notorious phrase, to "be interesting."[28] But what persists, despite the lack of anchoring commitments, is the rhematic opposition between "bad" materialist rhetoric and "good" idealist dialectics, between the social ("community values") and the Arnoldian suprasocial ("man's best self"). Even the postmodern celebrant of institutions must locate their foundations on transcendent ground.

Hence the burden of Coleridge's "connected style": to lead us from the de-

tails of syntactic discrimination to the largest tissues of connection between readers, their state, and their God. As the *Friend* made all too clear,
however, the self-conscious connected style could hardly negotiate the
channels of public reading Arthur Young called "circulation." The cultural
crisis of the 1790s forced writers to see that the possibility of alternative
readings merged with the possibility of alternative social orders. If circulation provided Arthur Young a model for cultural reproduction in 1792, it
did not satisfy the Coleridge who had struggled within and without the institutions of circulation—the journals and reviews and the whole publishing process whose humiliating rewards he totaled up in his "literary life."
The circulation of discourse is vulnerable not only to radical dissemination
that drains Truth into theories and principles into positions. It is also vulnerable to endless counterfeit circulations, the tributaries of the public
journals which aspire, like *Blackwood's Magazine,* to the centralized pooling
of all minds into one great Mind that is paradoxically weightless, grounded
in little more than a speculative faith. In this sphere of public discourse,
the genuine cultural profit of circulation can hardly be distinguished from
its false substitutes. "It is an unsafe partition," Coleridge tells readers of the
leading journals gathered as audience of the *A Lay Sermon,* "that divides
opinions without principle from unprincipled opinions" (*Lay Sermons,*
126). The circulation of texts cannot strengthen that partition; something
more must be required to guarantee "an earnest *endeavor* to walk in the
Light of your own knowledge" (121).

In a curious note to chapter 11 of the *Biographia,* Coleridge withdraws
imaginative energy from the deadening world of print to keep it circulating
and recirculating in the mind:

> "A person, who reads only to print [as Coleridge quotes Herder], in all
> probability reads amiss; and he, who sends away through the pen and
> the press every thought, the moment it occurs to him, will in a short
> time have sent all away, and will become a mere journeyman of the
> printing-office, a *compositor.*"
>
> To which I may add from myself, that what medical physiologists
> affirm of certain secretions, applies equally to our thoughts; they too
> must be taken up again into the circulation, and be again and again re-
> secreted in order to ensure a healthful vigour both to the mind and to
> its intellectual offspring. (*BL,* 1:231)[29]

Severing the connection so important to writers like Arthur Young, Coleridge withholds a real, life-giving circulation of thought from its official in-

stitutions. And, just as the publishing institutions deplete the writer's energy, so their high-revving engines exhaust their audiences, producing out of their cycles an ultimately meaningless blur of pure motion.

But if from the early eighteenth century all texts could be said to "circulate" in the new economy of publishing and periodical literacy, one text, properly speaking, never circulates. Centered on innumerable hearths, the Bible forms a collective textual feast of which every reader, in every condition, partakes "according to his eating": "The hungry have found food, the thirsty a living spring, the feeble a staff, and the victorious warfarer songs of welcome and strains of music; and as long as each man asks on account of his wants, and asks what he wants, no man will discover aught amiss or deficient in the vast and many-chambered storehouse." So too does the cottager or the artisan come to nourish himself at this ideal communal text "where he that gathered much had nothing over, and he that gathered little had no lack."[30] Diverse of meanings yet unified with Meaning, host of innumerable ways of reading without ever shredding into innumerable texts, the Bible forms a model of reading *before* circulation. Here there is no excess, nor any "lack," but a perfect harmonizing of a diversely whole text and a differential but communal body of readers. But the increasingly complex circulatory networks of discourse and, no less important, the ideological divisions among audiences have transformed the Bible into a conflicted scene of interpretation. That congress by which a reader once read according to his wants and understood according to his needs—in which the textual position of reading and the social position of the reader were in perfect accord—has now been disturbed, so that the Bible's readers now occupy either a point wholly outside it or a point wholly within it. If Coleridge's nineteenth-century "Reading Public" collectively and luxuriantly misreads, these two particular misreadings of the exemplary text reveal what it must mean to read properly.

According to *The Statesman's Manual*, standing wholly outside the Bible means performing an Enlightened reduction; remaining wholly within it means claiming an irrational inspiration. The philologist Johann Eichhorn's reading of Saint Paul shows how the Enlightened misreader reduces a complex, highly figurative passage from to "the negative pole" of interpretation: "It only means so and so!" This mode of the higher criticism has its characteristic rhetorical form: "The Figure of Speech, called Meiosis, by which Mountains are turned to Mole hills or a Mountain Text made to bring forth the blind Mouse (Mus typhlus) of a Socinian!! 'It *only* means so and so.' "[31] But the sublimely mountainous text is not only reduced; it is also transcoded, shifted into the intellectual and verbal accents of another discourse whose progeny include the radical audience of England and the liberal skeptics of the middle class. Reductively translated or redacted into the circulatory streams of the major middle-class magazines and reviews, the Bible thus reduced loses its earlier place as the focus of all readings; compelled into one interpretive mode—the meiotic or reductive—it loses its protean strength to reward others.

At the opposite interpretive pole, the "positive," or hyperbolic, reading exclaims, "It is a mystery: and we are bound to believe the words without presuming to inquire into the meaning of them." At its most ludicrous, this reading takes the form of "text sparring," when ignorant religionists "quote an unconnected sentence of half a dozen words from any part of the Old or New Testament." This "textual magic" claims "the whole written by inspiration." "The mysteries, which these spiritual lynxes detect in the simplest texts, remind me of the 500 nondescripts, each as large as his own black cat, which Dr. Katterfelto, by aid of his solar microscope, discovered in a drop of transparent water."[32] Far from Eichhorn's flattened reductive reading, this reading interprets uncontrollably by "reading in" with a vengeance, taking its own magnifications for daunting religious icons. The text that once anchored all its readings in a complexly diverse balance of desires and fulfillments according to the social positions of its readers, now veers between the absurdly hyperbolic reading that, like Dr. Katterfelto's surprised stare, finds in the texts its own reflections, or the devastatingly reductive reading that eventually finds its way into influential texts of the middle class.

Read as either excessive or lacking, Scripture can hardly serve the delicate ecology of readings where every man partook of his share. But an explicitly interpretive reading, neither reductive nor dumbfounded before the text, may restore "the fellowship of the mystery of the faith as a spirit of wisdom and revelation in the KNOWLEDGE of God, the eye of the UNDERSTANDING being enlightened" (Statesman's Manual, 46). Symbolic interpretation displaces the rhetorical reading that distinguishes literal from figurative and thus turns the Scripture's richest terms—water, flesh, blood, birth, bread—into mere metaphors and hyperboles, vehicles from the childhood of man for tenors now too ineffable to hear. Words become not mere signs but "things, & Living Things too"—when interpreted symbolically—because they resist the power of merely philological interpretation to squeeze the life out of them. Perhaps most important, symbolic interpretation collapses the historical barriers between its first ancient readings and its present, unencrusted reception: "to contemplate the ANCIENT OF DAYS, his words and works, with a feeling as fresh as if they were now first spring-ing forth at his fiat" (ibid., 25). Coleridge shows no interest in reconstruct-ing originary meanings for ancient audiences. The text's only meaning is its meaning now, at this historical moment; the old text must be made con-temporary by an immense effort of reading. Moreover, symbolic interpreta-tion contains its own validating principle: it always arrives at something uninterpretable, and it only succeeds when it comes up short against the barrier to meaning that guarantees meaning. Such interpretation main-tains the "life" of canonical words by a foreseen procedural failure. These words cannot be either an old mystery or a new mole hill. Neither mute nor loquacious, neither mystified nor confident of its total success, sym-bolic interpretation shifts between being authoritative and humbled, in-sightful and blind at the same time.

As the exemplary discipline for this reading, the connected style of the *Friend* and *The Statesman's Manual* deploys its "hooks and eyes of intellec-tual memory" to wrench the old, sedimented text free of its ancient moor-ings. These include, of course, all the readings to which it has been subjected, the deadening philological and the credulously stupified read-ings alike. Jerome Christensen points out how the connected style is con-tinually self-deferring, its sense deferred not to the end of the period but to the next period, and the next, and so on.[33] If this is a "continuous sublime" rather than Kant's momentary, ecstatic sublime, it marks a decisive passage of that reader who, abstracted from an audience by being abstracted from its reading habit, now struggles to "make sense" of a discourse that seems to merge him with the very process of writing.

Yet our contemporary preference for the "writerly text" should not ob-scure the fact that the "obscure" style does not seek a perpetual sublimity, an exalted reading experience, for its own sake. Coleridge does not abstract the reader from his original audience merely to leave him flailing in the fog of the serial sublime. Raised up and out of a situated social audience and into the solitary labyrinth of the obscure style, the Coleridgean reader should ultimately arrive at that which qualifies him to undertake the ardu-ous task of interpretation. This is a qualification, however, that no merely external certification of the professional can provide. The would-be cleric, like the Wedding Guest of "Rime of the Ancient Mariner," must pass from a secular community to a spiritual institution, as the Wedding Guest passes from a marriage feast to the "kirk" by means of the tale he hears. To make that passage, the Wedding Guest also shifts modes of discourse, from the secular song of wedding to the prayer he will murmur in the holy place where "each to his great Father bends." The clerisy as a cultural institution must be more than a collection of rules and certifying procedures, more than a body of readers and writers bound by a certain law. It must—if Coleridge's great cultural project is to succeed—be the correspondence of a social formation to an internalized, evanescent formation in which any of its members realizes in his act the whole outside him that echoes the greater whole within him. So loud and compelling is that echo that evidence of its material foundation, its law and procedures of unparalleled cultural authority which rule out all other readings of the social and cultural text, seem to vanish in its roar.

Coleridge's master plan for the making of an English clerisy, *On the Constitution of Church and State,* was not written in the obscure style. Rarely, in fact, was Coleridge so explicit about the crucial distinction to be made between the existing middle-class public and the special audience to which all his thought was now turned. The Notebooks of 1829 record this complaint:

> Alas! I have to address Men who have never distinctly or consciously referred their opinions to Principles, much less traced the several steps of the ascent; and yet in order to produce any *effect,* to make any immediate and general impression, I must state such positions only and urge only such arguments, as the Reader (or Hearer) will immediately see the full force of, and recognize as a previous Judgement of his own. In short, I dare not pretend to inform, instruct, or guide.[34]

Not readers of the *Friend* or *The Statesman's Manual,* this audience must be treated according to the logic of the reading habit formed by the *Quarterly* and *Edinburgh* reviews or *Blackwood's* and the *New Monthly* magazines. All signs must have earlier referents in such earlier reading acts. If the obscure style defers its signified until a point which can only be recognized as the *Idea* itself—the ultimate self-certification of the clerisy—the present style must refer itself back to the despised institutions of circulation while trying to prepare ground for the cultural state that would transcend it. Written from 1825 to 1829, *On the Constitution of Church and State* betrays the hesitancy of its author between a language already discredited by the high argument it urges and the properly "connected" language he dare not use.

The men of learning who are to compose the new nineteenth-century clerisy shall be organized, like their seventeenth-century model, into a nucleus of high clerics, instructing other members of the order, "cultivating and enlarging knowledge already possessed," overseeing the physical and moral sciences. Around it forms the larger part, scattered or "distributed" among the parishes of England, each cleric acting as "resident, guide, guardian and instructor" (*Church and State*, 42–44) The clerisy will operate as a nucleus with its local orbits; each orbit forms again the center of a larger sphere of influence, until the whole nation—and by indirection, the whole of Europe—shall be as a great series of teachers and audiences radiating outward from the symbolic field of the high-clerical core. This is the pattern followed by the Anglican clergy, whose members form in the *Biographia Literaria* the exemplary alternative to the poor, conflict-wracked man of letters:

> That to every parish throughout the kingdom there is transplanted a germ of civilization; that in the remotest villages there is a nucleus, round which the capabilities of the place may crystallize and brighten; a model sufficiently superior to excite, yet sufficiently near to encourage and facilitate, imitation; *this*, the unobtrusive, continuous agency of a protestant church establishment, *this* it is, which the patriot, and the philanthropist, who would fain unite the love of place with the faith in the progressive melioration of mankind, cannot estimate at too high a price.... The clergyman is with his parishioners and among them; he is neither in the cloistered cell, nor in the wilderness, but a neighbor and a family-man, whose education and rank admit him to the mansion of the rich landholder, while his duties make him the frequent visitor of the farmhouse and the cottage. (*BL*, 1:227)

The productive influence of the clergy shifts imperceptibly from the mind to the land, from a moral place to actual, regional places roused to active life by the power of the model. Likewise, the learned clerisy will transform every region and village into an audience for its discourse. In the *Biographia Literaria* Coleridge longingly compared the clergyman to the man of letters who is sorely divided between the nexus of workday/family and the fugitive, after-hours realm of one's calling and one's belated attention to Self. But the clergyman suffers no schism between practice and principles; he is at the same time worldly and ideational, showing up to comparative ridicule the mere writer who suffers the world of publishing with its increasingly unintelligible practices (*BL*, 1:178–79, 224). Transfused into the cleric, the man of letters recovers the union of practice and principles, not a merely idealistic quest for the dawning of the Idea, but a real, active, practical mode of being in the world without being divided within oneself. The neighboring cleric knows personally all classes from land baron to cottager; neither priest nor prophet, discoursing from a remote point above them or prophesying from an alien point outside them, the cleric moves fluidly among them, *almost* as if he were a circulating text, passing from hand to hand, class to class, hearth to hearth. Yet he is not a circulating text, nor does he bear one. Rather he bears within him the National Church, the institution that is neither church nor state, yet embodies the authority of the one and the personal freedom of the other.

Among the aims of the classical seventeenth-century clerisy—to guard past civilization, perfect and add to contemporary culture, "diffuse through the whole community the knowledge needed for its rights and duties," and make England the model of Europe in its "general civilization"—Coleridge marks "diffusion" as the most crucial function of the nineteenth-century clerisy. To "diffuse" culture has become a markedly different question for the nineteenth-century cleric, whose seventeenth-century example could "diffuse" culture from the highest to the lowest level, down through the social ranks, to listeners and readers who had not yet been organized in any alternate way, who did not yet compose a "Reading Public." What created that public also destroyed the older clerisy:

> As a natural consequence of the full developement and expansion of the mercantile and commercial order, which in the earlier epochs of the constitution, only existed, as it were, potentially and in the bud; the students and possessors of those sciences, and those sorts of learning, the use and necessity of which were indeed constant and perpetual to the *nation*, but only accidental and occasional to *individuals*, gradually detached themselves from the nationalty and the national clergy, and passed to the order, with the growth and thriving condition of which their emoluments were found to increase in equal proportion. Rather, perhaps, it should be said, that under the common name of professional, the learned in the departments of law, medicine, &c., formed an intermediate link between the established clergy and the burgesses. (*Church and State*, 50)

If the mercantile order that unhinged the classical clerisy also gave rise to a commercial reading audience, reconstituting the clerisy faces the immense difficulty of confronting the now fully articulated reading audiences that by 1829 were reading not only *Blackwood's Magazine* but the *Mirror of Literature, Amusement, and Instruction,* not only Coleridge's *Friend* but Cobbett's *Political Register.* The "established clergy" and the "burgesses" cannot accomplish that. They now form immovable, well-nigh permanent orders or social classes. But the "professionals" are still a migratory, indeterminate social formation who, if they once sundered the older clerisy in their new attachments to capital, can also become the restorative agents of a new clerisy. This sector of the middle-class reading public can be detached from its audience to form a new audience that generates the texts it reads and, what is more, teaches others how to read them in turn.

The public division among audiences has made essential the forming of a new National Church. In a socially precise description, Coleridge recalls how the English constitutional state divides equally between landed interests—conservative major land barons and the more liberal minor barons or franklins—and the corporate interests of the mercantile, manufacturing, distributive (or shopkeeping), and professional sectors. These forces of Permanence, or Law, and Progression, or Liberty appear to be balanced, even if they favor the power of Law and landowners, until they are disrupted by the very forces that will shortly be ratified by the 1832 Reform Bill:

> Roads, canals, machinery, the press, the periodical and daily press, the might of public opinion, the consequent increasing desire of popularity among public men and functionaries of every description, and the increasing necessity of public character, as a means or condition of political influence—I need but mention these to stand acquitted of having started a vague and naked possibility in extenuation of an evident and palpable abuse. (*Church and State,* 29)

The material communications of new transport systems and the semiotic communications of the daily and periodical press combine as forces of "circulation" to jolt the constitutional balance of the state. Worse, the state is about to *incorporate* these unsettling forces through the legislative recognition of the Reform Bill. This makes all the more necessary a separate institutional body that can correct the course of state without being subject to its progressive corrosion.

The state embodies men and women only in their collective, hierarchic forms as *classes,* while the church represents them purely as individuals. But between the external, class-structured state and the internal, democratic ethos of the church, the clerisy forges a parodoxical collective-within-the-individual just as it inserts the individual into a larger collective. This collective must itself be classless, detached from the class structure the state both embodies and administers. It must be a destructured state, an institution whose clerics filter down to the middle-class public interpretations that give certain acts of the mind and certain uses of language the apparent power to free one from class determination and its mental fetters. In place of the state's laws and its overt power to reward and punish, the institution adopts professional protocols and their severe discipline. Unlike the state's inability to withstand criticism from within its own ranks, the clerical institution incorporates self-criticism, at least as much as will prove its maxim that those who argue most powerfully against the profession's protocols are its most thorough professionals. Yet one protocol cannot be violated: there must always be a redemption in *reading*.

For the clerisy is above all an audience. Its members authoritatively interpret texts. By doing so, they establish interpretive procedures for others. As the clerisy assumes the body of the humanist academy in the nineteenth and twentieth centuries, its members will write and read one another's work. Indeed, the ideal of exchanging the roles of writer and reader celebrated in the eighteenth-century periodicals reappears in the idea of the clerisy, the penultimate textual community. But this is no longer the social exchange of reading and writing imagined in journals of the older middle class. At the heart of the clerisy lies a text that cannot be written, and thus an "audience" that cannot be touched or seen. To become clerics, certain readers have to be drawn from social audiences. And once abstracted from an audience that existed outside himself, the clerical reader must finally realize, in the power of symbolic interpretation, the audience *within* himself:

O what a mine of undiscovered treasures, what a new world of Power and Truth would the Bible promise to our future meditation, if in some gracious moment one solitary text of all its inspired contents should but dawn upon us in the pure untroubled brightness of an IDEA, that most glorious birth of the God-like within us, which even as the Light, its material symbol, reflects itself from a thousand surfaces, and flies homeward to its Parent Mind enriched with a thousand forms, itself above form and still remaining in its own simplicity and identity! O for a flash of that same Light, in which the first position of geometric science that ever loosed itself from the generalizations of a groping and insecure experience, did for the first time reveal itself to a human intellect in all its evidence and all its fruitfulness, Transparence without Vacuum, and Plenitude without Opacity! (*Statesman's Manual*, 50)

"The God-like within us"—this capacity to recognize the Idea cannot belong to the merely individual reader. It must belong, rather, to a greater whole realized within the clerical interpreter. It must be a collective apprehension embraced within the single breast. Entirely impersonal, the greater whole within is confirmed by the cleric's membership in the institution outside him. This apprehension is hardly possible for the floating middle-class reader of *Blackwood's* or the *Monthly Magazine*, whose notion of belonging to something greater than himself is purely notional. What will empower the clerisy in its cultural work is the capability to realize from within what ordinary audiences only fitfully recognize outside themselves, a collective apprehension of an Idea. Coleridge contrasts the intellectual operation of this clerical, constitutive audience with the merely ideological operations of all others. They are gripped by ideas and ideologies, whose collective character binds the individual reader to mere "conceptions":

> The latter, *i.e.* a conception, *consists* in a conscious act of the understanding, bringing any given object or impression into the same class with any number of other objects, or impressions, by means of some character or characters common to them all. *Concipimus*, id est, capimus hoc *cum* illo, —we take hold of both at once, we *comprehend* a thing, when we have learned to comprise it in a known *class*. On the other hand, it is the privilege of the few to possess an idea: of the generality of men, it might be more truly affirmed, that they are possessed by it. (*Church and State*, 13)

Ordinary theorists and conceptualizers perform those intellectual operations that classify them in their act of classifying. Only those who escape the classifying operation altogether can also escape being classified; only they can go *beyond* ideology. These few are not individuals situated in one or another "class"; they have individuated themselves out of any class.

Beyond classification and beyond ideology, the clerisy also goes beyond representation. The Idea, like the English Constitution, cannot be written.

Here, even the exemplary text of the Bible does not constitute the ultimate text of the clerical audience. This text can be interpreted but not written; it is borne solely within the audience that "reads" it. Indeed, its interpretations are the only palpable evidence that it exists, and only the clerisy may render them, just as only the enlightened Englishman can understand the Constitution that makes him English:

> But a Constitution is an idea arising out of the idea of a state; and because our whole history from Alfred onward demonstrates the continued influence of such an idea, or ultimate aim, on the minds of our fore-fathers, in their characters and functions as public men; alike in what they resisted and in what they claimed; in the institutions and forms of polity which they established, and with regard to those, against which they more or less successfully contended, and because the result has been a progressive, though not always a direct, or equable advance in the gradual realization of the idea; and that it is actually, though even because it is an *idea* it cannot be *adequately*, represented in a correspondent scheme of means really existing, *i.e.* as a *principle*, existing in the only way in which principles can exist—in the minds and consciences of the persons, whose duties it prescribes, and whose rights it determines. In the same sense that the sciences of arithmetic and of geometry, that mind, that life itself, have reality; the constitution has real existence, and does not the less exist in reality, because it both *is*, and *exists as*, an IDEA. (*Church and State*, 19)

The Constitution is unrepresentable, unable to be written; its "text" amounts to all the statements made in its defense, but even in sum, none of these are fully "adequate" to it. What sustains the clerisy can, likewise, nowhere be found in the sum of its written texts. Collectively it is an inexhaustible reader: its text can never become "only so and so!" Hence that collective reader speaks and writes a language that can never fully be represented by others, either. The clerisy must be unrepresentable by any other social audience whose discourses the clerisy itself can always represent. It lies beyond the reach of all classifications and ideological frames. It wrests from "ideology" the power and autonomy of the Idea itself. It can be attached to no social formation, no class of men themselves blinded by their own will to classification. Grasping the Idea, Coleridge's projected clerisy both transcends and recontains the intense struggle over signs waged by all other social audiences in the nineteenth century.

III. SHELLEY: WHAT FATE OF READING?

One Romantic writer did not believe reading redeems us. When he directed the same argument to different classes in the contrasting poetic styles of *Prometheus Bound* and the "Mask of Anarchy," Shelley implied what, unlike Wordsworth and Coleridge, he never produced—a theory of social reading. Those poems, as I have argued in the previous chapter, accentuate rather than elide the social and textual frames within which they must necessarily be read. Here there is no palimpsest of limited class discourses that translucently allows the "human" to reveal itself. In the Romantic theory of Wordsworth, Coleridge, and their modern interpreters, reading itself assumes an almost intolerable burden: to redeem the humanist subject against the threat of his extinction by his own instruments. But in the practice of the most visionary of nineteenth-century poets, the subject-reader coincides with a social audience, for whom to read is not to be redeemed but to be empowered.

Like Wordsworth, Shelley diagnosed, in his "Defense of Poetry," the thinness of contemporary writing which Peacock had seen as a mere literary entropy before the powers of rational calculation. Like Coleridge, Shelley saw that in the emerging class conflict between the propertied and the propertyless, reading and writing themselves were becoming crucial social and political acts. Both Wordsworth and Coleridge, however, conceptualized the audiences they wished to shape in terms that are finally class-transcendent, whether by invoking a language of the poor and the mingling of styles, or by molding a small intellectual audience who reads within a classless cultural realm. Both Romantic theories of language, reading, and social class presuppose a redemption in reading which Shelley implicitly refuses. For Shelley, reading and writing *as acts* do not offer escape from or transcendence of an early-nineteenth-century class-structured, commodified, and technologized social order. Language can only clarify the intellectual, social, and political frames or codes that constitute the cultural order while being formed by it. *Prometheus Unbound* presents as utopian possibility a world that stands against the class-divided world of the present, while the "Mask of Anarchy" admonishes its audience of reformers to cast off the blinders that prevent their purposive activity in a real historical world. These poems clarify what is at stake in their audiences' struggle against power, but they do not entertain the fiction that such readers may overcome that power simply by reading itself. Rather, Shelley's political poems explore and clarify the conditions under which the subjects of power might become fully human in acts of mind and will that lie beyond the scope of any poem.

Postscript

Their Search for Readers and Ours

I want to suggest here that the productive disarray of early-nineteenth-century relations among writers, ideologies, discourses, and social audiences has a more immediate parallel to our own efforts to forge new, sometimes disruptive cultural connections. Those writers—among them Shelley, Wordsworth, Coleridge, Cobbett, Young, Wooler, Wilson, Carlyle, Smith, Redding, Stevenson, Chambers, Paine—struggled to forge readerships in what now appears to have been a transitory, personal world of reading and writing far removed from the mass audiences and institutionalized discourses of the modern "consciousness industry" and its ideologies. The phenomenon of the *un*sought mass audience also first appeared in the early nineteenth century: Lord Byron and Walter Scott awakened to something hardly imaginable to the writers who thought and wrote in terms of a deliberately formed compact between writer and audience. The new mass public Byron faced could not be shaped, imagined, or directed. This vast, unsolicited audience asked of the writer that he perform, construct myths of "the author," become a public event in his own right; toward it, Byron adopted a stance of personal revelation and offered intimacies to a faceless public he professed to disdain. This historically new relation of the writer to his audience coincided with the effort to make publics I have described here, but in its cultural logic it was well beyond the problem of writers who had to think strategically about forming their audiences. From the mid-nineteenth to the mid-twentieth centuries, that massive cultural machinery has required another kind of analysis, the functionalism of an Anglo-American sociology of culture and the *Ideologiekritik* of the Frankfurt School. We are still compelled to speak largely in the languages of these cultural critiques, even as powerful new modes of cultural analysis now emerge.

The newly self-conscious middle-class and radical artisan publics that emerged after 1790 began to represent at least two possible relations between reader and audience. Either the reader's social belonging must be declared in an increasingly class-conscious radical discourse that helped give rhetoric its bad name by the very explicitness of its rhetorical assumptions, or the individual reader must be defined as a textual presence in a discourse where he constitutes himself as a "reader" by becoming aware of his distinction from all social, collective formations that he learns to "read" as a social text. The reader could also be constructed between these collective and individual stances. The mass writer of the 1820s and '30s represented his reader as a particular human type by means of innumerable representations of crowds, eccentrics, and other visually and ethically marked human varieties. Such human types mediated between the lonely reader discovered at the beginning of such a text—alienated from the crowd, repelled by the atrocity, fascinated by the inexplicable—and that great collectivity in which this reader will ultimately discover his place, humanity as such. The "human" becomes a utopian value in the nineteenth century when it is sought everywhere that it is most explicitly denied. Silencing both argument and dialogue, mass discourse replaces individual and political speech with the human murmur it tirelessly purports to echo, a voice we have come to know as the mouthpiece of commodities in their perpetual drone.

I have called Coleridge's conception of audience the most "complex" in the nineteenth century partly because it had to square with these emerging discourses and the relations between writer, text, reader, and audience they enacted. Arnold's remnant clerisy is far more resigned and removed from the fray of social discourses than Coleridge's activist clerisy, who will radiate outward from the Logos to hunker down with the cottager and illuminate the landlord. No floating reader of the social text, the nineteenth-century cleric must transform those quotidian languages from which he has been delivered. Without the state's authority to silence a dissident language, now lost, or the church's power to remoralize a language of commodity trade, now diminished, the clerisy governs by reading, interpreting, and mediating the sacred word in its journey among the profane languages of the nineteenth-century social text. Its combination of cultural strategies is unique. It borrows from the eighteenth century's world of public discourse the practice of exchanging the roles of reader and writer (the cleric is both). It assumes the distinction of the middle-class reader from the social realm of ranks and classes, while it makes audiences for its own discourse by means of its lectures, popularized research, and arbitration of cultural standards. No less important, the clerisy adopts the pedagogical if not the polit-ical stance of radical discourse. What the clerisy most implacably opposes is the degradation of moral life into the mean terms of the cash nexus. But, as Robert M. Maniquis argues, the clerisy paradoxically resembles the mass audience in its sense of being classless, opposing to the "presumed classless-ness of the commodity" the equally presumed classlessness of educated souls who read, think, and write.[1] Coleridge draws for his complex model of the clerisy upon the practices of all these public audiences, shaping from their disparate networks of cultural connection a new way to mediate the most perplexing contradictions of the nineteenth century.

Viewed historically, the audiences of the early nineteenth century constitute reading cultures; hence they raise the questions posed by all cul-tures whom the human sciences attempt to comprehend. To the largest questions—how did readers understand the texts they read? how were those texts used?—historical evidence offers few and scattered answers. These cul-tures remain, despite their occasional similarity to reading cultures of our own time, distinctly opaque insofar as we cannot penetrate the minds of all those readers who left no mark of their understandings, no trace of the doubtless ingenious ways they must have recombined, retranslated, or sim-ply resisted the interpretive and ideological patterns framed by their texts. We ourselves need to resist the ambition to reclaim those lost understand-ings in some consummate act of historical recovery. A certain blank space in cultural memory must not be filled, the space of an otherness that marks an unbridgeable difference between their reading and ours. There is a for-mal analogy, if only that, between the alienness these reading cultures must have experienced between themselves and the kind of otherness with which they confront us. Hence they can be located only at those borders where they contest the readings of other audiences in social space, marking some of the key incommensurates of a whole culture. This is why a histori-cal discourse about past cultures must be a social discourse—as though the differences marked in the social space of "their" cultures prevent their im-minent absorption into "ours."

The early-nineteenth-century search for audiences, however, makes more visible our own, posed now in rather different terms and largely within the academy. Semiotic historicism, a social anthropology seeking "the interpretation of cultures," an intellectual history fascinated by the passage of signs between "elite" and "popular" cultures, the "new histori-cism" in literary criticism—all these academic subdisciplines turn toward the past to recover in historical acts of reading what appears increasingly elusive in our own time: something like a genuine "response." "For discourse (and therefore for man)," Bakhtin once wrote, "nothing is more frightening than *absence of answer*."[2] The current interest in Bakhtin's own work, whatever its other motives, may also reflect a generalized crisis of response in Western societies, where "dialogue" becomes a theoretical object sought out in texts and historical reconstructions. According to Jean Baudrillard's dark comedy of postmodern "simulations," response must be manufactured by pollsters and advertisers in closed-circuit paradigms while its constituent mass audience sits raptly fascinated by its televised collective representations.[3] We may well lament the lost voices of the older democratic participation now being furiously simulated in the media—or we may instead pay Baudrillard's Beckett-like respect to the silence of the masses, which cautions us against false resurrections of the "dialogic" itself. If Bakhtin's concept indeed has historical value, it may be to mark a definitive loss, while at the same time it points to a new, yet largely unformed tissue of social and intellectual connection that remains to be made.

In any event, Northrop Frye's "public critics" and Gramsci's "organic intellectuals" have largely disappeared, and with them both the older middle-class intelligentsia distinct from the universities and the radical intelligentsia allied to movements of the working class. Mass culture and university culture face one another as institutional monoliths, each articulating Lyotard's "postmodern condition" and Habermas's "legitimation crisis" in its own way.[4] The older discursive space, defined in the nineteenth century by the kinds of discourses and audiences I have described in this book, seems to have narrowed down to exclude such now quaint figures as the "independent intellectual" or the genuinely oppositional "avant-gardes." When Stanley Fish celebrates the professionalism of the culture of critical discourse, he makes the same point as Baudrillard makes in his rather different, despairing prognosis of the "implosion of meaning in the media." Both, despite the clear difference between their political intents, itemize the loss of critical sites in the victory of institutional control.[5] Hence the recurring search for invisible sites, something like the resistant "practices of everyday life" investigated by Michel de Certeau, or the recovery of suppressed historical "readings" in the work of contemporary cultural historians.[6]

All this lends some support to Lyotard's claim for the end of the the "great narratives" of knowledge and liberation that now seem to be winding down like failing old clocks. It is worth recalling that in the early nine-teenth century, the new middle-class, radical, mass, and clerical audiences were in fact among the first readers of those great narratives. What they read configured the projects of knowledge and freedom in textually distinc-tive shapes. The mythical "useful" knowledge of the mass writer, the strate-gic knowledges gathered by the radicals, the aspirations to a collective central Mind envisioned by writers for the educated middle class—such projects of knowledge entailed programs of freedom as well as exercises of power, even where freedom was imagined purely within the act of "read-ing" itself. Coleridge's clerisy would equip itself to measure these claims for knowing and acting. But if one of the enduring functions of the clerical academy has been to give the floating middle-class reader a philosophical and interpretive "ground"—so he might "walk in the Light of his own knowledge"—today that purpose seems clouded with doubt as many clerics now call for what must be the most thorough rethinking of the clerisy's in-tellectual and social function since Coleridge first imagined the National Church at the end of the Romantic age.

For neither the clerical nor the mass-cultural institutions of textuality turn out to be so "monolithic" after all; each knows its own self-division, its multiple audiences, its ideological and interpretive languages. At present the "institution" and its practices are the primary topics of cultural criticism itself. Often this avowedly "social" criticism seeks to fortify its own institutional base by driving a wedge between critical thought and a canny institutional self-consciousness. Richard Rorty's "North Atlantic cultural conversation" and Stanley Fish's "professionalism" empower a frank drive toward purely institutional readings and their rewards. The bur-den of those intellectuals who still avow a critical consciousness must therefore be to fashion what models, tools, or weapons of criticism can be deployed *between* the clerical institutions they work within and the com-peting languages that constitute the larger social text.

Such criticism will have to include a wary response to the newest prod-ucts of clerical thought, including the kind of cultural history now being urged widely among the human sciences. Rorty, Fish, and Clifford Geertz represent a powerful new rationale for clerical work: local knowledges, the power of vocabularies, a nominalist historicism, a social hermeneutics. One learns a great deal from these pragmatic models, even as one maneu-vers against their effort to reduce all questions of power, knowledge, and freedom to the language games best played from within a purely institutional frame. In the name of diversity, localism, and a pragmatic suspicion of totalizers, this "postmodern bourgeois liberalism" sponsors a cultural history that increasingly reads back our current, sign-saturated condition onto historical cultures for whom the relation of signs to social practice was vastly different from our own.[7] But even the more critical uses of semiotic history will have to take seriously Wlad Godzich's charge that those who practice semiotics in the academy perform an invaluable service for the intensified sign-production of consumer society itself. Contemporary sign producers of all types require a semiotic expertise to unpack the meanings of everything from advertising to high-cultural texts—demonstrating, if nothing else, the unbroken continuity of certain authorized forms of "meaning" itself. Godzich's suspicion parallels Robert Maniquis's argument that nuclear strategists' demonstrate a semiotic sophistication equal to any poststructural theorists, and far more consequential.[8] What both these arguments urge is that latter-day clerics take their "critical" function seriously enough to engage those discourses beyond the university that exert fantastic power upon the moral, social, and political tenor of everyday life.

Engaging such discourses surely means, in the present context, abandoning that hypostatized "reader" who was elaborated in Romantic writing at the beginning of the nineteenth century and who has emerged as the textual hero of a postmodern criticism that claims to have given up all its Romantic faiths. It is no longer plausible to read the texts of the past as though they had always been written for the modern interpreter. Even the foundational texts of British Romanticism acknowledged in the intense friction of their language the pressure of contrary readings and resistant texts. Their engagement, if not their solutions, remains ours. The cultural practices of the past can hardly confirm us in our own institutionalized, mass-mediated times. They only remind us that there is no comfort in discourse, no refuge in reading, no alternative to the colliding languages of the social text.

Notes
Index

Notes

PREFACE

1. Introduction, *On Signs*, ed. Marshall Blonsky (Baltimore: Johns Hopkins Univ. Press, 1985), vii.

INTRODUCTION

1. I have been informed by, among others, Natalie Zemon Davis, *Culture and Society in Early Modern France* (Stanford: Stanford Univ. Press, 1975); Carlo Ginzburg, *The Cheese and the Worms: The Cosmos of a Sixteenth-Century Miller*, trans. J. and A. Tedeschi (Baltimore: Johns Hopkins Univ. Press, 1980); Clifford Geertz, *Negara: The Theatre-State in Nineteenth-Century Bali* (Princeton: Princeton Univ. Press, 1982), and *The Interpretation of Cultures* (New York: Basic Books, 1973); Peter Burke, *Popular Culture in Early Modern Europe* (London, 1978); Robert Darnton, *The Literary Underground of the Old Regime* (Cambridge: Harvard Univ. Press, 1982); Miriam Usher Chrisman, *Lay Culture, Learned Culture: Books and Social Change in Strasbourg, 1480–1599* (New Haven: Yale Univ. Press, 1982).

For an important discussion of the issues raised in these areas, see Roger Chartier, "Intellectual History or Social History? The French Trajectories," in *Modern European Intellectual History*, ed. Dominick LaCapra and Steven L. Kaplan (Ithaca: Cornell Univ. Press, 1982), 13–46.

2. Meyer H. Abrams, *The Mirror and the Lamp* (New York: Oxford Univ. Press, 1953), 25.

3. Morris Eaves, "Romantic Expressive Theory and Blake's Idea of the Audience," *PMLA* 95 (1980): 784–801. The "Romanticism" elaborated in the work of Northrop Frye, Harold Bloom, Geoffrey Hartman, and their students is perfectly represented in Eaves's skillful essay, which weaves the historical problem of audiences into the folds of Romantic idealism and, in particular, Frye's habit of arranging cultural relationships in six ultimately circular phases. For a very different, materialist view of Blake's struggle with audiences of the 1790s, see Paul Mann, "Apocalypse and Recuperation: Blake and the Maw of Commerce," *ELH* 52 (1985): 1–32.

4. Jerome J. McGann, *The Romantic Ideology: A Critical Investigation* (Chicago: Univ. of Chicago Press, 1983), 1.

5. Frank Kermode, "Institutional Control of Interpretation," in *The Art of Telling* (Cambridge: Harvard Univ. Press, 1983), 168.

6. For reasons I will explore in this book, the discussion about institutions grows partly out of earlier "reader-response" theory, particularly Stanley Fish, *Is There a Text in This Class?* (Cambridge: Harvard Univ. Press, 1981), and his respondents; see also *The Politics of Interpretation*, special issue of *Critical Inquiry* (September, 1982); and, for a recent, polemical discussion, Daniel Cottom, "The Enchantment of Interpretation," *Critical Inquiry* 11 (1985): 573–94. For a wider historical and political enquiry centered in Western Germany, see Peter Hohendahl, *The Institution of Criticism* (Ithaca: Cornell Univ. Press, 1982).

7. Geertz, *Negara*, 122–24.

8. Lynn Hunt, *Politics, Culture, and Class in the French Revolution* (Berkeley and Los Angeles: Univ. of California Press, 1984); cf. François Furet, *Interpreting the French Revolution*, trans. Elborg Forster (Cambridge: Cambridge Univ. Press, 1981).

9. Fredric Jameson, "Science versus Ideology," in *Marxists and the University*, ed. Robert M. Maniquis, a special issue of *Humanities in Society* 6 (1983): 283.

10. See Gareth Stedman Jones, *The Languages of Class* (Cambridge: Cambridge Univ. Press, 1984), 90–179. On the more general crisis of Marxism in recent years, see Perry Anderson, *In the Tracks of Historical Materialism* (London: New Left Books, 1984).

11. Jean-François Lyotard, *The Postmodern Condition: A Report on Knowledge*, trans. Geoff Bennington and Brian Massumi (Minneapolis: Univ. of Minnesota Press, 1983).

12. See Pierre Bourdieu, "Conclusion: Classes and Classifications," in *Distinction: A Social Critique of the Judgment of Taste*, trans. Richard Nice (Cambridge: Harvard Univ. Press, 1984), 466–84, and my discussion below.

13. Marx, *The German Ideology* (New York: International Publishers, 1947), 27.

14. I refer, of course, to the models proposed by Wolfgang Iser, *The Implied Reader* (Baltimore: Johns Hopkins Univ. Press, 1978), and Stanley Fish, *Self-Consuming Artifacts: The Experience of Seventeenth-Century Literature* (Berkeley and Los Angeles: Univ. of California Press, 1972); somewhat modified, they would also be extended to Hans Robert Jauss's work in *Toward an Aesthetic of Reception*, trans. Timothy Bahti (Minneapolis: Univ. of Minnesota Press, 1982).

15. Robert Darnton, "Readers Respond to Rousseau," in *The Great Cat Massacre, and Other Essays in Cultural History* (New York: Basic Books, 1984), 215–56. I should add that apart from the mistaken effort to link Ranson to the textual models of *Rezeptiontheorie*, this is a splendid study of how an eighteenth-century reader might have read.

16. Dominick LaCapra also raises questions about Ginzburg's approach in *History and Criticism* (Ithaca: Cornell Univ. Press, 1985), ch. 3. Tony Bennett puts Ginzburg's work to use in "Texts, Readers, Reading Formations," in *M/MLA* 16 (1983): 3–17: "I venture the concept of the 'productive activation' of texts as a means of displacing, rather than of substituting for, the concept of interpretation and the particular construction of relations between texts and readers that it implies" (3). Menocchio's reading of the Bible and Renaissance texts thus becomes an

example of such a formation. But the resulting "reading formation" seems to me wholly intertextual, and it does not resolve the question of whether a reading like Menocchio's was eccentric or central to his own culture.

17. Mann, "Apocalypse and Recuperation," 8. See also Peter Burke, *Popular Culture in Early Modern Europe,* on cultural mediators.

18. For the following arguments I refer to V. N. Voloshinov, *Marxism and the Philosophy of Language* (New York: Seminar Press, 1973), and M. M. Bakhtin, *The Dialogic Imagination,* trans. Caryl Emerson and Michael Holquist (Austin: Univ. of Texas Press, 1981), esp. "Discourse in the Novel," 259–422.

Interpretations of Bakhtin's work are as contested today as the social languages he brilliantly restored to critical view. His later work has led many, including his translators, to seek in his work the true, unconstrained "dialogue" of self and other—a post-Saussurean Martin Buber whose inner ear records the great dialogue of the "I" and "Thou." See, for instance, Michael Holquist, "The Politics of Representation," in *English Institute Essays,* ed. Stephen Greenblatt (Baltimore: Johns Hopkins Univ. Press, 1980), and Nina Perlina, "Bakhtin and Buber: The Concept of Dialogical Discourse," *Studies in Twentieth Century Literature* 9, no. 1 (1984). A secular-humanist Bakhtin appears in Tzvetan Todorov, *Mikhail Bakhtin: The Dialogic Principle,* trans. Wlad Godzich (Minneapolis: Univ. of Minnesota Press, 1984).

But this pluralist, theological Bakhtin does not square easily with the earlier scholar-activist who collaborated with Voloshinov to write—against both Saussure and Stalin—"Sign becomes an arena of the class struggle." My reading here assumes that early and late Bakhtin texts were not incommensurate; the relation of social to individual uses of language remains constant, though differently articulated, in both. For a sharp exchange between materialist and theological readings of Bakhtin, see essays by Ken Hirschkop and Gary Saul Morson in *Critical Inquiry* 11 (1985): 672–86.

19. On the "habitus," see Bourdieu, *Distinction,* 101–2 ff. An earlier and fuller explanation appears in his *Outline of a Theory of Practice,* trans. Richard Nice (Cambridge: Cambridge Univ. Press, 1977), 72–95.

20. Jon Elster, *Sour Grapes: Studies in the Subversion of Rationality* (New York: Cambridge Univ. Press, 1983), esp. 104–6. In *Making Sense of Marx* (Cambridge: Cambridge Univ. Press, 1985), Elster conducts a complex campaign against functionalist explanations within Marxism, using G. A. Cohen's work, an explicit defense of Marxist functionalism, as a chief foil (see Cohen, *Karl Marx's Theory of History: A Defense* [New York: Oxford Univ. Press, 1980]).

CHAPTER ONE: CULTURAL CONFLICT, IDEOLOGY, AND
THE READING HABIT IN THE 1790S

1. Jean-Paul Sartre, *What Is Literature?* trans. Bernard Frechtman (New York: Philosophical Library, 1949), 87–88; Walter Benjamin, "The Author as Producer," *New Left Review* 62 (July–August 1970).

2. Arnold Hauser, *The Social History of Art* (New York: Vintage, 1957), 3:52–

53; R. D. Altick, *The English Common Reader: A Social History of the Mass Reading Public, 1800–1900* (Chicago: Univ. of Chicago Press, 1957), 40. Among other classic accounts of the eighteenth-century public, see Ian Watt, *The Rise of the Novel* (Berkeley and Los Angeles: Univ. of California Press, 1957), 35–59; Raymond Williams, *The Long Revolution*, rev. ed. (New York: Harper & Row, 1966), 156–213; Leo Lowenthal, *Literature, Popular Culture, and Society* (Englewood Cliffs, N.J.: Prentice-Hall, 1961), 55–76. For skepticism about the pervasiveness of reading in the eighteenth century, see R. M. Wiles, "Middle-Class Literacy in Eighteenth-Century England," in *Studies in the Eighteenth Century*, ed. R. F. Brissenden (Canberra: Australian Univ. Press, 1968), 49–65.

3. Lowenthal, *Literature, Popular Culture, and Society*, 52.

4. Peter Hohendahl, *The Institution of Criticism* (Ithaca: Cornell Univ. Press, 1982), 44–82; Terry Eagleton, *The Function of Criticism: From "The Spectator" to Post-Structuralism* (London: Verso, 1984), esp. 9–37. Both follow Jurgen Habermas, *Strukturwandel der Offentlichkeit* (Frankfurt, 1962).

5. Hohendahl, *Institution of Criticism*, 52–53.

6. Erich Auerbach, "La Cour et la ville," trans. Ralph Manheim, in *Scenes from the Drama of European Literature*, ed. Paolo Valesio (Minneapolis: Univ. of Minnesota Press, 1984), and *Literary Language and Its Public in Late Latin Antiquity and the Middle Ages*, trans. Ralph Manheim (Princeton: Bollingen, 1964).

7. On the making of female audiences in the eighteenth-century journals, see Kathryn Shevelow, "Fathers and Daughters: Women as Readers of the *Tatler*," in *Gender and Reading*, ed. Elizabeth Flynn and Patricinio Schweickart (Baltimore: Johns Hopkins Univ. Press, 1986), 107–23, and Shevelow, *Fair-Sexing It: Women as Readers and Writers in the Early English Periodical* (forthcoming).

8. *Spectator* 271 in *The Spectator*, ed. Donald F. Bond (Oxford: Clarendon, 1965), 2:555. On late-seventeenth and early-eighteenth-century periodical practices, see Bond's introduction, 1:xxxvi–xliii.

9. Lennard Davis, *Factual Fictions: The Origins of the English Novel* (New York: Columbia Univ. Press, 1983).

10. The following account draws from several articles in *The Bee*, vol. 1 (1790–91): "Prospectus," vii–xii; "On the Advantages of Periodical Performances," 10–14; "On the Advantages of Miscellaneous Reading," 35–37; and "Further Remarks on the Utility of Periodical Performances," 167–71. Further references to these essays appear in the text.

11. Hohendahl, *Institution of Criticism*, 53; Eagleton, *Function of Criticism*, 10.

12. Robert D. Mayo, *The English Novel in the Magazines, 1740–1815* (Evanston: Northwestern Univ. Press, 1962), 162–63, 175; Crane Brinton, *The Political Ideas of the English Romanticists* (1926; rpt. Ann Arbor: Univ. of Michigan Press, 1966), 211–12. In *An Open Elite? England, 1540–1880* (Oxford: Clarendon, 1984), Lawrence Stone challenges the view that aristocrats mingled with *haut bourgeois* in a long-tenured "open elite." I cannot judge the weight of his argument here, but Cave's *Gentleman's Magazine* surely projects such interclass traffic and contributed, at least, to the sense that England's were fluid class borders.

13. Edward Said, *The World, the Text, and the Critic* (Cambridge: Harvard Univ. Press, 1983), 48. This is Said's response to Paul Ricœur's opposition between "circumstanced speech" and an "uncircumstanced text" (Said, 33–35). What is important to see, however, is that while today the notions of discourse as "democratic exchange" and discourse as an unequal power relationship are surely antagonistic, they were entirely compatible in the eighteenth century. The "public sphere" *was* a power relationship, despite Habermas's effort to idealize it. Eagleton seems both to recognize this fact and to try to preserve the public sphere as a critical measure of later discursive relationships.

14. Daniel Defoe, "Of the Trading Style," in *The Complete English Tradesman* (London, 1841), 2:19.

15. *The Periodical Press of Great Britain and Ireland* (London, 1824), 24 (the work is anonymous); William Chambers, "Magazines of the Last Century," *Chambers' Edinburgh Journal*, n.s., 18 (1852): 336.

16. "On the Reciprocal Influence of the Periodical Publications and Intellectual Progress of This Country," *Blackwood's Magazine* 16 (1824): 521.

17. Albert Goodwin, *The Friends of Liberty: The English Democratic Movement in the Age of the French Revolution* (Cambridge: Harvard Univ. Press, 1979), 176–77, 196.

18. Thomas Paine, *The Rights of Man*, ed. Henry Collins (Harmondsworth: Penguin, 1969), 175.

19. See Pierre Bourdieu, "The Economy of Linguistic Exchanges," *Social Science Information* 16 (1977): 645–68.

20. Marilyn Butler, "Introduction," *Burke, Paine, Godwin, and the Revolution Controversy* (New York: Oxford Univ. Press, 1984), 2.

21. John Gazley, *The Life of Arthur Young, 1740–1809* (Philadelphia: American Philosophical Society, 1971), 12.

22. Constantia Maxwell, "Introduction" to Arthur Young, *Travels in France during the Years 1787, 1788, and 1789* (Cambridge: Cambridge Univ. Press, 1929), xvii. Further references to the *Travels* will use the more recent edition by Jeffrey Kaplow (Garden City, N.Y.: Doubleday, 1969). No complete edition of the *Travels* has been published since the second, two-volume edition (Bury St. Edmunds, 1794), but Kaplow's is the most balanced and accurate.

23. On Wordsworth's bewilderment in revolutionary France, see also James K. Chandler, *Wordsworth's Second Nature: A Study of the Poetry and Politics* (Chicago: Chicago Univ. Press, 1984), esp. 42–79.

24. Defoe quoted in Max Byrd, *London Transformed: Images of the City in the Eighteenth Century* (New Haven: Yale Univ. Press, 1978), 15; Thomas De Quincey, *The English Mail Coach and Other Essays* (London: Everyman, 1961), 1, 9. On the senses of circulation in Defoe and John Cary, see Maximillian Novak, *Economics and the Fiction of Daniel Defoe* (Berkeley and Los Angeles: Univ. of California Press, 1962), 29–30. For the importance of circulatory metaphors for nationalist thinking and imperialist dreams in the nineteenth century, see Robert M. Maniquis, "Lonely Empires: Personal and Public Visions of Thomas De Quincey" in *Literary Mono-*

graphs, vol. 8, ed. Eric Rothstein and Joseph Anthony Wittreich, Jr. (Madison: Univ. of Wisconsin Press, 1976), 49–127.

25. Marx, "Money; or, the Circulation of Commodities," in *Capital*, trans. Samuel Moore and Edward Aveling (New York, 1906), 106–61; cf. also Marc Shell, *The Economy of Literature* (Baltimore: Johns Hopkins Univ. Press, 1978). Like many economists since, Marx relied frequently upon the accuracy of Young's calculations, but less gratefully called him "that unspeakable statistical prattler. . .the Polonius of political economy" (*Capital*, 386).

26. *Modern London: Being the History of the Present State of the British Metropolis* (London, 1804) (anonymous, printed for Richard Phillips), 438–39.

27. Pierre Bourdieu, *An Outline of a Theory of Practice*, trans. Richard Nice (Cambridge: Cambridge Univ. Press, 1977), 89, 183–84, and Bourdieu, *Distinction: A Social Critique of the Judgment of Taste*, trans. Richard Nice (Cambridge: Harvard Univ. Press, 1984), 114–15.

28. Gazley, *Life of Arthur Young*, 341.

29. Young's term "disseminate" has little evident relation to Jacques Derrida's widely circulated trope of "dissemination," and the two should not be confused here. Derrida's signs disperse and defer meanings, while Young means by "disseminate" something more like "dispense" fixed principles. But Young also means that radical discourse escapes the network of circulation that accrues meaning within the practices of English discourse, and the resulting "propaganda" subversively runs out of cultural control. In this limited sense, Young's sense of "disseminating" discourse shares with Derrida's usage the overtone of a quasi-sexual subversion of an acceptably ordered architecture of meanings. Cf. Derrida, *Dissemination*, trans. Barbara Johnson (Chicago: Univ. of Chicago Press, 1981).

30. *Spectator* 10 in *The Spectator*, 1: 44–47; Coleridge, "Consciones ad Populum" in *Lectures 1795 on Politics and Religion*, ed. Lewis Patton and Peter Mann (London: Routledge & Kegan Paul, 1971), 43.

31. *Spectator* 69 in *The Spectator*, 1: 292–96.

32. Coleridge, "Consciones ad Populum," 43.

33. For the importance of "accidentality" in Coleridge's argument with Wordsworth's preface, I have learned from Jerome McGann's paper "The *Biographia Literaria* and the Contentions of English Romanticism," delivered at the Coleridge Symposium, UCLA, 16–17 November 1984.

34. See Kelvin Everest, *Coleridge's Secret Ministry: The Context of the Conversation Poems* (Sussex: Harvester Press, 1979), 120–21.

35. His bemused account appears in *Biographia Literaria*, ed. Walter J. Bate and James Engell (London: Routledge & Kegan Paul, 1983), 1:184–85.

36. *The Watchman*, ed. Lewis Patton (London: Routledge & Kegan Paul, 1970), 375.

37. "Preface," *Monthly Magazine* 1 (1796): iii.

38. "On the Reciprocal Influence," 518–25.

39. "Are Mental Talents Productive of Happiness?" *Monthly Magazine* 3 (1797): 358–59.

40. *The Watchman,* ed. Lewis Patton (London: Routledge & Kegan Paul, 1970), 374–75.

41. E. P. Thompson, *The Making of the English Working Class* (New York: Pantheon, 1964), 177.

42. *Politics for the People* 1 (1794): 13.

43. *The Cabinet* 2 (1795): 116.

44. Wordsworth had copies of the *Oeconomist* sent to him along with the *Monthly Magazine.* It is clear that Losh was seeking as an audience those, as Wordsworth wrote to James Fox, whose "little tract of land serves as a kind of permanent rallying point for their domestic feelings, as a tablet upon which they are written." *The Letters of William and Dorothy Wordsworth,* ed. Ernest de Selincourt, rev. Chester L. Shaver (Oxford: Clarendon, 1967), 1:314–15.

45. *The Oeconomist* 2 (1799): 373–74.

46. *The Oeconomist* 1 (1798): 4; Raymond Williams, *The Country and the City* (New York: Oxford Univ. Press, 1973), 61.

47. Sartre, *What is Literature?* 71.

48. "Literature of the Day: The New Magazine," *The Metropolitan* 1 (1831): 22.

49. Ibid., 19.

50. James Montgomery, "A View of Modern English Literature," *The Metropolitan* 2 (1831): 355.

51. Fredric Jameson, *Marxism and Form* (Princeton: Princeton Univ. Press, 1971), 333: "From the dialectical point of view the whole concept of *stylistics* as a separate field is a profoundly contradictory one, for it implies that style, or language perceived as style, is everywhere an essential and constitutive component of the literary work of art."

CHAPTER TWO: READING THE SOCIAL TEXT

1. William Hazlitt, review of *The Statesman's Manual, Edinburgh Review* 27 (1816): 450; Coleridge, *Lay Sermons,* ed. R. J. White (London: Routledge & Kegan Paul, 1972), 36–37. Hazlitt's confidence owed something to his entire absorption in the reviewing apparatus, including the *Edinburgh Review, New Monthly Magazine,* and Leigh Hunt's *Examiner* and *Liberal.* On Hazlitt's institutional involvements, see David Bromwich, *Hazlitt: The Mind of a Critic* (New York: Oxford Univ. Press, 1983), 104 ff., and Herschel Baker, *William Hazlitt* (Cambridge: Harvard Univ. Press, 1962), 191–228.

2. *Lay Sermons,* 119.

3. *Biographia Literaria,* ed. James Engell and W. Jackson Bate (London: Routledge & Kegan Paul, 1983), 1:177–78.

4. [Francis Jeffrey], "State of the Country," *Edinburgh Review* 32 (1819): 294.

5. Marx, "The Fetishism of Commodities," *Capital*, trans. Samuel Moore and Edward Aveling (New York: Modern Library, 1906), 81–96.

6. John Clive, *Scotch Reviewers: The "Edinburgh Review," 1802–1815* (London: Faber & Faber, 1957), 143–44.

7. On the journals' individual prices, see R. D. Altick, *The English Common Reader* (Chicago: Univ. of Chicago Press, 1957), 319.

8. Neither William Gifford's *Quarterly Review* nor John Scott's *London Magazine* had a comparable impact upon the middle-class audience. James Mill's *Westminster Review* presents a different problem: a small, quasi-radical audience within the greater middle-class public. It deserves a closer and rather different kind of analysis than I undertake here.

9. Harold Perkin follows the tangled threads of *Blackwood's'* political economy in *The Origins of Modern English Society, 1780–1880* (London: Routledge & Kegan Paul, 1969), 224 ff.

10. Roger P. Wollins, "Blackwood's Edinburgh Magazine," in *British Literary Magazines, 1789–1836*, ed. Alvin Sullivan (Westport, Conn.: Greenwood, 1983), 47.

11. [William Stevenson], "On the Reciprocal Influence of Periodical Publications and the Intellectual Progress of This Country," *Blackwood's Magazine* 16 (1824): 518, 524–25.

12. [John Wilson], "Observations on Coleridge's *Biographia Literaria*," *Blackwood's Magazine* 2 (1817): 3.

13. Roland Barthes, "Style and Its Image," in *Literary Style: A Symposium*, ed. Seymour Chatman (London: Oxford Univ. Press, 1971), 3–10; see also Barthes, *S/Z*, trans. Richard Miller (New York: Hill & Wang, 1974), 100; William Hazlitt, "On Familiar Style" (1821), in *The Complete Works of William Hazlitt*, ed. P. P. Howe (London: Dent, 1930–34), 8: 247.

14. Sidney Smith's essays in the *Edinburgh Review* represent that older, balanced style still being written in many of the middle-class journals. But John Wilson was no doubt chief architect of *Blackwood's'* emphatic program of intellectual power and its prose styles. By training a philosopher and by vocation a lawyer, Wilson began writing and editing *Blackwood's* in mid-1817; he wrote some 500 essays for the journal over the next 30 years. In 1820 he would be named, in a disputed appointment, to Dugald Stewart's old chair of philosophy at the University of Edinburgh. Wilson brought academic philosophers like Alexander Blair to write for *Blackwood's*, opening channels between the university and the newer middle-class journals, and making this journal, in its first ten years, a public site for the search for Mind. For a lively if uncritical account, see Mrs. Oliphant's *Annals of a Publishing House: William Blackwood and His Sons* (London, 1887), 1:257–60.

15. "On the Analogy between the Growth of Individual and National Genius," *Blackwood's Magazine* 6 (January 1820): 375.

16. Following Julia Kristeva, Peter Brooks argues the relation between gesture and anaphora in nineteenth-century melodrama in *The Melodramatic Imagination* (New Haven: Yale Univ. Press, 1976), 70 ff.

17. Carlyle, "Characteristics," in *A Carlyle Reader*, ed. G. B. Tennyson (New York: Modern Library, 1969), 76.

18. See, for instance, "The Passing Crowd" in *Chambers' Edinburgh Journal* 1 (1832): 33, and my analysis of this essay in Chapter 3, below.

19. [Alexander Blair],"Thoughts on the Advancement and Diffusion of Knowledge," *Blackwood's Magazine* 16 (1824): 26.

20. Michel Foucault, *The Order of Things*, a translation of *Les Mots et les choses* (New York: Pantheon, 1971), 251.

21. "On the Reciprocal Influence," 524–28.

22. Henry Stebbing, "Unpublished Lectures on Periodical Literature, No. 3," *Athenaeum* 1 (1828): 335.

23. See Albert O. Hirschman, *The Passions and the Interests: Political Arguments for Capitalism before Its Triumph* (Princeton: Princeton Univ. Press, 1977), 100–116.

24. Herbert Marcuse, "The Affirmative Character of Culture," in *Negations*, trans. Jeremy J. Shapiro (Boston: Beacon Press, 1968), 88–133. To the *Athenaeum*, the middle-class audience and its writers seem unable to recognize "that periodical works are, indeed, the prepared channels in which we may plumb the stream of our individual humanity, the open cisterns in which we may see the collected fountain that springs from our own country's soil" ("Unpublished Lectures," 337).

25. I have used Fredric Jameson's notion of "positive" and "negative" hermeneutics differently than he employs them in "Reification and Utopia in Mass Culture," *Social Text* 1 (1978). There he uses it to modulate the Hegelian "hermeneutics of suspicion" and rectify the Frankfurt School's one-dimensional critique of mass culture as sheer manipulation. But my purpose here is to show that middle-class ideologies are not themselves one-dimensional but constantly self-correcting.

26. For the details about such practices of nineteenth-century publishers, see John Sutherland, "Henry Colburn, Publisher," in *Publishing History* (forthcoming), and, for a broader view, Sutherland's *Victorian Novelists and Publishers* (Chicago: Univ. of Chicago Press, 1976).

27. "Tokens of the Times," *New Monthly Magazine*, n.s., 13 (1825): 86–92; "Advertisements Extraordinary," ibid. 23 (1828): 209–14. An example of the latter: "How delicious is the style of George Robins in his advertisements! how flowery his language! how rich, copious and luxuriant his descriptions! —'a mansion *seated*,' not standing like vulgar mansions, but '*seated* on a beautiful lawn'—the lawn is thus identified with the house—a sort of cottage-chair for the mansion to repose in (they must be sadly off for cellar room)"(213).

28. [Cyrus Redding], "The Philosophy of Fashion," *New Monthly Magazine*, n.s., 7 (1823): 238–44.

29. Redding, quoted in the *Wellesley Index of Victorian Periodicals*, 3:165.

30. [T. C. Morgan], "Life in London," *New Monthly Magazine*, n.s., 11 (1824): 226–30. Books and journals of the early 1820s abound with the phrase "life in London," popularized by Pierce Egan in his "Tom and Jerry" series, which portrays a comic English urban low life for the consumption of middle-class readers. That the

phrase is ubiquitous in these years helps confirm what Peter Brooks has argued about Paris in the 1830s, that the city has become a semiotic clearinghouse of "society" itself. Peter Brooks, "The Text of the City," *Oppositions* 6 (1983): 7–12.

31. For the peculiar logic of this nonstandard reasoning, see Jon Elster, *Sour Grapes: Studies in the Subversion of Rationality* (New York: Cambridge Univ. Press, 1983), esp. "States That Are Essentially Byproducts," 43–108.

32. [Horace Smith], "English Pride," *New Monthly Magazine*, n.s., 2 (1821): 136–37.

33. [William Maginn], "Fashionable Novels," *Fraser's Magazine* 1 (1830): 320. The escape from class typing was also being accomplished institutionally by the British universities as they transported young men out of lower-class backgrounds to make them bourgeois gentlemen. But as an act of social *reading*, the interpretation of the social text I have described here allows the reader to be both materially middle-class and ideologically classless. Later in the nineteenth century, the universities themselves would institutionalize this ineffable sense of being outside and above any class belonging. Cf. Ben Knights, *The Idea of the Clerisy in the Nineteenth Century* (Cambridge: Cambridge Univ. Press, 1978).

For a French example of reading the city as a social text, see "A Bourgeois Puts His World in Order" in Robert Darnton, *The Great Cat Massacre, and Other Essays in Cultural History* (New York: Basic Books, 1984), 107–44. Observing Montpellier, Darnton's historical interpreter "defined the position of the bourgeoisie negatively by reference to its hostile neighbors" (128). But the writers I discuss here do not simply omit to define the bourgeois; they define it critically to raise their readers somewhere above it.

34. This is indeed one of the crucial means by which a social group universalizes itself, so that it cannot be located in any particular sector of social space. "For each new class which puts itself in the place of one ruling before it, is compelled, merely to carry through its aim, to represent its interest as the common interest of all the members of society, put in an ideal form; it will give its ideas the form of universality, and represent them as the only rational, universally valid ones." Marx, *The German Ideology* (New York: International Publishers, 1947), 40–41.

35. Clive, *Scotch Reviewers*, 136.

36. Clive charts the *Review's* political shifts, ibid., 86–123.

37. Ibid., 120; Thomas De Quincey, "The French Revolution," *Blackwood's Edinburgh Magazine* 28 (September 1830): 556.

38. Clive, *Scotch Reviewers*, 143.

39. [Thomas Carlyle], "Signs of the Times," *Edinburgh Review* 49 (1829): 441. Among the "prophetic" works Carlyle reviews: *Anticipation; or, An Hundred Years Hence; Rise, Progress, and Present State of Public Opinion in Great Britain;* and *The Last Days; or, Discourses on These Our Times.*

40. As elaborated in Althusser's *For Marx*, trans. Ben Brewster (New York: Pantheon, 1970), 228–29, 251.

41. Christopher Lasch, *The Culture of Narcissism: American Life in an Age of Diminishing Expectations* (New York: Norton, 1979). *The Minimal Self* (New York: Norton, 1985) modifies the argument but heightens the rhetoric.

42. "The English Periodical Press," *Athenaeum* 1 (1828): 695.

43. Quoted in Walter Benjamin, *Charles Baudelaire: A Lyric Poet in the Era of High Capitalism* (London: New Left Books, 1973), 137.

44. Coleridge, *Lay Sermons*, 37. On the distinction between his own audiences, see the letter to T. G. Street, 22 March 1817: *The Statesman's Manual* "I never dreamt would be understood (except in fragments) by the general Reader; but of the second [A *Lay Sermon*] I can scarcely discover any part or passage which would compel any man of common education and information to read it a second Time in order to understand it." *Collected Letters of Samuel Taylor Coleridge*, ed. Leslie Griggs (Oxford: Clarendon, 1959), 4:713.

45. Coleridge to William Blackwood, 2 April 1819, *Collected Letters*, 4:931.

46. I refer to the argument of Michael Fried, *Absorption and Theatricality: Beholder and Painting in the Age of Diderot* (Berkeley and Los Angeles: Univ. of California Press, 1980). By "theatrical" Fried seems to have in mind the stances of both radical rhetoric and mass-cultural display. His defense of the viewer's "absorptive" relation to a painting relies on this undefined antagonist, which in Fried's earlier essays appears as postmodern art, the "theatrical" opposite of the absorptive late-modernist painting Fried upholds. Fried's is a loaded argument, too complex to summarize here. But it is worth pointing out that theorists of this kind of reader/spectator nearly always fabricate a hybrid antagonist, composed equally of radical discourse and mass culture. One thinks of André Bazin's deeply subjective viewer of Italian neorealism in *What Is Cinema?*, whom he opposes to both Sergei Eisenstein's viewer of *montage* and the spectator of the Hollywood film; more recently, Stanley Cavell's *The World Viewed: Reflections on the Ontology of Film* (Cambridge: Harvard Univ. Press, 1979) shares this tactic with Fried and Bazin. In literary studies the most relevant example is Stanley Fish's "self-satisfying" (theatrical) and "self-consuming" (absorptive) styles in *Self-Consuming Artifacts* (Berkeley and Los Angeles: Univ. of California Press, 1971). For the implications of this strategy, see the discussion of Coleridge in Chapter 5, below.

CHAPTER THREE: FROM CROWD TO MASS AUDIENCE

1. Walter Benjamin, *Charles Baudelaire: A Lyric Poet in the Era of High Capitalism*, trans. Harry Zohn (London: New Left Books, 1973), 120.

2. T. J. Clark, *An Image of the People: Gustave Courbet and the Second French Republic, 1848–1851* (Greenwich, Conn.: New York Graphic Society, 1973), 15.

3. Scott Bennett conducts a complex financial analysis of England's largest mass journal in "Revolutions in Thought: Serial Publication and the Mass Market

for Reading," in *The Victorian Periodical Press: Samplings and Soundings*, ed. Joanne Shattock and Michael Wolff (Toronto: Univ. of Toronto Press, 1982), 225–60. Bennett's rigor and interesting results show the new seriousness with which periodical writing has recently been taken. But inevitably Bennett's method betrays its critical aim: to quantify any ideological analysis out of existence and portray nineteenth-century mass culture as an innocent discourse meant merely to enrich its readers' lives. "Too often we take conflict and its resolution to be the sole substance of history. Mass markets develop through consensus, not conflict" (252). Bennett speaks blithely of the "freedom to choose" and the "fundamental commitment to freedom in the mass reading market." Claims like this depend on taking Charles Knight's self-promotions as historical truth; but one can hardly miss the calculated self-justifications on every page of Knight's work.

4. Charles Knight, "Cheap Publications" (1819), quoted in his *Passages from the Life of a Working Man* (New York, 1874), 151–52. For Knight's account of his doomed *Plain Englishman*, see pp. 150–64.

5. Richard K. Altick, *The English Common Reader* (Chicago: Univ. of Chicago Press, 1957), 266. The *Mirror*, contemporary observer James Grant reported, "was to be seen everywhere. It was amazingly popular." Grant, *The Great Metropolis* (London, 1837), 2:349–50. The *Hive* appears to have established the mass journal's anthological style. Its more stimulating essays—"Execution by the Knout" or "Barbarisms of the American Indians"—approach the style of the later Victorian "penny dreadfuls," but were evidently nowhere near as popular as the *Mirror's*.

6. *Mirror of Literature* 2 (1823): 10.

7. The "style" of the mass journals displays the effusion of encyclopedic codes and cultural "stereotypes" that Roland Barthes believed form the very basis of literary styles themselves. See "Style and Its Image," in *Literary Style: A Symposium*, ed. Seymour Chatman (New York: Oxford Univ. Press, 1971), 3–10; and *S/Z*, trans. Richard Howard (New York: Hill and Wang, 1974), 184–85.

8. "Modern Phrases," *Mirror of Literature* 4 (1824): 174. Compare the catalog of dialect translations in Pierce Egan's popular *Life in London* (London, 1821), a book whose expensive color-plate production and binding as well as tone suggest that its audience was thoroughly middle-class, gazing amusedly at the linguistic eccentricities of London's subclasses. Louis James has reprinted a representative selection in *English Popular Literature, 1819–1851* (New York: Columbia Univ. Press, 1976), 145–49.

9. *The Mirror of Literature* 4 (1824): 172–76.

10. Richard Hoggart, *The Uses of Literacy* (Boston: Beacon Press, 1957), 123.

11. "Life in London," *Mirror of Literature* 3 (1824): 173, an article evidently inspired but not adapted from Egan's *Life in London*.

12. Defoe, *The Farther Adventures of Robinson Crusoe* (London, 1719); *Spectator* 465 in *The Spectator*, ed. Donald F. Bond (Oxford: Clarendon, 1965), 4:143; Wordsworth, *The Prelude* (1805), 7. 280–309. On the shapes assumed by the

eighteenth-century writer's crowd, see also Max Byrd, *London Transformed: Images of the City in the Eighteenth Century* (New Haven: Yale Univ. Press, 1978).

13. The English mass writer's rendering of such spontaneous social knowledge resembles the task of the French physiologue, who in the 1830s and 1840s cataloged the Parisian crowd in similarly cheap, pocketable journals. The popular physiologies, as Walter Benjamin describes them, "investigated types that might be encountered by a person taking a look at the marketplace. From the itinerant street vendor of the boulevards to the dandy in the foyer of the opera-house, there was not a figure of Paris life that was not sketched by a physiologue. . . .They assured people that everyone was, unencumbered by any factual knowledge, able to make out the profession, the character, the background, and the lifestyle of the passers-by. In these writings this ability appears as a gift which a good fairy bestows upon an inhabitant of the big city" (*Charles Baudelaire*, 35).

14. Or, as in many French instances, the noisy crowd treats the execution as carnival: "If the crowd gathered round the scaffold, it was not simply to witness the sufferings of the condemned man or to excite the anger of the executioner: it was also to hear an individual who had nothing more to lose curse the judges, the laws, the government and religion. The public execution allowed the luxury of these momentary saturnalia, when nothing remained to prohibit or punish. Under the protection of imminent death, the criminal could say everything and the crowd cheered." Michel Foucault, *Discipline and Punish: The Birth of the Prison* (New York: Pantheon, 1975), 60.

15. "Execution by the Knout," *The Hive* 2 (1823): 102.

16. "The Passing Crowd," *Chambers' Edinburgh Journal* 1 (1832): 33.

17. Friedrich Engels, *The Condition of the Working Class in England*, ed. W. O. Henderson and W. H. Chaloner (Stanford: Stanford Univ. Press, 1958), 30–31.

18. See, for a different view of the "popular," T. J. Clark's analysis of those who "define themselves by their difference from the popular *but also their possession of it*, their inwardness with its every turn of phrase. These are the connoisseurs of popular culture, its experts, its aestheticians; but that expertise is a way of establishing imaginary distance and control. It is the power of the petite bourgeoisie over the proletariat." Clark, *The Painting of Modern Life* (New York: Knopf, 1984), 237.

As we shall see, William Chambers meant his *Journal* for working-class readers and was disappointed to find that he was reaching only "shopkeepers and tradesmen." Clark's point would help explain why: the shopkeeper "mingles" in this crowd while he also possesses it.

19. "Reading for All," *Penny Magazine* 1 (1832): 1.

20. On the faith in technology promoted by the mass journals, see Celina Fox, "Political Caricature and the Freedom of the Press in Early-Nineteenth-Century England," in *Newspaper History*, ed. George Boyce, James Curran, and Pauline Wingate (London: Constable, 1978), 226–46.

21. Gas lighting had just been declared "safe" by Parliament in 1822, but

there were disturbing questions about its impact on the public. The utility developed once the Gas-Light and Coke Company earned its charter in 1810. London had one gasometer in 1814, at least 50 by the mid-1820s. Sir Walter Besant, *London in the Nineteenth Century* (London, 1909), 316–18.

22. "The Gas Light Works," *The Hive* 2 (1823): 161–62.

23. On the preindustrial crowd, see George Rudé, *The Crowd in History: A Study of Popular Disturbances in France and England, 1730–1848* (New York: Wiley, 1964), 195–269.

24. Raymond Williams, *The City and the Country* (New York: Oxford Univ. Press, 1973), 68–69, 142–43.

25. "The Mechanism of Society," *Bristol Job Nott* 1 (1832): 143. Now almost unknown, the *Job Nott* combined the explicit antiradicalism of the *Anti-Jacobin* (1797) and the *Anti-Cobbett* (1817) with the mass journals' discourse. Job Nott himself is a caricature of Thomas Wooler's Black Dwarf, but his language mocks Cobbett's. This journal offers ample proof that nineteenth-century mass discourse was not a naive effort to spread information among the English or have them reach "consensus, not conflict" (Bennett, *Victorian Periodical Press*, 252); it reacted to the conflict posed by radicalized working-class readers and built its "consensus" on their defeat.

26. Williams, *The City and the Country*, 68.

27. *Spectator* 69 in *The Spectator*, 1:292–96.

28. Quoted in G. A. Cranfield, *The Press and Society* (London: Longman, 1978), 116, 145.

29. Marx, *The Eighteenth-Brumaire of Louis Bonaparte* (New York: International Publishers, 1963), 124.

CHAPTER FOUR: RADICAL REPRESENTATIONS

1. Erich Auerbach suggestively traces the shift of meaning from *le public* as "state" to the public as "audience" in "La Cour et la ville," trans. Ralph Manheim, in *Scenes from the Drama of European Literature*, ed. Paolo Valesio (Minneapolis: Univ. of Minnesota Press, 1984). In England, the "public" as state (*OED*, sense 2) becomes rare after the seventeenth century, but James Thomson still uses it to describe a nascent civilization: "Then gath'ring men their natural powers combin'd / And form'd a Public to the general good / Submitting, aiming and conducting all." "Autumn," *The Seasons* (London, 1803), p. 133, lines 96–98.

2. The crowd's moral economy, argues Thompson, was based on a "consistent traditional view of social norms and obligations, of the proper economic functions of several parties within the community, which, taken together, can be said to constitute the moral economy of the poor." "The Moral Economy of the English Crowd in the Eighteenth Century," *Past and Present* 50 (1971): 79.

3. Coleridge, *The Collected Notebooks*, ed. Kathleen Coburn (London: Routledge & Kegan Paul, 1973), 3:3317, 4311.

4. Bakhtin, "Discourse in the Novel," in *The Dialogic Imagination*, trans. Caryl Emerson and Michael Holquist (Austin: Univ. of Texas Press, 1981), 285. My emphasis.

5. For greater detail on political stances and journals of these radical writers of the 1790s, see Olivia Smith, *The Politics of Language, 1791–1819* (Oxford: Clarendon, 1984), chs. 2 and 3; E. P. Thompson, *The Making of the English Working Class* (New York: Pantheon, 1964), 603–779; Albert J. Goodwin, *The Friends of Liberty* (Cambridge: Harvard Univ. Press, 1979), 208–67; and Chapter 1, above.

6. For a useful contrast between styles of middle-class and plebeian radical discourse, see Thompson, *Making of the English Working Class*, 746–49.

7. Patricia Hollis, *The Pauper Press* (New York: Oxford Univ. Press, 1970), estimates that each copy of the largest radical journals reached ten readers. For a thorough study of William Hone's journals and caricatures in this period, see Olivia Smith, *The Politics of Language*, ch. 5.

8. A detailed chart of income and occupational categories dividing "producers" from "parasites," published in the *Crisis* (1834), appears in *Class and Conflict in Nineteenth-Century England*, ed. Patricia Hollis (London: Routledge & Kegan Paul, 1973), 6–8.

9. See Gareth Stedman Jones, "Rethinking Chartism," in *The Languages of Class* (Cambridge: Cambridge Univ. Press, 1984), 106–7.

10. In addition to Olivia Smith, Thompson, and Goodwin (n. 5, above), see J. Anne Hone, *For the Cause of Truth: Radicalism in London, 1796–1819* (Oxford: Clarendon, 1981); I. J. Prothero, *Artisans and Politics in Early-Nineteenth-Century London* (Baton Rouge: Louisiana State Univ. Press, 1979); and Gwynn Williams, *Artisans and Sans-culottes* (New York: Norton, 1969).

11. Thompson, *Making of the English Working Class*, 746–49.

12. Bakhtin, *Dialogic Imagination*, 284. But it is *Rabelais and His World* (Cambridge: MIT Press, 1973) that most thoroughly demonstrates how one culture imbricates itself within another. For its implications in social and intellectual history, see Roger Chartier, "Intellectual History or Social History? The French Trajectories," in *Modern European Intellectual History: Reappraisals and New Perspectives*, ed. Dominick LaCapra and Steven L. Kaplan (Ithaca: Cornell Univ. Press, 1982), 13–46.

13. "We are so made as to be affected at such spectacles with melancholy sentiments upon the unstable condition of mortal prosperity, and the tremendous uncertainty of human greatness; because in those natural feelings we learn great lessons; because in events like these our passions instruct our reason; because when kings are hurl'd from their thrones by the Supreme Director of this great drama, and become the objects of insult to the base, and of pity to the good, we behold such disasters in the moral, as we should behold a miracle in the physical order of things. We are alarmed into reflexion; our minds (as it has long since been observed) are purified by terror and pity; our weak unthinking pride is humbled, under the dispensations of a mysterious wisdom. —Some tears might be drawn from me, if such a

spectacle were exhibited on the stage. I should be truly ashamed of finding in myself that superficial, theatric sense of painted distress, whilst I could exult over it in real life. With such a perverted mind, I could never venture to shew my face at a tragedy." Edmund Burke, *Reflections on the Revolution in France*, ed. Conor Cruise O'Brien (Harmondsworth: Penguin, 1969), 175. On Burke's revolutionary theatre, see also Ronald Paulson, *Representations of Revolution* (New Haven: Yale Univ. Press, 1983), ch. 2

14. "Intellectual vernacular" is Smith's term, in *The Politics of Language, ch. 3*.

15. Thomas Paine, *The Rights of Man*, ed. Henry Collins (Harmondsworth: Penguin, 1969), 175; Eric Foner, *Tom Paine and Revolutionary America* (New York: Oxford Univ. Press, 1976), xv–xx, 214–20. Paine addressed both middle-class and artisan readers in America; he tested the English audience with Part One of *The Rights of Man*, which met with middle-class readers' anger and artisans' enthusiasm.

16. On contemporary reaction, see David Hawke, *Paine* (New York: Harper & Row, 1974), 224–25, 240; Smith, *The Politics of Language*, 57–67.

17. William Hazlitt, "On the Difference between Writing and Speaking," in *Collected Works of William Hazlitt*, ed. P. P. Howe (London: Dent, 1930–34), 12:275.

18. Said defines a "beginning" as a "reversal, change of direction, the institution of a durable movement that increasingly engages our interest: such a beginning *authorizes*; it constitutes an authority for what follows from it. With regard to what precedes it, a beginning represents . . . a discontinuity (whether or not decisively enforced)." Edward Said, *Beginnings: Intention and Method* (New York: Basic Books, 1975), 34.

19. Jean Starobinski, *1789: The Emblems of Reason*, trans. Barbara Bray (Charlottesville: Univ. Press of Virginia, 1982), 55.

20. This analysis unavoidably recalls Jacques Derrida's notion of the "supplement" in *Of Grammatology*, trans. Gayatri Spivak (Baltimore: Johns Hopkins Univ. Press, 1976), 141–64. Like Arthur Young's opposition between discourses that "circulate" or "disseminate," Paine's metaphors involve constituting and deconstituting those "radical" limits of discourse itself. I want to stress that such figures appear in these historical texts without any help from latter-day French radical thinkers. They also force us to *historicize* categories that appear on our own cultural scene as avant-garde, as historically unprecedented. The Rousseauist "supplement" Derrida brilliantly analyzes reappears as a political figure not only in Paine, but in Brissot, Robespierre, and other French ideologues. For a stance indebted to this line of analysis, see Lynn Hunt, *Politics and Culture in the French Revolution* (Berkeley and Los Angeles: Univ. of California Press, 1984), chs. 1–3.

21. On resistance to Paine's arguments within the corresponding societies, see Goodwin, *Friends of Liberty*, 174–77.

22. Curiously omitted from Pierre Bourdieu's discussion in *Distinction* (Cambridge: Harvard Univ. Press, 1984) is the impact of radical political writing, reading, and action upon "cultural capital." Do radical activities, for example, reinforce cultural capital by incorporating radical criticism within established institutions? Or,

as Derrida implies, does radical criticism from within such institutions hollow out cultural capital?

23. On the relations between Burke's historicism and Coleridge's, see James K. Chandler, *Wordsworth's Second Nature* (Chicago: Univ. of Chicago Press, 1984), 237–38.

24. I quote from Olivia Smith, *Politics of Language*, 53. Compare Barbara Herrnstein Smith's discussion of epigram and antithesis in *Poetic Closure* (Chicago: Univ. of Chicago Press, 1968), 168–70, 196–210. The epigrammatist "holds the reader at a distance, addressing him directly but not inviting him to share experiences" (208). This is Paine's stance toward readers, in contrast to the invitational stance in Arthur Young's prose.

25. "Reader-response theory" and its cognates thus renew the Aristotelian claim to transform the reader/audience by implicating it in the "action" of the text, denying the possibility of a Brechtian space of reflection that historicizes the audience's own position in regard to the text and its historical subjects. This is why the characteristic "historicizing" moves of *Rezeptionkritik*, in works like Wolfgang Iser's *The Implied Reader* (Baltimore: Johns Hopkins Univ. Press, 1974), merely stretch out in a chronological sequence the premise of a reader perfectly adequate to the text, the "implied" reader. Such a reader can never be historicized; he displaces historical reflection.

26. Arthur Young, *Travels in France during the Years 1787, 1788, and 1789*, ed. Jeffrey Kaplow (Garden City, N.Y.: Doubleday, 1969), 287.

27. See, for example, John Holloway's rhetorical analyses of John Henry Newman, for whom "exposition, as it develops, actually becomes proof," and of Matthew Arnold's "value frames," which "envelop the main assertion in clauses which invite the reader to view it with favour or disfavour, and suggest grounds for the attitude he is to adopt." *The Victorian Sage* (1953; rpt. New York: Norton, 1965), 8, 215–19. Such indirect modes of guiding readers are only more self-conscious, intricate strategies of the kind Young adopts in *Travels in France*.

28. *Black Dwarf* 1 (1817): 145.

29. Quoted in Raymond Williams, *Culture and Society, 1780–1950* (Garden City, N.Y.: Doubleday, 1958), 14.

30. Antonio Gramsci, "The Formation of the Intellectuals," in *Selections from the Prison Notebooks*, ed. Quentin Hoare and Jeffrey Nowell Smith (New York: International, 1971), 5–14.

31. See Richard Hendrix, "Popular Humour and 'The Black Dwarf,' " *Journal of British Studies* 16 (1976): 108–28.

32. *Black Dwarf* 1 (1817): 3.

33. V. N. Voloshinov, *Marxism and the Philosophy of Language* (New York: Seminar Press, 1973), 23.

34. *Gorgon*, no. 1 (1818), 1.

35. *Republican* 1 (1819): 49.

36. *Black Dwarf* 3 (1819): 550–51.

37. On Wooler's theatrical background, see Thompson, *Making of the English Working Class*, 736. In the *Dwarf* Wooler often reviewed political melodramas like *Oroonoko*: "We can hardly afterwards contemplate that the mere force of will could give such energy to language, such inspiration to the sentiment, as Mr. Rae effects in his questions to the slave, who cursed himself and his masters, for having been some years in bondage—"*And do you only curse!*" went like electricity through every bosom. . . .Everyone should see this representation, the friend of freedom to open his soul to congenial daring—the sons of despotism, to learn the power of freedom." *Black Dwarf* 1 (1817): 48.

38. See especially "Appendix: The Curse" in Robert Elliott, *The Power of Satire* (Princeton: Princeton Univ. Press, 1960), 285–92.

39. Peter Brooks, *The Melodramatic Imagination* (New Haven: Yale Univ. Press, 1976), 201, 203.

40. Thompson, *Making of the English Working Class*, 676, 770–74.

41. "An Appeal to the Public in Favour of the Working Classes," *Gorgon*, no. 17 (1818), 129–30.

42. Thompson, *Making of the English Working Class*, 674–75.

43. James Sambrook, *William Cobbett* (London: Routledge & Kegan Paul, 1974), 84–86, 88.

44. On parodies of Cobbett in the journals, see George Spater, *William Cobbett: The Poor Man's Friend* (Cambridge: Cambridge Univ. Press, 1982), vol. 2.

45. Hazlitt, "Character of Cobbett," in *Collected Works*, 8:53.

46. "Mr. Cobbett," *Athenaeum* 1 (1828): 97.

47. Hazlitt, "Character of Cobbett," 52.

48. William Cobbett, *Rural Rides*, ed. George Woodcock (Harmondsworth: Penguin, 1967), 315. Woodcock's edition follows the 1830 text Cobbett gathered from his previous *Political Register* articles.

49. *Cobbett's Political Register* 32 (1817): 358–61.

50. Quoted in Sambrook, *Cobbett*, 174.

51. For a survey of critical readings of Cobbett, see Martin J. Weiner, "The Changing Image of William Cobbett," *Journal of British Studies* 13 (1974): 135–54.

52. Cobbett, *Rural Rides*, 401–2.

53. Cobbett's medieval faith is much stronger in works like *A History of the Protestant "Reformation"* (1824–26); see also Sambrook, *Cobbett*, 136–42.

54. Raymond Williams, *The Country and the City* (New York: Oxford Univ. Press, 1973), 112.

55. In this purely formal way, Cobbett's strategy bears resemblance to the "historical trope" of Hegelian Marxism, as Fredric Jameson defines it in *Marxism and Form* (Princeton: Princeton Univ. Press, 1971), 6–10.

56. Alice Chandler, *A Dream of Order: The Medieval Ideal in Nineteenth-Century English Literature* (Lincoln: Univ. of Nebraska Press, 1970), 59–82.

57. "Mr. Cobbett," 97–98.

58. *Letters of Percy Bysshe Shelley,* in *The Complete Works,* ed. Roger Ingpen and Walter E. Peck (New York: Gordian Press, 1965), 10:27, 58, 147.

59. "A Philosophical View of Reform," in *Shelley's Prose,* ed. David Clarke (Albuquerque: Univ. of New Mexico Press, 1954), 244.

60. "Essay on Life," *Shelley's Prose,* 173.

61. "A Defence of Poetry," *Shelley's Prose,* 278.

62. For recent discussions, see Michael Henry Scrivener, *Radical Shelley* (Princeton: Princeton Univ. Press, 1982), 196–210; P.M.S. Dawson, *The Unacknowledged Legislator: Shelley and Politics* (Oxford: Clarendon, 1980), 65–75; Timothy Webb, *Shelley: A Voice Not Understood* (Atlantic Highlands, N.J.: Humanities Press, 1977), 101–5; Art Young, *Shelley and Nonviolence* (The Hague: Mouton, 1975), 140–46; Gerald McNiece, *Shelley and the Revolutionary Idea* (Cambridge: Harvard Univ. Press, 1969).

63. For a fuller treatment of the problem of language in *Prometheus Unbound,* see Susan Hawk Brisman, "Unsaying His High Language: The Problem of Voice in *Prometheus Unbound,*" *Studies in Romanticism* 16 (1977): 51–86.

CHAPTER FIVE: ROMANTIC THEORY AND ENGLISH READING AUDIENCES

1. Coleridge, *The Statesman's Manual,* in *Lay Sermons,* ed. R. J. White (Routledge & Kegan Paul, 1972), 38.

2. Wordsworth, "Preface to *Lyrical Ballads,*" *The Prose Works of William Wordsworth,* ed. W.J.B. Owen and J. W. Smyser (Oxford: Clarendon, 1974), 1:129.

3. For a representative collection, see reviews by the *Critical Review, British Critic, Edinburgh Review, Eclectic Review,* and particularly the *Annual Review,* collected in John O. Hayden, ed., *Romantic Bards and Scotch Reviewers* (Lincoln: Univ. of Nebraska Press, 1971), 3–38.

4. Wordsworth to John Wilson, June 1802, in *Literary Criticism of William Wordsworth,* ed. Paul M. Zall (Lincoln: Univ. of Nebraska Press, 1966), 71–72.

5. Coleridge, *Biographia Literaria,* ed. James Engell and W. Jackson Bate (London: Routledge & Kegan Paul, 1983), 2:58. Hereafter, *BL* in the text.

6. I quote this passage as representative of the reviewers' stance against theory; Lyall's review, in *Quarterly Review* 14 (October 1815): 201–25, appeared in March 1816, while Coleridge was drafting the *Biographia.* Reprinted in Hayden, *Romantic Bards,* 76.

7. Jean Baudrillard, "The Structural Law of Value," in *The Structural Allegory: Reconstructive Encounters with the New French Thought,* ed. John Fekete (Minneapolis: Univ. of Minnesota Press, 1984), 62.

8. Wordsworth to Catherine Clarkson, 4 June 1812, *The Letters of William and Dorothy Wordsworth,* ed. Ernest De Selincourt (Oxford: Clarendon, 1970), 3:21.

9. Michel de Certeau, "The Beauty of the Dead: Nisard," in *Heterologies:*

Discourse on the Other, trans. Brian Massumi (Minneapolis: Univ. of Minnesota Press, 1986), 123.

10. Wordsworth to Francis Wrangham, 5 June 1808, *Letters*, 2:247.

11. In a more restricted sense of the "dialogic," Don Bialostosky makes the parallel between Bakhtin's dialogism and Wordsworth's dramatic dialogues in *Making Tales* (Chicago: Univ. of Chicago Press, 1984). The result is not enlightening: what is most social and interesting in both Wordsworth's and Bakhtin's sense of the encounter between socially rooted languages gets lost in Bialostosky's purely individual "dialogue."

12. See M. H. Abrams, *Natural Supernaturalism* (New York: Norton, 1971), 397; cf. Erich Auerbach, *Literary Language and Its Public in Late Latin Antiquity and the Middle Ages*, trans. Ralph Manheim (Princeton: Bollingen, 1964).

13. From the *Monthly Review*, 2d ser., 78 (November 1815): 229.

14. Jerome McGann, *The Romantic Ideology* (Chicago: Univ. of Chicago Press, 1983).

15. 21 April 1832, *Table Talk*, Bohn's Standard Library (London, 1903), 158.

16. Coleridge to Humphry Davy, 14 December 1808, *Collected Letters of Samuel Taylor Coleridge*, ed. Leslie Griggs (Oxford: Clarendon, 1959), 3:143. This letter also makes clear that in the 1809 *Friend*, Coleridge's first attempt to organize what would become the clerisy, his mutual antagonists were the *Edinburgh Review* and *Cobbett's Political Register*.

17. The "connected" and "Anglo-Gallican" styles are most thoroughly discussed in Jerome Christensen, "The Method of *The Friend*," in *Coleridge's Blessed Machine of Language* (Ithaca: Cornell Univ. Press, 1981), 186–270. I have learned much from this absorbing, difficult chapter. But the discourse it reconstructs is misleadingly self-enclosed and gives us no sense of what Coleridge elaborated such stylistic oppositions *for*. Restricting himself to the 1818 *Friend*, Christensen makes it a philosophical (or, given his perspective, a grammatological) *summa* rather than, as in 1809, a first real intervention in England's existing cultural and social relations, as I have interpreted it here.

18. *Logic*, ed. J. R. de J. Jackson (London: Routledge & Kegan Paul, 1981), 23. To clarify Coleridge's definitions, I have combined his table with Professor Jackson's translations from the Greek.

19. "For the Friend," Christensen writes, "style is a matter of hermeneutics rather than rhetoric" (*Blessed Machine*, 211). This is a false choice; "meaning" cannot be discovered in language apart from the shared commitment to articulate it in a certain way (for example, in a "connected" style). That shared commitment is fundamentally a rhetorical one.

20. Roland Barthes, *Writing Degree Zero*, trans. Annette Lavers and Colin Smith (Boston: Beacon, 1967), 14, 25.

21. 12 September 1831, *Table Talk*, 139.

22. Coleridge to Southey, 20 October 1809, *Collected Letters*, 3:254.

23. See, for the politics of "Kubla Khan," Norman Rudich, "Coleridge's 'Kubla Khan': His Anti-Political Vision," in *Weapons of Criticism*, ed. N. Rudich (Palo Alto: Ramparts Press, 1976), 215–42.

24. "The very connectives of sentences, those last remnants of that logic, which from the time of Socrates or the elder Zeno had distinguished the literature of Europe from the cementless aggregates of the oriental Sages, have almost disappeared in modern French books, and are shunned by the Professors of fine style, the admirers of Gallican Point and Terseness, in England." Coleridge, "On the Catholic Petition. Letter II" (1811), in *Essays on His Times*, ed. David Erdman (London: Routledge & Kegan Paul, 1978), 2:306–7.

25. Coleridge, *The Friend* (1809), ed. Barbara E. Rooke (London: Routledge & Kegan Paul, 1969), 2:46.

26. Freud, "Jokes and Their Relation to the Unconscious" in *The Complete Psychological Works of Sigmund Freud*, trans. James Strachey (London: Hogarth Press, 1960), 8:115. I am indebted to Daniel Cottom, "The Enchantment of Interpretation," *Critical Inquiry* 11 (1985): 573–94, for extending the problem of "misreading" both to jokes and to social discourses as such.

27. Robert DeMaria, "The Ideal Reader: A Critical Fiction," *PMLA* 93 (1978): 466–67. In *Coleridge's Poetics* (Stanford: Stanford Univ. Press, 1983), 12–16, Paul Hamilton argues forcefully against these claims as they often appear in Coleridge criticism. But the Coleridgeans are not wrong to detect this aim in Coleridge's project; they simply "discover" the identity of reader and writer prematurely because, good Coleridgeans, they seek it everywhere.

28. Stanley Fish, *Self-Consuming Artifacts: The Experience of Seventeenth-Century Prose* (Berkeley and Los Angeles: Univ. of California Press, 1972), 17–19. See also *Is There a Text in This Class?* (Cambridge: Harvard Univ. Press, 1981) for the remark, later retracted, that critical claims need not be true, but only interesting.

29. Christensen makes a similar point in *Coleridge's Blessed Machine of Language*: "Each circulative model has the function of both identifying and indemnifying a processive space safely apart from the labyrinth of letters where a person first loses his way, then loses his memory that there is a way to lose. . . .The implicit justification of the apparent auto-affection of the physiological model is the economic principle of homeostasis, the conservation of the organism's health, vigor, and life" (167–68). But this is too simple: Coleridge is withdrawing one kind of "circulation" from another—the one Christensen rightly calls "imagination" from another world that also circulates, the world of public reading, whose intense social and political contests threaten what Coleridge must preserve from its motions. Typically, Christensen reduces that social world to a purely typographic one, the ghostly world of "letters."

30. *Confessions of an Inquiring Spirit* (London: Adam & Charles Black, 1956), 68–69, 76.

31. Annotation to Eichhorn, *Einleitung in das Neue Testament*, quoted in *Lay*

Sermons, n. 1, p. 45. On Coleridge's relation to the higher criticism, see Elinor Schaffer, *Kubla Khan and the Fall of Jerusalem* (Cambridge: Cambridge Univ. Press, 1975).

32. *Omniana* (London, 1903), p. 380.

33. Christensen, *Blessed Machine*, 215–16.

34. Notebook 38, fol. 25, quoted in John Colmer's Introduction to *On the Constitution of Church and State* (London: Routledge & Kegan Paul, 1976), lv.

POSTSCRIPT

1. Robert M. Maniquis, "Poetry and Barrell Organs: The Text in the Book of the *Biographia Literaria*," in *Coleridge and the Biographia Literaria: Text and Meaning*, ed. Frederick Burwick (forthcoming).

2. Quoted in Tzvetan Todorov, *Mikhail Bakhtin: The Dialogic Principle*, trans. Wlad Godzich (Minneapolis: Univ. of Minnesota Press, 1984), 111.

3. Jean Baudrillard, *Simulations*, trans. Paul Foss, Paul Patton, and Philip Beitchman (New York: Semiotexte, 1983), 12–13.

4. Jean-François Lyotard, *The Postmodern Condition: A Report on Knowledge*, trans. Geoff Bennington and Brian Massumi (Minneapolis: Univ. of Minnesota Press, 1984); Jurgen Habermas, *Legitimation Crisis*, trans. Thomas McCarthy (Boston: Beacon, 1975).

5. Stanley Fish, *Is There a Text in This Class?* (Cambridge: Harvard Univ. Press, 1981); Fish, *Change* (forthcoming); and Jean Baudrillard, *In the Shadow of Silent Majorities* (New York: Semiotexte, 1983).

6. Michel de Certeau, *The Practice of Everyday Life* (Berkeley and Los Angeles: Univ. of California Press, 1983); see also the work of Natalie Zemon Davis, Carlo Ginzberg, Tony Bennett, and others.

7. The phrase "postmodern bourgeois liberalism" first appears in Rorty's essay of that name (*Journal of Philosophy* 80 [1983]: 583–89) but has since been largely accepted to define the ethos shared broadly by Rorty, Fish, Geertz, and other post-Vietnam liberal thinkers. The new liberalism gives a semiotic inflection to the old; its enemy remains a class analysis of historical societies, as in Geertz's argument that we need a "poetics," not a "mechanics" of power. Clifford Geertz, *Negara: The Theatre-State in Nineteenth-Century Bali* (Princeton: Princeton Univ. Press, 1982), 121–36. The antiphilosophical argument Rorty has made famous would surely have a historical corollary: to write our histories according to what is "good" for us now rather than according to what we believe to have been true of the past. In this sense, a pragmatist historicism would regard the past as Geertz regards the cultures read by ethnographers, namely as an opaqueness we must make familiar. The politics of this strategy are well remarked in Michel de Certeau, "The Beauty of the Dead: Nisard," in *Heterologies: Discourse on the Other*, trans. Brian Massumi (Minneapolis: Univ. of Minnesota Press, 1985), 119–36.

8. Wlad Godzich, "The Semiotics of Semiotics" in *On Signs*, ed. Marshall Blonsky (Baltimore: Johns Hopkins Univ. Press, 1985), 421–47; Robert M. Maniquis, "Pascal's Bet, Totalities, and Guerilla Criticism," *Humanities in Society* 6 (1983): 257–82. The pungently critical use of social and historical semiotics in the work of de Certeau, the earlier Barthes, and the later Baudrillard remains exemplary.

Index

DESIGNED BY BRUCE GORE
COMPOSED BY POINT WEST, INC.
CAROL STREAM, ILLINOIS
MANUFACTURED BY EDWARDS BROTHERS, INC.
ANN ARBOR, MICHIGAN
TEXT AND DISPLAY LINES ARE SET IN GOUDY

Library of Congress Cataloging-in-Publication Data
Klancher, Jon P.
The making of English reading audiences, 1790–1832.
Includes bibliographic references and index.
1. Books and reading—England—History—19th century.
2. Books and reading—England—History—18th century.
3. England—Popular culture. 4. Romanticism—England.
5. English literature—19th century—History and
criticism. 6. Authors and readers—England. 7. England—
Social conditions—19th century. 8. English periodicals
—History—19th century. I. Title.
Z1003.5.G7K57 1986   028′.9′0942   86-22443
ISBN 0-299-10780-9

DATE DUE

8/5/92 DKC/UWR		
IL: 9037525		
DUE: 9/3/92		
OCT 3 0 2000		
ck 125/646		